# NEARLY OFF THE RECORD

The Archives of an Archivist

by

Berwick Coates

Published by Paragon Publishing, Rothersthorpe
First published 2016

© Berwick Coates 2016

The rights of Berwick Coates to be identified as the author of this work have been asserted by him in accordance with the Copyright, Designs and Patents Act of 1988.

All rights reserved; no part of this publication may be reproduced, stored in a retrieval system, or transmitted in any form or by any means, electronic, mechanical, photocopying, recording or otherwise without the prior written consent of the publisher or a licence permitting copying in the UK issued by the Copyright Licensing Agency Ltd. www.cla.co.uk

ISBN 978-1-78222-463-1

Book design, layout and production management by Into Print
www.intoprint.net
+44 (0)1604 832149

Printed and bound in UK and USA by Lightning Source

# Dedication

To all the thousands of pupils, teachers, parents,
ancillary workers, governors, celebrities, cooks, cleaners, groundsmen,
technicians, and the many others I have overlooked,
who, between them, knowing and unknowing,
have made West Buckland School what it is.

# CONTENTS

| | | |
|---|---|---|
| 1 | Introduction | 5 |
| 2 | Statement of intent | 7 |
| 3 | Up and running | 8 |
| 4 | People | 18 |
| 5 | Getting written about | 33 |
| 6 | More people | 50 |
| 7 | Who are we? | 61 |
| 8 | Living and learning | 73 |
| 9 | Records and records | 87 |
| 10 | Archive guide to emails | 107 |
| 11 | A spot of history | 109 |
| 12 | The shock of the new | 118 |
| 13 | Music and monarchs | 128 |
| 14 | Exmoor – first verse | 138 |
| 15 | Should do well | 141 |
| 16 | Well, how would you describe it? | 156 |
| 17 | Becoming an archive | 164 |
| 18 | Exmoor encores | 170 |
| 19 | We are all human | 183 |
| 20 | Songs of praise | 206 |
| 21 | You can't beat a good story | 215 |
| 22 | Assembly philosophy | 229 |
| 23 | Little tributes | 248 |
| 24 | What do you actually do? | 259 |

# 1. Introduction

AFTER FORTY YEARS IN the classroom, I was offered the job of school archivist. I had no professional qualifications and no experience. All I could offer was a wide knowledge of schools and education generally, a lifetime studying History, and a facility with words. Oh – and a great deal of apprehensive optimism (I was going to need every bit of that).

My life thereafter became a random mixture of trial and error, hope, experiment, and hand-to-mouthery. Of course I built up, as I went along, a certain amount of knowhow (I hesitate to call it 'expertise'), which had been quarried from surprises, mistakes, inadequacies, and the occasional piece of luck.

Early on, and perhaps fortunately, I groped my way to the truth that very few people on the premises knew much about an archive, or indeed were that interested. It was up to me to make everybody aware that the Archive (note the capital letter now) existed, and, having won a measure of their attention, to trumpet the virtues and value of an archive. So the publicity factor emerged, and I realised that this knack with words was going to be mighty useful.

Like Topsy, it growed, and I became adept at seizing any opportunity to spread the gospel. I wrote memos, I drafted articles for the press, I did public speaking, I took school assemblies, I produced reports for the school magazine, I gave lessons, I wrote scripts and scraps for concerts, theatre programmes, public event brochures – anything which offered the opportunity of what they call in the trade a 'plug'. I even got myself on the telly – once.

People would ask me for information about this and that. After I had researched and provided it several times, it occurred to me that there was a book waiting to be written. So I wrote it. Luckily, I found a publisher. Then, after a while, I thought, if I can write one book, I can write another. So I did that too. The addiction began to take hold. After a while, I gave in to writing a third.

That was several years ago now, and the craving has taken a grip again. But what should I write about? How much research would I have to do? Then it dawned on me: there it all was, under my nose – all those memos and articles and assemblies. Would they have any entertainment value?

I don't know, but I have enjoyed putting it all together. After all, it is a very lucky author who can write a book *knowing* that it will be a wow. For most of us humble mortals, it is a bit of a leap in the dark – a triumph of thick skin and furtive energy. I offer it therefore, as I said, with apprehensive optimism.

A final word: if you are particularly observant, you may notice a few examples of repetition. These pieces were written over a period of seventeen years, and inevitably I used the occasional good idea twice or even more. (That's one of the points of good ideas; they stand usage.) I decided to leave them in, because I did not want to upset the smoothness and momentum of the individual pieces, and this is, after all, only a miscellany, not a literary masterpiece.

## 2. Statement of Intent

How long have you lived in your present house? Ten years? Twenty? And how many people live there? Four? Five? Say six, with the cat. Think how much material you have accumulated about the past of that house and its six inhabitants in those ten or twenty years. And how interesting it is when you come across it.

Have you ever been up into your loft to look for something, and found yourself still there three quarters of an hour later because you have come across an old newspaper or a folder of fading photographs of Aunt Sarah and Uncle Charles taken on holiday fifty years ago? Well, exactly; you know what I mean.

Now – imagine a building with over 150 years of continuous occupation by over 8,000 people – with scores of cupboards, drawers, attics, barns, sheds, nooks and crannies.

A building that produces all sorts of material which people had not intended to keep, perhaps had not wanted to keep, or simply did not know they were keeping. To say nothing of all the official records, lists, catalogues, folders, files, minutes, albums which they thought *should* be kept.

It is the work of a school archivist – indeed of any archivist – to try and bring order to a collection like this, to make it intelligible to the present inhabitants, and to persuade those inhabitants that it is worth looking at.

Luckily most of us want, deep down, to know where we come from. We want to know what made us into what we are. So the past does matter; it helps us to make sense of our lives. And it is there; you cannot escape it and you cannot ignore it. You cannot get away from the past any more than you can pretend that your parents did not exist.

Knowing what is behind us helps up to face what is ahead of us. As President Chirac said at the commemoration of D-Day in 2004, 'There is no future without remembrance.'

Of course the past isn't everything; the present and the future matter very much. We want the pupils of West Buckland to look ahead, to take the world by storm, to reach up to the stars. But they also need to know where they come from.

The past and the Archive represent the school's roots. Without roots, nothing grows.

# 3. Up and Running

## A School in the Middle of Nowhere

WEST BUCKLAND SCHOOL REGULARLY takes in foreign pupils. Those who enter at sixth-form level usually have a fair command of English; those who come in earlier often have much less. So they need lessons – in English as a foreign language. The teacher of a group of Chinese twelve-year-olds once asked me to come in and give some simple lessons on the history of the school. That took care of the verbal side of it. Then she asked me to write a short piece which covered the same ground, using language and grammar which would be within their scope, and which could test their written English and comprehension. This was the result.

In 1852, a young priest called Joseph Brereton became the rector of West Buckland. He was one of eleven children of a priest in Norfolk, but, unlike most of his brothers and sisters, he did not enjoy good health. His lungs were weak. So he was educated at home until he was fifteen, and then he was sent to the famous Rugby School. He was a bright lad, and went on to Oxford University, but because of his poor health, he did not do as well as he had hoped in his exams. He could not become a university teacher, so he became a priest instead.

He worked in London at first, but the city was not kind to his lungs, so he looked for a job in a place where there was more fresh air. He found fresh air – plenty of it – in the small village of West Buckland, miles away from anywhere, in North Devon. He married Frances Martin, the 17-year-old daughter of another priest, and settled down in his new village. In the course of the next twenty-odd years, he fathered sixteen children. (What if his health had been strong?)

He found time for plenty of other things too, beside being a father and a priest. He was a keen horseman; he was a busy farmer; he set up, wrote, edited, and published a local magazine; he helped the village primary school; and he was on dozens of committees about absolutely everything.

In the course of his riding, writing, publishing, committee work, and so on, he met a young nobleman called Lord Ebrington, the son of the second Earl Fortescue, who lived at Castle Hill a few miles away. (The house, and the Fortescue family, are still there.) Brereton and Ebrington became close friends, and remained so for the rest of their lives.

It so happened that Ebrington had come to live in Devon because of *his* health. He had gone into politics in London, but he caught a very bad eye infection. In the end it forced him to retire, back to the family house in Filleigh. That was one coincidence.

The second coincidence was that both he and Brereton were interested in education. In the 1850's there was no national system of primary or secondary schools. Children from five to eleven went to the local village school if the church ran one, if they could afford it, and if their parents allowed them to go. A lot of working-class parents sent their children out to work as soon as possible, because they needed the money. A farm labourer in those days was paid about 65p. a week, which did not go far even with the much lower prices of the time.

There were not many secondary schools either. A lot of towns had grammar schools, and, dotted around the country, were the old and famous independent 'public' schools. But they all charged fees – in some cases very high ones. Nine ordinary children out of ten did not have a hope of getting in. Most of them had had a very poor primary education (or none at all), and so would not have been able to do the work. And of course their parents could not afford it.

Brereton wanted to do something for secondary education. He decided that the children of rich people were well looked after; there were plenty of public schools for them. The children of poor people could not afford the low fees of primary schools, most of them, so they certainly would not be paying the fees for secondary schools.

But a powerful *middle* class was growing up in Britain. Thanks to the many new inventions, factories, railways, farm machinery, and so on, more and more ordinary people were able to earn more money, if they were in the right place. They could live in better houses, buy better clothes, eat better food, own better furniture, drive in their own carriages, and make plans for the future. They no longer had to work hard simply to stay alive; they could work hard to have a better life. These people would be interested in sending their children (or at least their sons) to a school which would give a good education and allow them to get on even better than their parents had done.

So Brereton thought up a totally new idea – *secondary education for the middle classes.* The schools would offer simple boarding, practical teaching, and low fees. They would not teach old subjects like Latin and Greek, which was what the public schools did. They would teach new things like Maths and Science, which would be useful when the boys left school. There would also be the usual subjects like English, History, and Geography – maybe French or German, even Drawing if you paid extra. There would of course be religious education, but a boy would not be forced to believe strict Church rules. He would be shown the Christian life; he would be offered the Christian Faith; what he did with them was his own business.

Brereton also had ideas for girls' education, at a time when most people still thought that a girl's best place for learning was the home, where she learnt needlework, cookery, house management, good manners, and a little polite Christianity.

In many ways Brereton was a long away ahead of his time. But he was only a poor country priest. If he worked alone, he would get nowhere. This is where his new friend Ebrington came in. Ebrington was rich; he was powerful; he had been in Government work in London; he knew everybody. And – *and* – he was keen on education.

Between them they set up the West Buckland Farm and County School. It was started in November, 1858. They advertised, and persuaded three fathers in Bishop's Tawton (a village about ten miles away) to send their sons – James Waldon, Henry Dendle, and Henry Tyte. They raised a little money from investors. They appointed a young headmaster, Joseph Thompson, aged only twenty-one. Everything seemed to be coming along nicely, when they realised that there was a snag: they had some money; they had some pupils; they had a headmaster; the only thing they did not have was a school.

\* \* \* \* \* \*

A local farmer came to the rescue. A Mr. Miller had a farmhouse in Stoodleigh, just outside West Buckland. He allowed his house – or part of it – to be used as a temporary school. The parlour downstairs became the schoolroom, and a bedroom became the dormitory. For a few weeks, Mr. Miller's house *was* the West Buckland Farm and County School.

The farmhouse is still there, and members of the Miller family still live in it, and have sent their children to West Buckland right up until a few years ago. There is a plaque on the front gate recording the School's beginnings.

More pupils arrived, and in January, 1859 Brereton moved the School to Tideport, a farm he owned, also near the village. A barn became the schoolroom. Still more pupils came in, so a new wooden dormitory was built near the barn. It was opened on 24th May, Queen Victoria's fortieth birthday. Earl Fortescue offered to pay for it, and gave a prize for a young farmer who had given up farming for a year to attend the School. He was twenty-five. The Headmaster, Thompson, was twenty-two. It must the only time when a headmaster presented a prize to a pupil who was older than he was himself.

Before long, even the barn and the new dormitory were not enough, and some of the boys moved again to one of Fortescue's farms at Middle Hill, down the lane from the present School. But it was clear that the School could not go on moving from one farmhouse to another. They had to build something permanent.

Because of this success, Brereton and Ebrington were able to persuade more people to invest money in a new stone building. Ebrington provided a piece of land, on some rising ground about 650 feet above sea level, between the villages of East and West Buckland (he was the biggest landowner in the area). He offered to rent it to the School, and gave them the chance to buy it after five years. It stretched for eleven acres. (The School now has a hundred acres.) Ebrington's father, the second Earl, laid the foundation stone on 4$^{th}$ October, 1860. It can be seen on the wall to the left of one of the front entrances.

Most of the building is still there, except for the east end, which was destroyed by a fire in 1930. The Karslake Hall did not come till 1878, and the Memorial Hall was built after the fire.

A magazine called the *Illustrated London News* published an article about the opening, together with a picture. It estimated that the cost of the building would be 'about £2,000'.

Sadly, Earl Fortescue died only a few days before the opening of the School, and it was his son, Ebrington, who became the third Earl, who performed the opening ceremony.

Why was it called the 'Farm and County School'?

First, it was in farming country. Brereton had the idea of running the School as part school and part farm. The senior boys would be taught their lessons, and then would go out on to the farming land and put their lessons into practice. What they grew on the farm would be sold, and the profits of the sales would help to pay for the expenses of the School. In his dreams (and he was a great dreamer), Brereton may have had the idea that the School would one day be able to pay for itself. It never did. In fact, only a few years later, the 'farm' part of the School quietly died.

Why 'County'?

Another of Brereton's dreams was of a huge system of middle-class schools across the whole country. Schools like West Buckland. Each county would have several such schools, according to its size. This was why he called them 'county schools'. In the course of the next twenty or thirty years, he helped to set up county schools all over England – Somerset, Bedford, Gloucester, Hampshire, Sussex, Surrey, Durham, Suffolk, Norfolk. Most of them failed.

When the boys reached the age of about sixteen, he planned that they would go to county colleges. This didn't come to anything either. Brereton even got as far as setting up a special sort of advanced college for his county school boys in Cambridge University – Cavendish College. After about fifteen years that failed too.

But West Buckland did well. The new Headmaster, Joseph Thompson, was young and energetic, and the numbers grew steadily. He had been appointed without a degree. He was not a priest either. Nearly every headmaster of the public schools was a graduate of either Oxford or Cambridge, and he had a dog collar. Brereton wanted his school to be different. It was not going to be an expensive prison for the sons of gentlemen, where they learned Latin and Greek, the Bible, and very little else except bad habits like drinking, fighting, and bullying.

His boys would learn practical subjects – Arithmetic, Algebra, Geometry, Book-keeping, Surveying, Political Economy, Land Management – besides the usual ones like English, History, Geography, and of course the Bible. The fees would be low. An early prospectus said that the fees for a year would be twenty-five guineas. A guinea was £1.10. So twenty-five guineas was £27.50, for a whole year's teaching and boarding – which was low even by the standards of the time. Soon after he opened the senior school, he also opened a Prep. department, where the fees for day boys would be only four guineas – a year.

Pupils from the School were entered for the new public examinations which had been set up at Oxford and Cambridge universities in 1858 – the ancestor of GCSE. West Buckland came top of the national league three years running.

The School was popular and successful. Within ten years the numbers had climbed to over a hundred. It became quite famous as the first school of its kind in England. Other schools imitated it. Journalists wrote about it. Public school headmasters visited it. The author of *Tom Brown's Schooldays*, the most famous school story of the nineteenth century, came one year to present the prizes. Fortescue persuaded the Archbishop of Canterbury himself to come down for Speech Day in 1863. The Devon County School was on its way.

## Brereton's Creed

BURIED WITHIN THE REVD. Brereton's voluminous writings was this encapsulation of his philosophy of education, and showed that, for a nineteenth-century Anglican clergyman, he displayed a staggeringly broad view of how to educate children. This is how he summarised the ethos of his new school:

**'It is connected with no party, identified with no sect, dedicated to no saint, and signalized [sic] by no symbol except the motto "Read and Reap".'**

Cards on the table. It could have come out of the twenty-first century.

## The Religious Foundation

NO SCHOOL IN THE nineteenth century dared to announce that it intended to omit religious instruction from the curriculum. (Perhaps very few are so frank even today.)

What made Brereton so rare in 1858 is that he declared that no *denominational* beliefs were going to be thrust down his pupils' throats. These were the days – indeed this was the century – when more ink was spilt, and more invective hurled, over the topic of the place of religion in education than over almost any other matter a politician could imagine.

[Where quotations are given, they come from the Revd. J.L. Brereton's own writings, unless otherwise stated.]

The overwhelming impression given by Brereton is that he envisaged a 'broad' atmosphere in both schools and colleges which he had a hand in founding or organising. In his discussion of his county college, for instance, he estimated that 'two-thirds would avowedly be members of the National Church, and the rest would nearly all belong to one of those nonconformist bodies which have, next to the National Church, a traditional hold on the confidence of English families. A small minority might belong to the Roman Catholics and the Unitarians, and perhaps a few individuals might seek admission whose parents would not make profession of the Christian faith.' (*County Education, 1874*, p. 62.)

For this reason, he proposed to align his system of secondary schools with the county, not with the diocese, for fear that it might look like favouritism towards one particular brand of Christian belief. (*County Education, 1874*, p. 46.)

The county school should be run by a layman – 'the school should have a secular basis (i.e. be under a lay master), with so much of religious teachings, e.g. Scriptural Knowledge, as would be undisputed, with school prayers for all, and attendance at public worship, subject to the wish of parents; while a free opening (so far as the discipline of the school would allow), should be given to the special religious instruction of such public representatives of religious bodies as the directors of the school would sanction, and those bodies acting under the control of enlightened public opinion would be likely to nominate.' (*County Education, 1861*, p. 18.)

Brereton claimed that he had found acceptance for this arrangement – 'The school, it was well known, was started and encouraged by a clergyman of the Church of England; but placing full confidence in the qualification of the head master for all ordinary instruction, including Scriptural Knowledge, I had confined my own interference to special services in my church, for which I found that in the few cases of Dissenting parents, there was rather gratitude expressed than any suspicion or jealousy.' (*County Education, 1861*, p. 18.)

Lord Fortescue endowed a chaplaincy 'to be connected with a service in the Parish Church of East Buckland'. Though he made the first appointment himself, he 'entrusted it for the future to the trustees of the school, subject to the approval of the incumbent of the parish'. 'Our school, therefore,' said Brereton, 'without being in any offensive sense to Dissenters a Church School, but having the wider basis of a county character, and a lay master, has that provision which suitable to the fact that the great majority of the pupils are, and are likely to be, members of the Church of England, yet neither prevents Dissenters, by any offensive exclusiveness, from sending their sons to the school; nor deprives them of the opportunity, if they should desire other instruction than that of the masters and the endowed chaplain, of providing it through regular communication with the authorities.' Then he cannot resist adding the pious, even smug, hope that 'that communication will not be made so long as the master and the chaplain are animated with the true sense of their position, and do not forget that they are, towards the boys, the trusted representatives of the parents'. [And he may well have been right.]

Finally, there is the comment of Frederick Temple, Bishop of Exeter, which Brereton proudly quotes on p. 37 of his 1874 book on *County Education*:-

'As far as I have observed in speaking to a great many people of very different opinions, and very different parties, on this question, there is no school in the country which conciliates to itself a larger amount of favourable opinion, and at once disarms hostility more entirely, than this school at West Buckland. I believe that the course here pursued has, at any rate, succeeded in this respect, that it is confessed on all hands that the religious instruction given is really religious, and, on the other hand, I never yet heard of any one who could complain that there was any interference with the rights of conscience whatever.'

Frederick Temple (1821-1902) was an ex-HMI, an ex-headmaster (of Rugby and Kneller Hall), and a future Bishop of London and Archbishop of Canterbury, so his judgment must have carried a great deal of authority.

Which just about seems to wrap it up. Brereton's (and Thompson's) regime was to be one of broad-based Christianity, which was to open doors as well to nonconformists, Catholics, even secularists and Unitarians (which latter often incurred the greatest odium from their so-called Christian brothers). At the same time, they kept enough long-term control to head off any future possible threat of over-zealous tails wagging the dog. They made no secret either of their beliefs or of their desire for toleration, so no sectarian or freethinker could afterwards complain that the ideals of the school were not made clear.

In this respect, therefore, the School was light years ahead of its time.

Put that together with its ethos of middle-class education, modest fees, and modern curriculum, and we have an establishment of a remarkably pioneering character, a leader of national significance in several fields. Not bad going for a little country school in the back of beyond.

> Christianity of the Samaritan rather than that of the Pharisee. . . .

## 4. People

THESE PIECES (AND MANY others later in the book) were composed to be said out loud – to an audience of pupils, of both sexes and any age between eleven and eighteen.

A warning therefore: you will find many examples of a style which, to a perfectionist, might grate if one were taking it straight off the page – which of course you are. Effective written and spoken English are not necessarily the same. So please make allowances, and try to remember that these pieces are printed almost entirely from the spoken word. Think of the circumstances: the speaker up there on the stage and the distance between him and the listeners; the value of intonation, of variation of pace, of dramatic pause, even of repetition; changes of speed and volume – and more. They all contribute to the overall effect.

A young colleague once said to me that she got the impression, listening to me, that I was saying the words for the very first time, from a random collection of notes. Not so; every word was read. Moreover, there had been many drafts and re-drafts. They were designed, and my delivery was designed, to make it *sound* as if I was saying it for the first time. It needs work, and craft.

## The Revd. W. Watson

THIS SCHOOL IS 143 years old. In the course of that time, a lot of documents and pictures have accumulated about the history of the School. About three or four years ago, the Headmaster decided that it would be a good idea to collect all this material in one place, and to appoint a person specially to look after it. I am that person.

I should like to attempt three things – to give you some information, maybe to surprise you a just a little, and finally to offer a small challenge.

A boarding school like this – tucked away in the moorland countryside in the back of beyond – is often compared to a kind of enormous family. Families living in large houses in the back of beyond for a long time collect ancestors, and they put portraits of those ancestors on the walls – usually up and down a large staircase. Well, behind this hall is a large staircase. We don't have old ancestors, but we do have old headmasters. If you have kept your eyes open on that staircase, you will have seen a picture of one of them – Revd. Harries, who was Headmaster for 27 years. There is an engraved plaque about the very first Headmaster, Revd. Thompson, who was Head for 30 years. I shall come back to these portraits in a moment.

It may not surprise you to be told that, in 143 years, we have had 15 headmasters, including Mr. Vick [HM from 1997 to 2016]. But I think it might surprise you to be told that the first Headmaster, Mr. Thompson, was appointed at the age of 21. That was in 1858. In 1864, two more teachers were appointed – a Mr. Watson, who was barely over twenty, and a Mr. Thomas, who was nineteen. Well, you may say, young assistant teachers have to start somewhere. True. But these newcomers were not young probationers under the watchful eye of an experienced head of department. Watson became Second Master, and Thomas became Third Master. So we have a school of nearly 100 boys in the mid- to late 1860's, which was being run by three young men whose average age was about 24.

Watson went on to become the second Headmaster in 1867. The first Head, Thompson, went up to Cambridge University to read for a degree in Maths, and Watson was made Acting Head while he was away.

So, at twenty-four, Watson was teaching a full timetable, and running the School. At the same time, he decided to study in his spare time for a degree in Chemistry – and passed.

And he still wasn't finished. He wanted to be a head in his own right, and most headmasters in those days were clergymen. So he also studied for holy orders – while he was teaching, being a boarding school housemaster, an acting headmaster and reading for a chemical degree. Oh – and just before the end of all that he went courting as well. He married the niece of the priest at the village of Charles. Very successful marriage too – they had eleven children. He also became curate at East Buckland Church.

Now we come back to the family ancestors I was talking about. I thought it might be a nice idea to have a picture of each of those fourteen old headmasters – possibly up and down the staircase – just like those family portraits I mentioned. I have pictures of all of them – except one. Watson.

We had a picture once, but it was only lent by a member of his family, and was obviously given back. But I have the covering note that came with it. It came from Hilda Watson, his daughter, and there is an address. I have written to this address, and have been told that the house, in Exmouth, is now the site of a block of flats.

How then do I find a picture? This is where the challenge bit comes in.

We have the evidence of Watson's family and his wife's, which could possibly be traced by means of the Internet. Also on the Internet are the complete records of the censuses of 1881 and 1901. Watson later became Headmaster, in his own right, of a school in Norfolk – also founded by Revd. Brereton, who founded this one. If there is anyone out there who likes spending time scouring the Internet, and who relishes a chase, let them have a go at finding Revd. William Watson, who died in 1889. (There are death certificate records too.) What I would like is a picture – an authenticated picture.

Supply that picture, and we can put another family ancestor on the staircase – and, beside it, a tiny little plaque telling all about you who found it. Your own immortality.

If you are interested, come and see me – on Tuesday or Thursday mornings, in my office, just beside the Bursar's office. Get me a picture of William Watson, and I can offer you a place on the wall among the ancestors – for all time.

We are still waiting for this picture.

## William Arthur Knight

How do you make up your mind about a person? How do you judge a human being?

Just over a year ago, a gentleman came to the Archive Office to talk to me about his father, who had been a pupil at the School, and to give me a School Crest that his father had received. There is a copy in the main Entrance Hall. His name – father's, that is – was Arthur Pearce, and he had left in 1908. 1908. This man's father – not his grandfather; his father – had left the School 95 years ago.

The Headmaster during most of Arthur Pearce's time here was called Knight – William Arthur Knight. His photograph is on the wall above the staircase to the Memorial Hall. Take a look at him next time you are passing, and see if you agree with me. I think he gives the impression of being a little – um – severe – cold, steely eyes; a flat, frigid sort of expression; and a heavy, slightly droopy moustache. Oh – and there was also a story that his rule was so bleak and wintry that the School was known as The City of Dreadful Knight.

What I found out from Arthur Pearce's son did nothing to change this first impression. Arthur Pearce, apparently, used to tell his son stories about Mr. Knight's regular use of the cane. When he (Mr. Knight) was in a bigger temper than usual, little flecks of foam used to appear at the corners of his mouth; he would lean forward, and vow, through gritted teeth, 'I'll flog yer!' Worse still, Mrs. Knight was a flogger too. We all know that corporal punishment was common practice in the early twentieth century (Mr. Knight became Headmaster in 1900), but it would seem that he pushed it to extremes. It is quite possible that it was the reason for a concerted effort by many parties associated with the School to try and squeeze him out of the Headship. Which, in the end, they did.

So far, then, we have a clear picture of – at best a harsh disciplinarian, at worst a sadistic bully. But the rest of the record shows rather more than that.

He was a comparatively young man, for a start. Indeed, he became engaged shortly after he took office, and married shortly after that, and fathered two children, all during a six-year tenure of the headship. So was his bullying a symptom of a lack of confidence due to inexperience?

Then again, when he took over, the numbers in the School had fallen to 31. 31 – in a set of buildings designed to accommodate 180. Think of the worry and stress of trying to build the numbers back up again. And he succeeded too – got them up to the eighties. Nearly trebled in six years. Not bad – for a hateful bully.

He worked hard. He taught Maths – not a popular subject at the best of times. One Inspectors' Report recorded that his work-load was too heavy for a headmaster; he spent 27 hours a week in the classroom – which did not allow him enough time to keep his finger on the pulse of the School. How many headmasters teach for 27 hours a week today? How many *teachers* now spend 27 hours a week in the classroom?

In amongst this fearsome programme of instruction and administration, he found time for cricket and football; we have photos of him in the centre of school teams. He was a good player too.

He also built the first proper swimming pool – the one which is now covered over. He built a cricket pavilion. Still there. He began the School Reading and Debating Society – which, now renamed the Phoenix Society, will celebrate its hundredth anniversary this month [2003]. He set up a Rifle Club. He built Science laboratories.

Bully – maybe. Flogger – unquestionably. But think of the strain on a comparatively young man, trying to rescue this tiny, poverty-stricken school in the back of beyond. And boys were no more likely to be angels then they are now.

In 1901, the School magazine, the *Register*, contained an entry to the effect that the Headmaster had just become a father, and duly congratulated him. It also carried another paragraph which offered its sympathy to the Headmaster on the death of his son, only three days old. **Both entries were printed on the same page**. And this man, while having to console a grieving wife, and suffering the pain of the death of his firstborn son, had to go straight from a funeral in East Buckland churchyard, back to his work of rescuing a struggling school, and teaching another 27 hours a week.

Arthur Pearce was no doubt right in saying that Mr. Knight was a flogger. He told the truth. But it was not the whole truth. Headmasters – indeed all human beings – are much more than the memories of a single schoolboy.

## Brereton has an Idea

JOSEPH LLOYD BRERETON WAS born in 1822, one of eleven children of a country vicar in Norfolk. Because his health was not strong, he was educated largely at home, and did not go to proper school till he was fifteen. Then his father packed him off to Rugby, where the Headmaster was Dr. Thomas Arnold, a man with a legendary name in 19th century education.

At first he hated it, but when he got into the Sixth Form, he found he liked books and enjoyed learning. He was a bright lad, and destined for an academic career. He duly went up to Oxford, but poor health prevented him doing himself justice in the exams., and he settled for becoming a clergyman instead. He served as curate in Norwich and London, but his health let him down again – his lungs apparently were 'weak', as they said in those days – and he had to move to a healthier location – Paignton. There he kept himself going by giving private lessons.

Then in about 1852 he did three things which were to mould the rest of his life. First, he did some sucking up to important people, and was able to obtain the post of rector at West Buckland Church. Second, he got married, to the daughter of another clergyman. Her name was Frances – oddly the name of Brereton's own mother (food for thought there). She was seventeen; he was thirty. She was to bear him sixteen children, of whom eleven reached maturity.

Thirdly, he struck up a lifelong friendship with the son of the second Earl Fortescue, who became the third Earl on the death of his father in 1861. Each discovered that the other was extremely interested in education. Castle Hill, the Fortescue family home, was only a few miles away from Brereton's rectory; it is still there. So are the Fortescues. They discovered too that their respective talents fitted each other perfectly. Brereton had the ideas, the charm, the drive, the energy; Fortescue had the money, the connections, the clout – he knew absolutely everybody.

So what did they cook up? They cooked up the West Buckland Farm and County School, that's what they did. (And that is a whole assembly in itself.) They were so mad keen to get started – well, Brereton was; Fortescue was a bit more cautious – that by the end of 1858 they had raised some money, appointed a headmaster, collected some pupils – three, to be precise (and we know their names) – only to realise that they didn't yet have a school. For a few weeks they had to use a local farmhouse. That is still there too. The parlour was the classroom and the bedroom was the dormitory. They had two more temporary homes nearby before the first permanent buildings were set up – where they remain, right in the heart of the School. The second Earl Fortescue laid the foundation stone just before he died.

This is typical of Brereton. He would go rushing ahead, spending money and devising yet more elaborate schemes, and Fortescue would come along behind, complaining about the lack of planning and the huge bills.

One cannot go into detail here, but – just to give you some idea of Brereton's way of doing things – besides West Buckland, he set up, or was connected with setting up, schools in Somerset, Hampshire, Shropshire, Gloucestershire, Bedford, Norfolk, Suffolk, Surrey, and Durham. At least six of these failed. He set up a new Cambridge college; that failed. He set up an organisation for the education of girls – he was very fair-minded, and believed that girls should receive the same opportunities as boys – and that failed too.

The trouble was usually finance – or the lack of it. Brereton always went into elaborate details about his schools, and used miles of figures to 'prove' that they could not fail, but they usually did. But such was his charm, such was his energy, such was his obvious enthusiasm, that he conjured money out of a never-ending list of celebrities, including dukes and earls, even the Prince of Wales. I have read some of his writings, and, believe me, he is very persuasive. Even across the chasm of the years, you can still feel the tug on your cheque book. If you had been there, you can see yourself putting your hand in your pocket.

He spent fortunes – mostly other people's. Fortescue continued to complain, and they had numerous rows about it. But Brereton's charm usually patched it up, and Fortescue paid out yet again. He, Brereton, travelled thousands of miles on the new railways – weak lungs and all. He was actually injured in a bad train crash in 1882. He was responsible for a new station being built at Filleigh for the pupils of his school; he even gave a party for the navvies who built it.

He was also involved in setting up the first system of nation-wide examinations – the ancestor of GCSE. He pioneered the idea of education for the middle classes. He championed the education of girls, perhaps because he had seven daughters of his own. He believed in religious education being tolerant of other shades of belief besides the Church of England. Many of his ideas were way ahead of his time.

In his way, he was a great man. But, like many great men, he was absolutely impossible. For example, his own personal debts were so large that his family spent nearly fifty years paying them off. He didn't like his daughters getting married; they had to stay at home and help with his 'great work'. Only two got away – one of them married the first Headmaster, Thompson.

But remember that, amongst all the mistakes, all the faults, the failures, the infuriating traits of character, he also had one great success – West Buckland – us. Without Joseph Lloyd Brereton, we would not be here.

## The Four Houses

LIKE MOST PUBLIC SCHOOLS (and grammar schools for that matter, and no doubt many others), West Buckland operates on a 'house system'. The pupil body is divided into three, or four, or six houses (or whatever). It makes numbers more manageable; it provides a framework of athletic competition (if you are going to have team games or individual contests, you have to strive against somebody); and it offers a sort of nursery for those whose talent will later allow them to represent the school; it offers a channel of healthy rivalry; and it is another means of building the quality of loyalty. One way and another, it is reckoned to be a pretty good thing.

In the early days of the school, there were very few pupils, and they slept in just two dormitories. These dormitories were given names, for sheer convenience; they were Brereton and Courtenay. Brereton, obviously, after the founder, the Revd. JLB. [See above.] Courtenay was the family name of the Earls of Devon, and more than one earl has been a school benefactor over the years. About fifty years later, an energetic headmaster decided to follow in the steps of the more fashionable public schools, and re-classified them as 'houses'. Shortly afterwards, growing numbers allowed the creation of a third house, Fortescue (named, equally obviously, after Brereton's friend and fellow-pioneer, Earl Fortescue.) Finally, continuing growth of numbers allowed the creation of fourth house; in 1918, Grenville house was born, named after the famous sea-dog, who hailed from Devon. I don't know whether this is common practice but the tradition has grown up of referring to each house by means of the definite article – not 'Brereton and Fortescue' but 'the Brereton' and 'the Fortescue'.

Having 'done' an assembly about Brereton, it occurred to me that I could have more assembly ammunition with the names of the other three. And here they are.

## The Courtenays Survive Everything

THE FIRST COURTENAY HOUSE was not a house; it was a bedroom. Well, a dormitory if you insist. When the permanent School buildings were set up in 1861, there were to be two dormitories. They were to be called Brereton and Courtenay.

Brereton, obviously, because the whole idea of the School sprang from the fertile imagination of the Revd. J.L. Brereton. It was Brereton who gave the School its aim – to provide education for the middle classes. But why Courtenay?

Because Brereton knew that aims and ideas were not enough. The world would not listen to him unless he had people on his side who were important. He wanted a 'big name'. How about the Earl of Devon – whose name was Courtenay?

In the Devon of 1858, names didn't come any bigger than Courtenay. Though, looking at its history, one wonders why. The family mortality rate was truly astounding. Luckily there were an awful lot of them. There needed to be; they showed genius for getting into trouble. Just listen to this – and this is a shortened version.

Apparently the Courtenay family was documented in Normandy *before* 1066. That is nearly a thousand years. They were, it seems, into everything. The Norman Conquest, obviously. Like all respectable medieval noble families, they sent members to the Crusades. Three of them became Count of Edessa – roughly Syria today. One died as a result of a mine collapsing on him. Another was captured, blinded, and died in prison. Another Courtenay continued the tradition of sticky ends by getting himself killed at the siege of Jerusalem in 1187; apparently a piece of the wall fell on him. There was a much-married lady called Agnes Courtenay, who notched up four husbands, and various other 'relationships'. And then – and then – in the thirteenth century, luck turned a bit. Three Courtenays became, one after the other – I kid you not – Emperor of Constantinople. The last one was expelled, admittedly. But Emperor of Constantinople!

Another branch of the family – the one which came over with William the Conqueror, made its mark on the map of Devon. Look carefully, and you will find Sutton Courtenay, Wootton Courtenay, and Sampford Courtenay. Then I have to skip a bit, till another Courtenay was created Earl of Devon in 1335.

*Nearly off the Record*

It was after that that the Courtenays began to get into real trouble. No fewer than three of them managed to get themselves executed or killed in battle during the Wars of the Roses. They made such a good job of this family suicide that the whole senior line died out.

There was, however, a member of a junior branch of the family – Sir Edward Courtenay – who had chosen the right side to support – Henry VII. Henry re-created the Earldom of Devon. So the Courtenays were in business again.

Then the next Earl, Sir William, went and married a Yorkist, and the King was a Lancastrian. It cost him a spell in the Tower, but at least he escaped the block. His son Henry, however, did not learn the lesson of history, got involved in a rebellion, and lost his head in 1539 – courtesy of Henry VIII. His only son, another Edward, nearly made it to the top, because he was once considered as a possible husband for the Queen, Mary – Bloody Mary. Hardly an enviable status. However, he chose to get mixed up with another rebellion, was sent to the Tower, then got kicked out of England, and ended his days in Italy in 1556, with no heir. So the 2nd earldom was dead.

The Courtenays – what was left of them – retired to their seat at Powderham Castle, and for the next two or three hundred years kept their heads down and kept their heads on. They built up their castle and their fortunes – often by well-judged marriages. They were rewarded by being made Earls of Devon again, in 1831. The third creation.

In 1858 the Revd. Brereton was looking for a posh name to put on his company's prospectuses, and for a wealthy supporter to invest some money. What better choice, what more notorious name, than Courtenay? So Brereton set out to charm the Earl of Devon. And he was a great charmer. The charm worked. The Earl duly coughed up, and lent his support to this peculiar school – for the 'middle classes' (I wonder what the Earl thought of that) – in the back of beyond in a village nobody had ever heard of.

And when Brereton told him that it was proposed to name the second dormitory 'Courtenay', I wonder what he thought of *that*. Umpteenth Earl of Devon – descended from a thousand years of Norman nobles, famous medieval malefactors, castle proprietors, Counts of Edessa, and Emperors of Constantinople – and he was going to be 'honoured' by having a bedroom of schoolboys named after him.

## **Fortescue Lends a Hand**

THIS SCHOOL OWES ITS existence to a coincidence, and it is all to do with bad lungs and bad eyesight. I have told you about the Revd. Brereton, the School's founder. He came to Devon because of his health; his lungs were weak. The bracing air would be good for them. In the course of his priestly duties he met the man who would become Earl Fortescue on the death of his father in 1861 – let us for simplicity call him 'Fortescue'. Fortescue had been heavily involved in politics when he was young. But he contracted severe ophthalmia (an infection of the eye), which led to the loss of sight in it. He gave up politics, and retired to the family seat at Castle Hill, in Filleigh. Brereton and Fortescue met, as I said, and struck up a friendship which lasted all the rest of their lives. Out of this friendship was born West Buckland School – the fruit of weak lungs and a diseased eye.

Brereton brought to the project the energy, the drive, the ideas; Fortescue provided the connections, the clout, the class. He also provided the land; he rented 11 acres to the School, with the option to buy it in five years' time for £466. (The School campus now covers about 100 acres.)

He did more than that. He provided the money for a school chaplaincy; he set up a Fortescue scholarship for poorer boys; he began the tradition of the Fortescue Medal. This was to be awarded to a boy of the highest merit (no girls in the School then). The tradition still remains; the Fortescue Medal is still presented (and by no means every year) to boys or girls who, by their efforts both inside and outside the classroom, have brought distinction to themselves and to the School. It is the highest award in the School's gift. A few of you, sitting down there, will step up one day to receive it; when you do, perhaps you will remember this assembly.

In case you should think that the Fortescue family are famous only because they are associated with West Buckland School, let me fill you in. Remember the Courtenays, whose family went right back to the 11th century? Well, the Fortescues can claim the same. One of them fought beside William the Conqueror at the Battle of Hastings. But that was not all. Family tradition says that during the course of the battle he saved William's life, not once, but three times, by placing himself between William and his enemies. By being, if you like, a sort of shield. Very brave of him. You'll see the point of this in a minute. The Latin word for 'shield' is '*scutum*'. The Latin word for 'brave' is '*forte*'. So a 'brave shield' is '*forte scutum*'. '*Forte scutum.*' Hence 'Fortescue'.

Anyway, William was very grateful, and gave the man some land, and the Fortescues have never looked back.

When the School was nearly fifty years old, in 1907, a new headmaster was appointed. His name was Ernest Harries. 'Ernie' to all the boys. He was a man of great gifts, and before long he was raising the numbers of pupils. The original two houses – Brereton and Courtenay – it was decided, were not enough. There would be a third house. What more obvious name than 'Fortescue'? By the outbreak of the First World War, they were competing on level terms with the other two.

But remember that everything was on a much smaller scale then than it is now. Say about 120-odd – altogether. So, if there were three houses, that makes about 40 for each. Take two cricket teams – senior and junior – 22 – and over half the boys played cricket for their house. If rugby had been played then, three quarters of the entire school would have played rugby for their house. Take the *Exmoor*. There were three races – senior, under 15, and under 13. Take away the very smallest boys to act as markers; it meant that only about 10 boys from each house competed in their respective races. People say things about the 'family' atmosphere of the School now; how much more that must have been true in, say, 1910 or 1911, when Fortescue House was invented. And when they were all boarders. How much more it must have hurt when 56 old boys were killed in the First World War. Out of a school roll of less than 120.

Well – Fortescue. The family of Fortescue have continued to take an interest in the fortunes of the School. They have come to the rescue – several times – when the school finances were in a bad way. Every speech day, every big event, every big celebration – a Fortescue was there – six generations of them. The Fortescue family have had a member on the Board of Governors ever since the School began. A few years ago, I was talking to Lady Margaret Fortescue's daughter, Lady Arran, who has taken over as a governor from her mother. I asked whether Lady Arran's own daughter would continue the family tradition. 'Oh, yes,' she said. 'She has been told.'

## Grenville gets into Trouble again

THE GRENVILLE IS, so far as I can make out, the only house of the four which has a birth certificate. It appears on page 69 of the School magazine for November, 1918. The magazine, by the way, was called the *Register* then. It began in 1863, and continued until it was reorganised, enlarged, and re-named in 1998. Well, the Grenville and the *Register*.

On page 69, November, 1918, it said, 'A new House has. . . . come into existence.' That's it. No reason. No explanation. No account of how. 'A new House has come into existence.' Just like that. A sort of Big Bang. Or, if you are a member of the other three houses, a Little Bang.

So I thought, how did it come about? There must have been some discussion somewhere at a pretty high level. What about the Minutes of the Governors' Meetings? I looked them up. In the whole of 1918, how many Governors' Meetings were there? One – on 5$^{th}$ July. Well, only one recorded. Perhaps the fact that there was a war on had something to do with it. Anyway, what was in the Minutes?

A list of those who attended, naturally. One of them, incredibly, was the Revd. Joseph Thompson. Why incredibly? Because he was the first Headmaster, appointed in 1858. Now retired of course. But – he was still alive – in 1918 – sixty years later!

Then there was some stuff about numbers of pupils. The total was now 137. The Headmaster, Harries, had hoicked it up from about 80 in 1907. But he said nothing about creating a new house. Instead, he gave details of the numbers of ex-pupils serving in the Army – about 300 apparently. Two had won the DSO, 12 had got the MC. 37 had been killed. The total of deaths went up to 56 in the end.

There was a bit about the water supply. Apparently 'the water difficulty still existed'. No set of Governors' Minutes was complete without a reference to drains or water or sewage or wells or septic tanks or cesspits.

Apart from that, and a couple of votes of thanks, and a wedding present for the Headmaster – he was 50! – that was about it.

So what happened? It looks as if Harries, the Head, sat down one day and said to himself, '137 pupils – that's too many for three houses; we ought to start a fourth.' So he did. And there it was in the *Register*. I think he was the Editor as well, so he could put in what he liked. We have 500 pupils today [more now], and nobody has suggested creating a fifth house. Interesting.

The actual choice of the name Grenville was not a surprise. Grenville was a famous Devon name. There were several Grenvilles who got themselves into the history books, but the most famous, and obviously the one Harries had in mind, was Sir Richard Grenville, one of Queen Elizabeth I's gang of sea-dogs. Who were the sea-dogs? They were the sea-captains who made life miserable for the Spanish during the second half of the sixteenth century – raiding, pirating, illegal trading, capturing treasure ships, and generally being a pain in the neck for the best part of thirty years. And don't think they were true-blue, boy-scout heroes just because they were English. Oh, no. For the most part, they were ambitious, arrogant, ruthless, ornery, cussed individualists who were often as much embarrassment to the Queen as they were to the Spanish.

And it is possible to make a case that our Grenville was the most ambitious, arrogant, ruthless, ornery, and cussed of the lot. Just to show you – in 1591, he and his admiral, Howard, ran into an enormous squadron of Spanish warships sent to guard another treasure fleet which Grenville and Howard were trying to ambush. Howard decided that the odds were too great, and ordered a retreat. Well, he was outnumbered over four to one. Grenville, who was late because of getting sick sailors off the shore, found himself last to leave. Disobeying orders to go the long way round and avoid trouble, he thought he could slip between the two halves of the Spanish fleet. He couldn't. Hemmed in on all sides, grappled to a standstill, he fought off the Spanish for fifteen hours. His ship, the *Revenge*, sank two enemy ships, disabled two more, and caused hundreds of casualties. Severely wounded himself, he decided to blow up his ship rather than surrender. But for once he did not get his own way. His sailors – only about 25 remained on their feet – had him transferred to a Spanish ship, where he died three days later. The *Revenge*, what was left of her, was wrecked in a storm two or three days after that.

Honour and glory, maybe, immortality even. After all, here you are – the Grenville. But he could have saved all that trouble, and saved his ship, and saved his men, if he had done as he was told. What do you think? Was it worth it?

## 5. Getting written about

Items offered to the press have the obvious use and purpose of getting West Buckland in people's minds and keeping it there. What we call today 'maintaining the profile'. The trouble is that they have to be written in a particular style, which the newspapers demand. If you didn't offer it like that, they would rewrite the piece to make it conform to what they wanted. Such a style would not sit well here, so I have made the necessary changes, which ensure, I hope, that the pieces don't jar in any way.

## First Steps into the Past

WHEN I WAS APPOINTED to be School Archivist, there was no Archive; I had to go and look for it. I found it in all sorts of places. The likely ones were, of course, cupboards, drawers, lofts, and cubby-holes (in which a building like West Buckland abounds). The less likely ones were luggage chests, neglected office shelves, laboratories, cadet huts, barns, and once, quite literally, under the floorboards. Other material came trickling in from old boys, or rather from the descendants of old boys, who had found some of grandpa's bits and pieces that they had not known were there.

What did I get? Lots. Books, naturally, often very good ones – old prizes from long-past speech days. Old text-books, even old exercise books. Files, pupil lists, programmes, cadet training schedules, prospectuses, reports, accounts of inspectors' visits, old boys' dinner menus, governors' minutes, school magazines (which go right back to 1863), share certificates (the school began as a public company). Oh – and I don't know what.

Photographs, equally naturally. Thousands. Many, particularly the very old ones, in a staggeringly good state of survival. I took one to a shop in Barnstaple to have a copy made, and the man didn't believe me when I told him that the original had been taken in 1885. I was able to prove it by pointing out the first headmaster in the middle of the group, and we had other photos of Mr. Thompson, so the man had to accept my word – albeit with his mouth open.

Physical things too: early Fortescue medals [the highest award in the school's gift], old tools and gadgets (whose use has provoked a good deal of speculation), drums and bugles, even the leopard-skin used by the bass drummer. Some of the blazers are over seventy years old, and still wearable, though no self-respecting boy would be seen dead in them today. But two members of staff cheerfully wore a couple for the end-of-term sports day. So they were that good.

Then there are the curiosities – the unexpected ones, which often defy classification. For example, the first-ever balance-sheet of the Devon County School (West Buckland's early name), which showed that the Headmaster's salary in 1860 was £150 – a year.

There is a splendid menu and programme for the Devon County School Old Boys' Association annual dinner from 1907. The Edwardians ate well: there are eight courses listed. Listed in French too, *without* an English translation. So the Old Boys were presumably well educated as well as hungry. Not only that; they expected to be entertained too. There were twenty-three separate items, including five speeches and ten songs. God knows what time they staggered into the street outside the Holborn Restaurant.

The dinners were good value too. The 1937 Dinner at the Trocadero Restaurant in Piccadilly cost a huge fifty-two and a half pence – evening dress and all.

We have the actual letter from the War Office, dated March, 1909, authorising the then Headmaster, the Revd. Harries, to set up a cadet force, or Officer Training Corps, as it was called then. (You couldn't have pupils of a public school – even one buried away in the wilds of Devon – being called mere 'cadets'; everyone knew that they were of course going to become officers.) A grant was made for each cadet of £1.50. Harries, though a priest, eagerly doffed his dog-collar and put on his Sam Browne. Muscular Christianity, you see. Charles Kingsley, a Devon celebrity, would have approved.

The most interesting part of all this was when you were able not only to see what they wrote and what they looked like, but when you found something which gave you a glimpse into their minds.

For example, on 28th July, 1882, a pupil called Frederick Adams wrote home to his mother. The letterhead is printed in Gothic script (red), and the paper folds into a tiny envelope barely four inches by two. The handwriting is beautiful copperplate. And so formal. Not 'Hullo, Mum' but 'Dear Mother'. And it ends not 'Love, Fred' but 'I am yours Affectionately F. Adams'.

## It Should Take Some Beating

On 24th May, 1859, there was a meeting to celebrate the opening of a new dormitory at the School – which was known in those days as the West Buckland Farm and County School. Earl Fortescue made a speech of congratulation, and gave a special prize to a young farmer of twenty-five, who had taken a whole year out, away from his farm, in order to study at the School. That's the first record: does any other school have documentary evidence of a secondary school pupil over the age of twenty-five at all, much less one winning a prize?

Next, the Headmaster, Mr. J.H. Thompson, had been appointed the previous year, at the age of twenty-one. Which might qualify for a second record. At the very least there cannot be many headmasters who were appointed at that age. So when the opening of the new dormitory was celebrated in 1859, he was still only twenty-two.

So, can any school claim a speech day at which a pupil prizewinner was three years older than the Headmaster?

## League Champions

LEAGUE TABLES ARE NOTHING new in schools. Well, they are nothing new at West Buckland. There is evidence that they existed, and were boasted about, in the 1860's. So there is nothing new under the sun.

At that time, the school regularly entered candidates for what were known as the Oxford and Cambridge Local Examinations, or the 'Locals' as they were familiarly, and much more easily, called. It was the forerunner of GCSE, of the earlier 'O' Levels, and the even earlier School Certificate. In those days the school was an independent company, with directors instead of governors. In the Directors' Report of 1867, it was proudly announced that the number of boys who had received certificates was higher than at any school in the whole of England – for the third year in succession.

A later document declared that West Buckland's total number of certificates up to 1869 (the exams had started in 1858) was fifty higher than that of its nearest rival, and over a hundred higher than that of Manchester Grammar School.

This was a noteworthy achievement by any standards, and particularly for a school that was barely a decade old in 1869. No wonder the Directors shouted about it. Anybody else would have done the same.

The school had been set up, and was recognized, as a pioneer experiment; it was the very first county school in England to be dedicated to middle-class education. Before long similar schools were set up in Surrey, Suffolk, Sussex, and Durham along exactly the same lines. They are better known today as Cranleigh, Framlingham, Ardingly, and Barnard Castle.

For a glorious decade or two, the Devon County School was the leader in its field, and proud of it. And rightly so.

## Shakespeare Out Over

THE BARD MADE HIS debut on Exmoor on the evening of Monday, 25th July, 1881, at half-past seven – with *The Merchant of Venice.*

How do we know? Because I found the original playbill, which gives details of time, place, and cast.

This is supported by a photograph which has also come to light – of the cast in action during the famous 'pound of flesh' scene.

This is turn is confirmed by an entry in the School Magazine, the *Register*, for 1907, in which R.P. Chope, the boy who had played Shylock 26 years before, was recorded as donating several photographs to the School, including one of *The Merchant of Venice*, and dated '1881'.

It would be interesting to hear word of any earlier performance of Shakespeare in Darkest Devon. Say, *Hamlet* at Heasley Mill to celebrate the centenary of the Bard's birthday in 1664? Or *Henry V* in the open air at Dunkery as a loyal offering to the newly-crowned George III in 1760? Or *Romeo and Juliet* at Exford to mark Queen Victoria's wedding to Prince Albert?

Even if they can, it will be hard to match West Buckland's value for money. When *The Merchant of Venice* had finished, the playbill also advertised another extravaganza entitled *A Phenomenon in a Smock Frock.*

The locals may have found it difficult to conjure up any reaction at all to the former, but the latter should have given them something familiar to ponder on in the dog cart on the way home.

## Devon v. the World

HOW MANY SCHOOLS THESE days can make up their own rules to their favourite games? Well, West Buckland School could over a hundred years ago – or Devon County School, as it was known then.

The main game – the only game – in winter at Devon County School in its early days was football. Or 'foot ball', as it was first known. It evolved then into 'foot-ball', before emerging from the chrysalis as the word we are familiar with today. But the Rugby Football Union rules and the Association Football rules were only just beginning to spread. So the School made up its own.

A set of rules was published in an early School magazine. For instance, the players changed ends every time a goal was scored. The field could be up to 200 hundred yards long and 100 yards wide. There was no crossbar to the goals. There was no limit to the number of players on each side. Devon County School could not have been very popular with other local teams, because when they played matches at home, they compelled the visitors to play according to their own rules.

Because of the large numbers involved, there was a risk of injury, and the very youngest were left out of internal games. For the same reason, goals were not frequent. Bit like the Eton wall game, I should think.

Another result of having so many players was the problem of devising two teams which might be of roughly equal ability. One solution was to have 'First Half of the Alphabet v. the Second' It so happened that the two dormitories in the School were divided by the parish boundary, so, as a variation, the two teams could be 'East Buckland' and 'West Buckland'. Again, depending on where the boys' homes were, they would divide between 'Devon' and 'the World'.

There cannot be many sports in which Devon could take on the rest of the world – and beat them.

## Names to conjure with – here

WHEN I STARTED TO put together the Archive at West Buckland School, I soon became aware of the achievements of rugby players like Victor Ubogu and Steve Ojomoh – England internationals; of fencers like Charlotte Read, who captained the women's sabre team at the Commonwealth Games in Kuala Lumpur and won a gold medal; and of athletes like Jonathan Edwards, who mopped up just about every title, prize, and distinction in the triple jump

Talking to old boys soon gave me three more names – Herbert Jones, who won his rugby cap in 1950; Harold Gimblett, who played cricket for Somerset 329 times; and Bertie Hill, who rode horses for England in three separate Olympic Games.

Dust-laden photographs and yellowing early School magazines soon gave me yet two more, from the deep past. Harry Packer won his first rugby cap for Wales in 1891. And Harold Hilton was an international golfer of such skill and renown that he became Amateur Champion four times – in 1900, 1901, 1911, and 1913 – as well as Amateur Champion of the USA in 1911. More remarkable still, he became English Open Champion even before that – twice – in 1892 and 1897.

He would have given a modern health expert heart failure today. He must have been one of the earliest examples of a chocoholic. Throughout his tournaments, apparently, he was forever munching lumps of it. And when he was wasn't eating chocolate, he was smoking, even while he was putting.

I also found two members of staff who had represented their country. Mr. T.H. Judson, a master in the 1890's, played rugby for Wales, and a man who had represented Wales for football became Headmaster – in 1895. His name was J.B. Challen.

Mr. Challen was also a cricketer of county standard. During his headship, he played cricket for a local team. In one season, 1898, he scored 1,285 runs in only 15 innings, and his average was just over 85. Which was double that of the greatest cricketer in England – W.G. Grace himself.

## The Recipe for a long life

IF YOU WANT TO live to a ripe old age, become a boarding school headmaster. That is the message that has come out of the records in the Archive.

Out of 14 previous headmasters, only two are known to have died young, that is, before 60. At the time of writing, the present incumbent has served eighteen years. His two predecessors are still alive and, to my knowledge, in full vigour.

The very first, Revd. Joseph H. Thompson, left after 30 years' service because of his declining health, and lived on till he was 85. He even got married when he was turned 50, raised a family, and served as a parish clergyman for over thirty years – that is, *after* his retirement.

The most famous of the West Buckland heads, Revd. Ernest Harries, lived to be 86. He too embarked on matrimony when he was turned 50, and fathered three sons in two years. (Work that one out.) Old boys recalled that, when he was over sixty, he was still coaching rugby, and insisting that the boys should tackle him – hard.

His successor, Commander Westall, left the School after only five years, but lived to be 93. Leslie Stephens, who was Head during the 1950's and 1960's, lived to be 92.

This longevity seems to have affected almost anyone who sat in the Head's chair. There was a caretaker headmaster in 1952, who held office for only six months. He lived to be 88.

But the record is held by another caretaker headmaster, who took over during the worst time of the war – Mr. G.B. Smith. He had retired from the headship of Sedbergh because of his health, and he retired again from West Buckland, after only one year, for the same reason. He lived to be 95. And he was playing bridge the night before he died.

## A Heavy-Duty Author

LITERARY FIGURES ARE NOT very thick on the ground at West Buckland. The only two old boys with a national reputation are R.F.Delderfield – novelist, playwright, and historian; and Brian Aldiss – who has written in most forms about almost everything.

I can claim no credit for discovering a new one, except insofar as the discovery took place during my watch. In Corsica, of all places.

As so often happens, its genesis was the result of coincidence. We had a teacher of Modern Languages called Martine leBarth. One year, she was on holiday with her family at a camp site in Corsica, and got into conversation with a Mr. Armstrong. It turned out that he too had been at West Buckland, as a pupil in the 1960's. He now lives in Aosta, in Italy.

Before they parted, he presented Mme. leBarth with a copy of a book he had recently helped to produce, about the Scammell heavy goods vehicles. It is a sumptuous work, full of splendid illustrations, and with text in four languages. Even Mr. Aldiss has to arrange separate translations for his many books.

Mr. Armstrong's book, which weighs almost as much as the Scammells it describes, has been presented to the School Library. I doubt if its sales will match those of Mr. Delderfield or Mr. Aldiss, but purely as an article it is not easy to ignore.

Mr. Armstrong is very honest about his career at West Buckland. In a letter to me, he said his teachers 'realised right away that we [he and his brother] were not destined to distinguish ourselves academically'. They were, he admits, 'much more perceptive than we gave them credit for at the time'.

However, Mr. Armstrong does share one distinction with the two literary giants; they were all three members of the Phoenix Society, which succeeded the old Reading and Debating Society.

Which brings me, easily, to the next topic .

*The Archives of an Archivist*

## Mr. President, Sir

THIS ARTICLE, AND THE following one, were written not for a newspaper but for a monthly magazine about life on Exmoor – entitled, appropriately and predictably, *Exmoor*. There have been a few tweaks and additions.

How do you keep boys occupied out of lessons in a small, remote, obscure, poverty-stricken school in 1903? Mr. Knight, the Headmaster, had a problem. In fact, he had several.

His predecessor had left the school after a disagreement with the Governors (or the Directors, as they were then – the school was a shareholding company). Unfortunately, he had taken two-thirds of the boys with him to set up a new school in Barnstaple. When Mr. Knight took over, the numbers had fallen to thirty-one, in a set of buildings designed to accommodate over a hundred and fifty.

So he had insufficient pupils – though, to be fair, he did succeed in doubling that number in the next few years. He had insufficient facilities – no science laboratories, for one thing. No proper swimming pool for another. Worse, he had insufficient funds. The finances of the school company were in a bad way. In fact he spent most of his headship under the shadow of possible closure.

It never rains but it pours – in this case quite literally. A storm blew down the pavilion. The staffing difficulties were so great that he himself was spending twenty-seven hours a week in the classroom. There was a personal tragedy too: he lost his first-born son at three days old.

To complete his discomfiture, a team of inspectors said that, though the teaching was adequate, and the provision of games, there was next to no provision for any recreational or cultural activity.

Mr. Knight, to his credit, set about the task with the energy of the young man; he couldn't have been much beyond his mid-thirties, if that.

He persuaded one of his staff to start a Rifle Club. He set aside a spare room (no problem in such a cavernous school) as a Reading Room. He got a swimming pool built. Admittedly in the open air, but it was a marked improvement on the 'school pond' which they had had before. He conjured the funds out of the Directors to finance the first laboratories. He appointed the very first member of staff whose primary duty was to teach Science.

And finally, he set up a Reading and Debating Society, and induced the new Science teacher to run it. Perhaps this young man, newly appointed, knew what was good for him.

This new society held regular meetings and kept proper minutes. These minute books are still in the School Archive, and are complete, from foundation in 1903 right up to 1926. (More of that later.) Boys discussed current affairs; they read scholarly papers to fellow-members; and, of course, they debated.

The minutes make fascinating reading. Not only for the topics, but for the attitudes displayed, the knowledge as well as the ignorance, the strong points and the blind spots.

What did they debate? What you might expect – hunting, naturally; votes for women (no prizes for guessing that); the Yellow Peril (enough to get you in front of a tribunal today). But they could be surprisingly modern too; for instance, they discussed a Channel tunnel and reform of the House of Lords – in 1907! They could be light-hearted as well: 'Is it better to be a bigger fool than one looks, or to look a bigger fool than one is?'

The views they expressed pinpointed not only the era in which they lived – a male-orientated boarding school in a remote rural county. Their ignorance showed with every speech they made. But they also exhibited, albeit unconsciously, the unspoken values of their time – pride in the Empire; certainty of Britain's almost divine role to rule it; total loyalty to King and country; respect for bravery, loyalty, sacrifice, athletic prowess. Wariness, at the very least, of women. And so on.

One chauvinist, for example, suggested that a way of controlling the activities of suffragettes when they got out of hand at public meetings was to keep in some handy box a mouse, which could be let out at the appropriate moment. Even the fact that it was a joke was still an indication of attitudes in Edwardian England.

One has always to bear in mind that when debaters referred go 'The Great War', it was not 1914 they meant; it was the Boer War. And remember too that, when the 'real' 'Great War' did come, boys like these enlisted in their thousands – ignorance, chauvinism, up the Empire, and all. Fifty-six of them died, out of an average pre-war roll of less than 120.

But the Society survived the War, and was in full flow in the 1920's. Then, suddenly, in 1926, it was wound up. And we don't know why. The Headmaster, the Revd. Harries, was quite a ball of fire in his diminutive way, and had reformed pretty well everything in sight since his appointment in 1907. The War had tragically interrupted the flow, but by 1926 he was ready to turn his fearsome attention to the Reading and Debating Society, and appointed a committee to discuss its purpose and future. The result was, as I said, oblivion, and no reason was given – or at any rate no reason that has survived in the record.

However, Harries clearly believed in the value of debate (his name appears often in the minutes). Accordingly, a new society arose – from the ashes, you might say – of its predecessor. Predictably, then, it was christened the Phoenix Society (or, more simply, 'The Phoenix').

Its minutes are complete up to 1962. With one exception: there was a fire in 1930 and one of the casualties was the minute book of that period.

In the mid- to late sixties it seems to have fallen on bad times, and the record runs dry. However, it arose again (another Phoenix from some more ashes) in the 1970's, and has persisted ever since. In 2003, it celebrated its centenary. (That is, if you include the Reading and Debating Society.)

Debates today consist of four main speakers, after which the audience may put questions to either side, as teams or as individuals. Then come two-minute speeches from anyone on the floor of the house. There are regulations about what qualifies a pupil for membership. The members control the voting. Staff attend as honorary members, with no voting power. If there is time, there are further questions, and the proceedings end with final statements from Opposition and Proposition, and the members vote on two topics – the motion, and the best speeches.

Under normal conditions, a pupil who makes two main speeches over a period of time may be accepted as a full member, and the President awards him, or her, a Phoenix tie, or badge, according.

There is an annual Christmas dinner in some nearby hostelry, after which members make brief speeches on a topic declared only a short while before. A successful one recently was: 'What makes your bells jingle at Christmas?'

A recent development – a very recent development – has been to arrange a debate between the Phoenix and the Old West Buckland Association. If you stop to think about it, it seems such an obvious thing to do that it is remarkable that it has never occurred to anybody before.

A purist would find plenty to criticise in the content, structure, and delivery of the speeches, and it is also true that many a speech would be improved with more preparation and thought. But, for many of these boys and girls, it is the very first time they have stood up and formally addressed a group of other people. It is a splendid forum for learning in; one is safe in the knowledge that the audience has had to go through, or will have go through, the same experience as oneself, so they will be tolerant if nothing else. It is an ideal place in which to learn the rudiments of speaking as opposed to talking, of putting together a coherent argument, and of thinking on the feet.

An old member once remarked to me that, all things considered, the Phoenix experience was the one feature he most valued about his time in the school.

It was this boy (he is a family man now) who produced one of the finest spontaneous gestures of goodwill I have witnessed in a school. He had not had what you might call a distinguished career coming up the years, and one wondered how he would cope with sixth form work. In fact, he didn't cope very well, not to begin with. He was struggling.

Then he got interested in the Phoenix. He said to me that he had been to a debate out of curiosity, and after what he saw, he said to himself, 'I can do better than this.' And he threw himself into it – with success. So much so that he was elected President at the end of his first year. Members of staff were concerned that this absorption in a debating society would have a deleterious effect on studies which were already a bit – well, a bit dodgy, to say the least.

But everyone was wrong. Not only did he turn out to be one of the best presidents in years; his academic work picked up – growing confidence possibly, after the Phoenix success. He didn't set the Examining Board on fire at 'A' Level, but he got respectable enough passes to gain entrance to a university, and went on to do research. He is now a very successful businessman.

The incident I am about to describe took place during a debate at which he was presiding. It will be clear from other chapters in this book that West Buckland takes in a lot of pupils from foreign countries, mainly in the senior school. Some of them are keen enough to absorb the language to be willing to come to debates, and, when they are used to them, to speak. Here the members come up trumps; they are well aware of the foreigners' difficulties with the language, and well aware therefore that making a speech must be much more of an ordeal than it is for themselves.

They pay great attention; you can almost feel them *willing* the speaker to succeed. They encourage him with generous laughter at the jokes; and they are fulsome with their applause at the end.

On this particular occasion, the speaker was a boy from, I believe, the USA – which is quite rare. Obviously he did not have trouble with the language, but it was just as much of a challenge. He had never spoken at the Phoenix before. He rose to the occasion with great aplomb, and showed a level of fluency, and relevance, which was well above average.

The applause at the end was not only kind; it was genuine and appreciative.

The President got up from his chair, walked forward till he was standing in front of the speaker. He took off his Phoenix tie and gave it to him, amid redoubled applause.

## **Runs don't matter**

EXMOOR AND CRICKET DO not naturally go together. Somehow wild heather and sphagnum moss do not sit easily in the mind with batting creases and leg breaks. So an Exmoor cricket match must be something rather special.

And special it was, at West Buckland School on a summer weekend in August, 1885, when the Old Boys of the Devon County School (as it was then) returned to their *alma mater* for the annual Past v. Present cricket match.

An Old Boys' cricket day today is what it says – a day. Go to a Past v. Present at West Buckland in the 1880's and you would not get away for four days. The Old Boys began to arrive on Thursday, 6th August. They would soon have found their nostalgia antennae twitching because the weather laid on a real Exmoor welcome. As the official report said with true Devon stoicism, 'Thursday was a fine day, except for a thunderstorm in the afternoon, and a heavy one at night. On Friday the weather was somewhat threatening and rather cold, though it remained fine.'

The report devoted four of its six pages to the cricket. It was almost a ball-by-ball commentary. It marked every fall of every wicket, every change of bowling, every noteworthy incident. There were two innings on either side and a full scorecard was printed, complete with bowling analysis.

The game began on Friday morning, with twelve on each side. The Taplin family was well represented: one played for the School and five for the Old Boys. There were two masters in the School side, and two more masters acted as umpires (so the School had a sort of insurance policy if things got too bad).

There was a very relaxed attitude to the clock. For instance, the game did not start until 12.45 pm. Lunch, taken at 2.40 pm, lasted an hour and twenty minutes. But on Saturday, play began at 10.40 am. They spent half an hour between innings with a photographer. Lunch, taken at 1.50 pm, occupied an hour and fifty minutes. The Old Boys' second innings made the match a real nail-biter, but in the end the School won by a whisker – well, ten runs. 'No one could wish to see a better match, and it will be long remembered by those who saw it.'

Among the features of the cricket were three hits for five, including one that 'went past the new pavilion and half way across the field behind'. So it seems that there were no boundaries; everything had to be run. Which makes F.O. Taylor's hit for six seem prodigious. In the Old Boys' second innings Mr. Thomas 'went on to bowl slow underhands' and got a wicket! The scorecard also records that 'Mr. Thomas bowled a no-ball', which, if he were still bowling 'slow underhands', must have been quite a feat.

On Friday evening, there was a Dramatic Entertainment, while on the Saturday evening all the Old Boys attended a formal dinner in the Dining Hall. So did the entire school. Speeches were made, toasts drunk, songs sung. There was 'great cheering'. At the end, 'the whole party adjourned to the quadrangle, which had been lit up by a large number of Chinese lanterns.' They stood round 'the Archbishop's tree' (long story) and sang *Auld Lang Syne.*

On Sunday there were two church services. At the end of the second 'all joined in singing the hymn for Old Boys' Sunday, written for these gatherings at the School by the Rev. S. Childs Clarke, Vicar of Thorverton'. The Old Boys left on Monday morning.

It was not the thunderstorms that they would take away in their memories, not the dinner menu, not the lumps in the wicket, nor even the cricket itself, memorable though it was. It was the familiar faces, the familiar sights, the Chinese lanterns, the Archbishop's tree, the 'great cheering'. Runs really did not matter.

## 6. More People

### The Revd. Thompson Sends a Telegram

AT FIVE MINUTES PAST ten on the morning of 24th May, 1912, the Revd. Joseph Thompson went into the Post Office at Warkleigh in North Devon, and sent a telegram. It was received at twenty-seven minutes past ten at Filleigh Post Office, also in North Devon.

[I waved it in the air.] That piece of paper is over ninety years old. I don't suppose any of you has ever sent a telegram, much less received one. But once upon a time, my children, in the prehistoric past before mobiles and faxes and emails, and before everybody had a telephone – if you can imagine that far back – telegrams were the only way of getting a message to somebody in less than a day. The message was written out on a special form, and handed in to the Post Office clerk. The message was sent by wireless telegraph to the other Post Office, where another clerk typed it out, or in this case, because it was North Devon, wrote it out by hand. It was then given to a Post Office delivery messenger, who brought it in person – by motor cycle or bicycle – to the person to whom it was addressed.

This one was addressed to a Mr. Taylor, and it said: 'Afraid unable come Barnstaple please apologise Thompson.'

Now, you may say, 'Big deal. Who was this guy Taylor, and who the hell was the Revd. Joseph Thompson?' Well, I'll tell you. And I think I can also tell you – or at least suggest to you – why Thompson wasn't coming to Barnstaple that morning.

Taylor was a teacher at the school, and he was also the Secretary to the Governors. Joseph Thompson was the first Headmaster of the School. He was appointed in 1858, at the age of twenty-one. Twenty-one. In those early days the School was known as the Devon County School. He remained Head for the next thirty years, and watched the School grow from its original three pupils to over 150.

For years afterwards, he continued to atttend Old Boys' dinners, and was a familiar figure in his black clerical clothes, dog collar, and monocle. And he continued to take a passionate interest in the fortunes of the School. Understandably.

It had its ups and downs, and came near to being closed – twice. Then, after about 1907, it began to recover. Part of the recovery process involved the company that ran the school going into liquidation – going voluntarily bankrupt, it you like. The School was re-formed as an independent fee-paying establishment, with support from the Devon County Council. It was also given a new name – West Buckland School. The old Devon County School title slipped away into history.

The process took four or five years – don't ask me why. But the final meeting to complete the business – the final, ultimate, really, absolutely last meeting to wind up the affairs of the Devon County School was arranged for 24th May, 1912, in the liquidator's office in Barnstaple – Cross and Wyatt (they are still there). Thompson, as the first Headmaster, was invited to attend.

By this time Thompson was seventy-five years old. He had been retired from the headship for twenty-four years. He had built the School from nothing – well, from three pupils in a farmhouse. He had seen the new buildings rise, stone by stone. He had watched as the numbers and reputation of his School grew steadily, year by year. He had supervised the planting of every tree and every shrub on the grounds. Each one had been to commemorate a special event, and he knew them all. He had taken pride in the School's academic successes – when, for instance, the Devon County School came top of the national league in the Cambridge Local Examinations three times in succession. He had kept contact with generations of old boys, and now enjoyed the status of a sort of gruff great-grandfather.

Now – suddenly – they were going to change the School's name. His school. It wasn't going to be the Devon County School any more. His brain must have told him that the School was going to get a new lease of life under a new system. But his heart must have told him otherwise. It was a bit like a parent, after three or four decades, being told that his son was going to change his name. He would have to get used to the child he had nurtured and loved changing from Sam to Fred. His head must have told him that it was the same underneath, but his heart told him that it wasn't – not quite.

Was that why he sent the telegram to Taylor to say that he couldn't come? To the meeting that was going to write in the name 'West Buckland School', and cross out the words 'Devon County School'. It wasn't his school any more.

## **Edward Hamilton Southcomb**

IN 1904, A BOY entered the school from Cheltenham. He was nine years old. Not remarkable today, when, if you don't look where you're going, you can trip over little mites of three and four. But in 1904, there was no Prep. School at all. Most boys came in at about 11 or over. So this one was unusual.

But he went up the school in a quite normal way. Won a prize for Science in 1908. Was one of the first members of the Cadet Force when it was formed in 1909. The Headmaster at that time was crackers about cadets, and commanded it himself, despite the fact that he was a priest. So perhaps the boys didn't get much choice about whether or not they joined. Incidentally, they didn't call it the Cadet Force, or the CCF; it was the 'Officers' Training Corps' – of course.

He left when he was only fifteen, because his parents, for some reason we don't know, wanted to send him to Shrewsbury School. The Headmaster couldn't object, because Shrewsbury had been his own old school. And that, you might think, was that. But it wasn't.

After he left Shrewsbury, he went to work in a bank, and might have stayed there, if it hadn't been for a small matter called the First World War. Like thousands of other young men, and boys, he joined the Army – the Gloucester Regiment. Well, he had come from Cheltenham.

He secured a commission, so all that parading in the new Officers' Training Corps must have paid off. He became a Second-Lieutenant in the Manchester Regiment in November, 1916.

In March, 1917, he was sent to France, to what was commonly known as the 'Western Front'. It meant in fact that a line of trenches – a double line of trenches, English and German – stretched 450 miles from the Swiss border all the way to the North Sea. These trenches were protected by forests of barbed wire, mountains of sandbags, and hundreds of machine-guns – water-cooled machine-guns, which meant that the barrels never became too hot to allow firing. If required, they could keep shooting pretty well all day.

I expect you are by now getting ahead of me.

This young man was killed on 31$^{st}$ July, 1917. But you were not completely right; he was in fact killed by a sniper. Death was instantaneous. The record added, curiously, that this took place 'in the early morning', as if this somehow made it a bit better.

When all his possessions were packed up to send home to his family, they added up to a revolver and lanyard, a torch – with a battery, a compass, two watches – one without a glass, and an identity disc with chain and whistle. A parcel for his mother.

What made him special? Countless soldiers were killed out there. The names of 54,000 of them are carved on the Menin Gate at Ypres alone. At the battle of Verdun, a million men died. The school alone lost 56, out of an average school roll of barely 120. So why single him out of the 56?

Because of what he did before he went into battle for the last time. Remember I said that when he left, it wasn't the end of the story?

He made a will. He was only twenty-two. How many young men of twenty-two today feel it is necessary to make a will? In it he remembered his old school, the school he had left seven years before. He gave instructions that ten guineas – £10.50 in today's money – should be given to providing some trophy to be awarded for sport.

The School authorities put their heads together, and came up with the idea that it should embrace as many sports and as many houses as possible. When this boy had come to the School in 1904, there had been only two houses, Brereton and Courtenay. By now there were two more – Fortescue, and the youngest, Grenville, which was born in 1918.

They put the idea to the boy's family, who agreed. They didn't hurry about it, because the plan didn't come into action until 1924, seven years after this boy had died.

You are probably ahead of me again. [Well, they would be. You will see why below.] It was decided to create a trophy which would be awarded to the house which gains the highest total of points for the combined sporting competitions of the whole school year. It would take the form of a shield.

And there it is. And here he is. [Both shield and photograph were on show on my table. I held them up.] We shall put the two together as soon as I can persuade Mr. Parker [the school maintenance manager] to fix them on the wall [which he did].

So you will know his name by now – Southcomb. Edward Hamilton Southcomb. His shield will be presented this year for the 84th time [2007]. Edward Hamilton Southcomb, killed in action, aged twenty-two, on 31st July, 1917 – 'in the early morning'.

## Sam Howells

IF YOU CLIMB THE big stone staircase outside the Memorial Hall, half-way up you will see a headmaster who may remind you of Hitler. Now, there may be those among you who think all headmasters are like Hitler. But this man really did look like Hitler.

It was the moustache. What they used to call a toothbrush moustache – quite fashionable before the War. But because Hitler wore one like it, the temptation is to think that every man who wears one is like him. But I am not talking about Hitler.

I am talking about Mr. S.E. Howells – Sam Howells. He was always known to his pupils as 'Sam', though not of course to his face. He was Headmaster from 1941 to 1952. I am talking about him first because we have just put his picture up on the wall. And secondly because he died on 6th June, 1952 – exactly fifty years ago yesterday. Incidentally, he was the only headmaster in the School's history to die in office. Lung cancer – he was a very heavy smoker.

He came to the School in 1918 – in the last year of the First World War. He had some weakness in his health – never mind the smoking – which prevented him from doing military service. Today we cannot realise the enormous pressure on young men to join up in the First World War – to fight, to serve their country – and the burden of shame and frustration that lay upon those who could not. Sam had to bear that all his life.

He taught English, and, later, Biology. An odd combination. He did not have glittering degrees or diplomas. I believe he taught himself Biology, and started the subject in the School practically from scratch. He was not a sportsman – that health trouble again.

But he was an outstanding teacher. I have spoken to a lot of old Old Boys, who remember his classes very clearly. One or two claim that they can still recite poetry he taught them nearly sixty years ago. Such was his influence that, when he had finished teaching you, you stayed taught.

He also had a reputation for fierce discipline. Perhaps it was the Hitler moustache. It certainly wasn't his voice. Apparently, he couldn't say his r's correctly. They came out as w's. He was fond of comparing naughty boys to tiny, restless birds. So, when he was particularly cross, he would shout at a class of juniors, 'You wetched little spawwows!' But nobody dared laugh. However, when some of his ex-pupils saw him in action years later, when they themselves were adults, they were surprised to discover that he was not so fierce after all.

Sam in time became Deputy Headmaster, and would no doubt have continued to be so had it not been for the War – for Hitler, the real Hitler. The Headmaster left to join the Army, and the next Headmaster had to retire because of ill health. So a desperate board of governors invited Sam to take over as Headmaster for the rest of the War. Which he did. He went on, as I said, until 1952, when his consumption of Gold Flake cigarettes caught up with him, and he was diagnosed with lung cancer. Hundreds of boys would talk of Sam's Gold Flake suit because it smelt so much of stale tobacco. [Gold Flake was a common make of cigarette.]

What Sam did between 1941 and 1952 was what hundreds of deputy heads did all over the country – take over the school at a bad time – blackout, bombing, food rationing, shortages of staff (all the young, fit ones had joined up), shortages of practically everything – petrol, building materials, paint, books, paper. Their job was to hold a school together. Sam did just that, with no fuss and a great deal of common sense and humanity. These caretaker headmasters were usually men in their middle years who had not particularly wanted to be heads – certainly not in wartime. But they accepted what had to be done, and they got on and did it. They are the unsung heroes of the profession.

If, after this assembly, you go and have a look at Sam – halfway up the staircase – you will probably think he is a bit funny. But then most teachers are, aren't they? – one way or another. After what I have said, you may think he was an old-fashioned, smelly bully of a man who is now just a face on the wall. But you cannot put the full force of a teacher into a picture on the wall, or into a talk like this. To get the full force, you had to be there, and the men who were there say he was a great teacher.

Most of us are prepared to learn from anybody who has the ability to teach us. If it were possible for Sam to come back and teach you, I fancy that you would be kept in order, you would be kept busy, and you would learn. Moustache or no moustache, 'spawwows' or no 'spawwows', he would make you mind, he would make you work, and he would make you remember. And isn't that what all teachers are supposed to do?

## The Man Who Could not Stop Doing Good

WHEN YOU CAME BACK to School at the beginning of this term, you might have noticed something simply because it wasn't there. I'm talking about the buildings which housed the Library and the classrooms for Art and Technology. But did you ever notice something which was there, over the door of one of those old classrooms – a brass plaque? And did you ever read what it said – 'The Pearse Chope Workshop'. And did you ever wonder about it? I am sure you all did, many times. All those little gatherings of pupils in the quad and the tuck shop, constantly asking each other, 'Who was Chope?'

Well, I am about to satisfy the nagging curiosity which has kept you awake so often, so late, night after night – the Great Puzzle: who on earth was Pearse Chope?

Richard Pearse Chope, actually. He was a great benefactor of the School. But not quite like any other benefactor. He spent his whole life doing good for the School, continually, unstoppably, relentlessly. He was like some kind of human dynamo – a man of awesome talents and fearsome energy – a combination of Leonardo da Vinci and Napoleon, determined to do us good. He was like the tide coming in. He was so clever too it made you sick. I'll tell you what I mean.

He was born in Hartland, in 1862. His father sent him to the fairly new Devon County School – us, here – in 1874. In the Cambridge Local Junior Examinations (the ancestor of GCSE) he came top – not just in the School, but in the whole of England. He later came top – in all England – in both the Cambridge and the Oxford Senior Examinations. He took part in the first Shakespearean performance in the School of which we have a record – *The Merchant of Venice*, in 1881. He was Shylock, naturally. He was chosen to be Head Prefect, and it will, by now, come as no surprise to you to be told that he also won a Fortescue Medal.

He went up to Cambridge University to read Maths – which in any period of history and in any university is no soft option. He got a First, of course.

He went to work in the Government Patent Office – the office concerned, as the name suggests, with issuing patents for inventions. The work he did there ran into over 100 volumes of printed material. During that period, he found time to edit a weekly trade journal.

Back home in Hartland, he was a keen amateur historian and

archaeologist, and published a stream of articles on local history. He built up his family's farming estates to over 1,000 acres. He assisted the Professor of Comparative Philology at Oxford in the compiling of the *The English Dialect Dictionary*. He himself was an expert on the Devon dialect, and he gave hundreds of lectures and recitations on it and in it. He wrote articles for the local paper, *The Hartland Chronicle* – over 200 actually. He helped, and paid for, a lot of restoration in his local church. He founded, and ran, a local dramatic society, and performed with it. Needless to say, he was a churchwarden and a local magistrate.

All this, remember, over two hundred miles from London, where he worked. Think of the commuting he had to do. And there was no railway to take him anywhere near Hartland.

He was a constant presence at every Old Boys' Dinner and every Social Evening. He served as Treasurer and President. During his presidency he trebled the membership. He served on the Governing Body of the School. At the Old Boys' annual Gathering every Whitsun, guess who read the lesson in East Buckland Church. In nearly every surviving group photograph from that period, guess who in the middle of the front row.

He showered on the School an endless cascade of gifts, books, pictures, prizes, and 'useful' ideas. He presented a splendid collection of glass slides of the many inventions he had been concerned with, and many more from earlier times. We still have them. He wrote interminable articles for the School magazine, which the editors very bravely tried to shorten to manageable proportions. He designed a cover for the School magazine, which was in use till 1965. He compiled, every year, a General Knowledge Quiz for the boys, and presented a prize for it, which was awarded at Speech Day. I've seen some of them. They were fearsome. I suggest that a quiz between contestants from both staff and pupils would throw up some very odd results. The General Knowledge Prize continued to be awarded right up to, again, 1965.

There was something unstoppable about this man, so much so that one wonders what was driving him. Was it that, all the time, he was searching for some kind of immortality? And he got it – at last – in 1935, two years before he died, with that brass plaque over the door of 'his' workshop. The Pearse Chope Workshop. And now it has gone. Perhaps, when the new one is built, we owe it to him to put it back.

## A Rose on Exmoor

ON ONE OF THE walls of the Memorial Hall are three venerable portraits in ornate frames that look as if they have been there since the Middle Ages. Actually, it is only a century and a half. Two of them are of the school's founders, the Revd. J.L. Brereton and Earl Fortescue. The third is of Brereton's wife Frances.

Once upon a time, my children, there lived a girl called Frances. She lived in a country vicarage with her mother and father. She was growing up to be so beautiful that it looked as if she was going to be surrounded by crowds of handsome, vigorous, rich suitors who would strew their treasures at her feet, and kneel there themselves with proposals of marriage. Her father and mother must have waited with pleasure for the time when she should make her choice of the handsomest, strongest, and richest.

Instead, she went and married a priest with poor health and next to no money at all. And she was only seventeen. He was twenty-nine. How did he do it?

Do clergymen normally sweep teenage girls off their feet? I wouldn't have thought so. Not now, and not in the middle of the nineteenth century either. In fact even less in the nineteenth century, because everything was so much more formal, more correct, more respectable. Look at the clergymen you happen to know; do any of them strike you as the Great Lover, the Great Heartthrob? The image doesn't fit, does it?

So what did this ardent priest have going for him? Certainly not money; *his* father was a clergyman too. He was no dashing swashbuckler either – no trace of Robin Hood or the Three Musketeers. In fact he came down to the country for his health; he had always suffered from weak lungs. This had prevented him working hard enough to get a good degree at Oxford, so he had to give up his ambitions to become an Oxford don. He had to make do with being a priest – in a tiny village church in the back of beyond. So he had taken refuge in the sticks as a sort of failure.

What on earth then did she see in him? Remember, she wasn't plain, and desperate. On the contrary, she was beautiful. The perfect English rose. She could have had anybody.

Well, for a start, he too was unquestionably handsome. Dishy, you might say. A high, noble-looking forehead. A long classical nose. Well-formed facial features. A good head of fine hair. From pictures of him it looks as if he trained the curls at the sides. So perhaps he was vain too. But girls will often put up with a little vanity in return for the attention of somebody so dishy.

He was also charming. He must have been, because he was absolutely brilliant at conjuring money out of potential investors for his many elaborate projects. If you have ever tried to get money out of anybody, for anything, even when they owe it to you, you will know how very difficult it is.

But above all, he was alight with imagination. He was incandescent. His mind boiled with ideas and plots and plans and schemes and projects; he was unstoppable. Being with him must been rather like living with the Big Bang.

Whatever the reason, she was bowled over, and married him. Neither of their families thought the marriage was a good idea. So she must have been pretty determined too.

Whether she lived to regret her decision we don't know. I don't think she kept a diary. In any case, in those days, people didn't go and get divorced when they felt a bit fed up. You stuck it out. You had to be respectable, especially if you were a clergyman's wife. And divorce was not respectable.

So she stayed in her village rectory, and did what clergymen's wives did – good works, and more good works. Raising a family too. And it was some family. Her husband had come down to the country because he suffered from bad health. And they had sixteen children. Sixteen. Heaven knows what would have happened if he had had good health.

Sadly five of these children died young. But she raised the rest. I shouldn't think she had time for much else. Even if she had servants – and she probably did – children still need loving. Servants may have done a lot of the work, but there was still the company and the story-telling and the general simply being there. To say nothing of running the vicarage. And think of all those pregnancies – sixteen. And it was quite likely that she had one or two miscarriages as well – women in those days often did.

What must her life have been like? Did she travel much? Did she socialise much with many of the celebrities her husband met on his travels and endless meetings and conferences? Remember he was a busy village priest too. Did she get time to read much, to have hobbies, to visit friends, to entertain, even to relax? We don't know.

But one thing she did find time for was to have her portrait painted. By one of the leading painters of the day, George Richmond. And there she is [dramatic gesture from the speaker towards the portrait on the wall], the perfect English rose. Frances Brereton, wife of the founder of the school. Isn't she lovely?

When that picture was done she had already had eight children. Eight more to go. You will not surprised to be told that she did not live as long as her husband. There he is beside her. They make a handsome pair. At least they *look* a handsome pair. I wonder what the truth really was?

# 7. Who are we?

## Roots and Fruits

IF EVER A SCHOOL sprang from the soil of its surroundings, the West Buckland Farm and County School did in November, 1858. Created by the local rector, the Revd. J.L. Brereton, and the local aristocrat, the second Earl Fortescue, it began offering lessons in a farmhouse on the edge of the village. Within a dozen years, it had a permanent home, it boarded 100 pupils, and it had topped the national examination league more than once.

It would be foolish to claim that the school's history since has been one long chronicle of unbroken triumph. Of course it has had its ups and downs. But over the years it can feel proud of its achievement, and of its originality. It was the first secondary school to cater specifically for ordinary children of ordinary people. Christian teaching was deliberately non-denominational. Pupils were encouraged to respect and enjoy their rural surroundings. It offered a modern curriculum half a century ahead of the hitherto permanent diet of Greek and Latin elsewhere. In the days before nation-wide government systems of education, it identified itself closely with its locality. Its very remoteness produced a remarkable *esprit de corps* among its 'inmates'.

Much of this ethos survives today. Few schools can claim a broader social mix than West Buckland ('ordinary children of ordinary people'). Not only do our pupils come from practically every kind of background in Devon and elsewhere in England; we have also welcomed, over the years, pupils from nearly sixty foreign countries.

This diversity enriches the social and cultural life of the School. No religious allegiance is enforced, but we do try to teach tolerance and understanding of another person's beliefs and customs ('deliberately non-denominational').

Close to Exmoor and the sea, we live in glorious countryside, which provide endless opportunities for a huge range of sport and other outdoor activities ('respect and enjoy their rural surroundings'). From West Buckland's earliest days, pupils have enjoyed a remarkable level of robust health. Exmoor weather has also taught generations of boys and girls the virtues of flexibility, patience, and resilience.

Indoors, the challenges are thick on the ground – in the Humanities, the Sciences, and the Arts ('a modern curriculum'); in the cadet force; and in lunchtime and after-school clubs and activities. There is more to school than examinations, but it is also a fact that healthy, well-taught young people with a variety of interests and a balanced life tend to succeed in these too. We are proud of our academic achievements; nearly all our sixth formers go on to further academic study, mainly on demanding university courses. There is no scope on Exmoor for giving pupils a hothouse treatment.

The School continues to maintain strong links with the Devon countryside. Our largest single group of families derive their livings from farming and other rural occupations. We encourage pupils to engage in conservation and community work, which gets them out of school and into meeting local people, who in their turn improve their own understanding of what really goes on in a school like ours ('identified itself closely with its locality').

West Buckland has always had a strong boarding tradition. This allows many children extra time in the day to benefit from what the School has to offer – time that would otherwise be eaten into by travel in a large rural county. For foreign pupils, of course, boarding is the only option. The School has long since rejected the old notion that Tom Brown dormitories and Colditz wash-basins in some way shape the character. Purpose-built boarding houses meet all the standards of civilised living that are demanded by the modern world. This is backed up by a dedicated boarding staff who are aware and around all the time. Leavers – both staff and pupils – pay tribute to the family atmosphere that the School generates ('remarkable *esprit de corps* among its inmates').

The future presents exciting prospects in which the School's original ethos is still relevant. It is vital that we continue to provide yet more opportunities for 'ordinary children of ordinary people'. It is equally vital that we provide bursaries and scholarships for some of these 'ordinary children' of modest means to enjoy them.

We can now offer a continuous education for a boy or girl from the age of three to eighteen – an awesome commitment for both school and parents. But families from half-way round the world send their children here – into the second generation sometimes; in Devon into the third and fourth generation – evidence that we can appeal to parents anywhere.

Not only do we bring *in* children from all over the world; when they leave, the majority of our sixth-formers go *out* all over the world in their 'gap' year and later, and do absolutely everything. We like to think we have prepared them for much, much more than passing exams. Old Boys, from the first days of their Association in the 1880's, used to look back fondly on their time at the Devon County School – Colditz wash-basins and all. Almost unbelievably, there is evidence in the Archive that this fond sentiment has been expressed by boys who were pupils at the school for barely more than a year. We hope that boys and girls who leave West Buckland School now will have memories of a rich and varied (and more comfortable) life here, which, quite often, was a lot of fun too.

[If you are particularly quick on the uptake, you will detect a – shall we say? – promotional element in the above. And it must be admitted that this is a shot of the school's best side, and is intended to be. But it does not follow that every other side is bad.]

## 150 Brochure

[IN 2008, WEST BUCKLAND celebrated its 150th anniversary. Understandably, this provoked a good deal of looking back and gazing fondly on tradition and achievement. And why not? It is indeed a record to be proud of.]

A HUNDRED AND FIFTY years ago, secondary education for ordinary people did not exist.

Two men in North Devon, the Revd. Joseph Lloyd Brereton and Earl Fortescue, decided to do something about it. Their idea was a nation-wide system of county schools, where the fees would be modest, the curriculum would be modern (lots of Science and Maths), and where pupils would not suffer discrimination for their religious views. They would be given a sound Christian education of course, but it was to be the Christianity of the Samaritan, not of the Pharisee. In the days of privileged public schools for the sons of gentlemen, the stranglehold of Latin and Greek, dog-collared Oxbridge headmasters, and rigid denominational Bible-beating, their inspiration was a beacon in the gloom of mid-century mindsets.

Many of these new schools, sadly, did not survive. But West Buckland did, though not without a lot of ups and downs, which is to be expected in a century and a half of history. It has changed, but not completely out of recognition. It has grown from its original three pupils to nearly 700; it has developed its curriculum to take account of the growth of learning and of technology; its campus has expanded from 20 acres to 100. But its commitment to toleration and a broad intake continues: it has accepted pupils from over fifty foreign countries, and it is dedicated to providing as many opportunities as it can to children from less fortunate backgrounds. It continues to offer the best of the world to ordinary children of ordinary people. As one ex-pupil recently wrote, 'The special thing about West Buckland is that everyone is made to feel the same way, at ease with the person they are and valued because of it.'

One feels that the Revd. Brereton and Earl Fortescue, after 150 years, would have approved.

## Not in my time

OLD BOYS WHO RETURN to West Buckland after forty or fifty, even sixty or more years, generally notice two things: one, that a lot has changed; and two, that quite a lot hasn't.

The latter of the two is, perhaps, no surprise. After all, you could not do away with the solid, unchangeable front façade, which, over 150 years after its construction, still looks, from the road, pretty jolly sensational – the sort of façade which, you like to believe in your fantasies, every country independent school ought to look like. (The bits behind are another matter.)

By the same token, they would find the rugby field familiar, the quad, the tennis courts, the *Exmoor* – oh, lots more. And, naturally, the weather. That hasn't changed since Adam and Eve.

But, my word, they would notice a great deal of other things too – sights, sounds, smells, tastes, activities, and attitudes.

Sights? Obviously, the new buildings, some of which obtrude into the line of vision the moment one gets out of the car (as opposed to arriving, as one did, after the two-mile walk from Filleigh Station, which was obligatory and unavoidable) – 'blocks' and 'centres' for everything – Science, Arts and Drama, Sports, Library, 'Learning', and of course the much-vaunted new boarding accommodation – the by-now famous *en-suite* facilities.

Sounds? Female voices in 'new' games like rounders and netball; practice for the jazzband; rehearsals for the chamber choir; the clank of scaffolding and the chug of diggers always, it seems, engaged on something.

Smells and tastes? We have come a long way from the food which one old boy described to me as 'universally grey' – two hot choices for lunch, a salad set-up with a dozen dishes to dig into, and a 'pasta bar' (with a name like that, one almost hopes for a glass of Asti Spumante on the house with the ravioli). To say nothing of an Aladdin's cave of a tuck shop. Hardly grey now.

Activities? Golf, camping, public speaking, speech and dama (and a regular mopping up of prizes in local competitions), full-scale productions of major musicals, living in snow caves on holidays, abseiling, stargazing. A far cry from a chancy film show on a wet Saturday evening, dependent upon a rackety 8mm. projector.

*Nearly off the Record*

What has happened since those old boys left? One scarcely knows where to begin: little crocodiles of nursery pupils, gumshields, laptops and ear-plugs, computer games and texts instead of conkers and marbles, and the new trinity of the modern world – Google the Father, Amazon the Son, and Facebook-and-Twitter the Holy Ghost. Worship still goes on; it's just the deities that are different.

Attitudes? Because of space, one example will have to suffice. Old boys I have spoken to have often mentioned the prevalence of bullying. Some admitted that nearly everybody got bullied, in one way or another, at some time or another. Well, no school could ever claim that it had eliminated bullying. But I bet that West Buckland, fifty years ago, did not enjoy the compliment recently bestowed upon it in an inspectors' report that it was far ahead of most schools of its type in the level of the care and respect that its pupils showed *for each other*.

A change worth noting, I should have said. And a change that one would not see, hear, smell, or taste. But if you kept your antennae out, you would sense it.

## Foreign Legion

OVER THE YEARS, WEST Buckland has played host to pupils from nearly sixty foreign countries. These young people arrive at the school with little more than the clothes they stand up in. In the case of one Nigerian boy, quite literally; he was wearing nearly every item of clothing he had packed in his suitcase because he was so cold.

But they have to tackle a great deal more than the cold, and quickly – West Buckland horizontal rain and cross-country runs; scrambled egg and rhubarb crumble; cricket and the Royal Family; *Strictly Come Dancing* and *The 'X' Factor*.

Besides learning to cope with a foreign weather system, foreign diet, a foreign culture, and foreign TV, they have, of course, to learn a foreign language. After all, that is one of the reasons why their parents sent them here in the first place. How do they manage? Well, like any human group, they are a mixed bunch, and their levels of success are bound to be mixed. As Damon Runyon said of his guys and dolls on Broadway, they 'do the best they can'.

But on the whole, by and large, and taking things all round, they don't do too badly. A Japanese boy has played cricket for the First XI. The Secretary of the Phoenix Society one year was Hungarian. Part of the School's website page was designed by a Lithuanian. One scorer for the cricket team was Chinese. We have had head boys from Hong Kong, Thailand, and Uganda.

These young people do pretty well when they leave school too. By now integrated into West Buckland, and armed with some solid English, they have won entrance to, and distinction in, Oxford, Cambridge, London, Manchester, and similar prestigious establishments, in both undergraduate and postgraduate courses. Some have gone on to represent England on the sports field.

Since education is a two-way business, the school has also had to learn. They have come to appreciate these students' impressive work ethic, their sense of purpose, and (obviously) their talent, to say nothing of the evocative cultural colour that they can bring with them. It can also become a feat merely to read the register. Try these names for size: Lacava, Zaouk, Ongsaranakom, Yim, Chewprecha, Wing-Yiu, Gergely, Quaishi, Sayidzadeh, Wijesekeva, Tantisuvanichkul. Oh – and Karnasuta (I wonder what his nickname was).

## Why do you come to old members' dinners?

I WAS ONCE INVITED to be the chief guest at the annual London dinner of the Old West Buckland Association. It had formerly been simply the 'West Buckland Old Boys', but the advent of girls in the 1970's and 1980's necessitated a slight shift of 'correct' text.

I took the chance to give a plug for the Archive. However, when it came to composing the text, it suddenly became quite a formidable task to think of something to say which was in any way 'news' to these gentlemen who all had much more experience of the school than I did.

Mr. President, ladies and gentlemen – I must thank you for the compliment implicit in your invitation to me – a non-ex-pupil – to address you on what is essentially a private occasion. For a group who share the common experience of having come through West Buckland, I must say you look a surprisingly untraumatised, well-integrated bunch of old campaigners, fellow-sufferers, survivors, and walking wounded.

How can I say something fresh, something comforting, something uplifting, to such a seasoned audience who have seen everything, who have been through the fire, who have gazed into the abyss? What can I say about an institution – West Buckland – that is a name to conjure with even in the SAS – the Sadistic Arts Society?

The answer, obviously, lay in research. Research on the Association – the O.W.B.A. And what do I find? So many groups and gatherings which also possess the same initials. It was a good job I found out what they stood for before spending further time in fruitless study of them.

For instance, OWBA stands for Out-of-Work British Architects. No mileage there. Then there was a little-known Government department. You have heard of the Milk Marketing Board. I bet you haven't heard of the Oyster and Whitebait Authority. I tried again, and came across a very discreet organisation – Over-Weight Businessmen Anonymous. Perhaps one or two of you have acquaintances who have confided to you their membership. There is an obscure standardising department of the United Nations, dedicated to the smooth running of the world's industry – the Oriental and Western Ballbearing Agency. Common knowledge to you engineers, I have no doubt.

Finally, there was one which very nearly caught me out completely – the Organisation for the Worldwide Banning of Alcohol – or 'Owba'. Their officers are well known, as is the American TV drama series which championed their activities – 'The Man from Owba'. Their number one

*The Archives of an Archivist*

agent was played by that popular Irish actor, Kenneth O'Branagh. Who has not heard of 'OWBA – 1 Ken O'B'?

But I digress.

I am a historian by inclination. I am a teacher by trade. I am now an archivist by occupation. As a historian I believe that we are all potential enjoyers of history, because everyone wants to know where he or she comes from. As a teacher, I have spent a lifetime showing people how they can indeed enjoy that history. As an archivist, I work (within the stern limitations of the funds allowed to me) to make everyone associated with the School, past and present, more aware of its history and its place in their lives. At all times – as historian, as teacher, or as archivist – I try to stress balance and perspective.

If history does nothing else, it makes you grateful that you are alive in the $21^{st}$ century, and not the $18^{th}$ or the $12^{th}$; makes you pleased you are here in 2002, and were not here in 1902 or 1862.

You – all of you here – are fond of the School – I presume. But I put it to you that there are features of its history which you may not have relished at the time had you been there.

Do you regret, for instance, not having been at the School during the scarlet fever epidemic of 1864? Do you regret the fact that you didn't have to spend every Easter and Michaelmas holiday at the School before the 1870's, because the railway line had not been opened, and it was too far for you to go home if you lived outside the West Country? Do you regret not having been at the School in 1899, when the Headmaster left, taking two-thirds of the boys with him to start another school, leaving behind a pitiful rump of 31 pupils in a building designed to accommodate 180?

Do you regret having missed Prize Day in 1865, when the reports of the speeches ran to 31 pages in the *Register*? Aren't you glad you didn't receive prizes that day like Bacon's *Essays*, Scott's poems, Hymns Ancient and Modern, Russell's *Crimean War* (both volumes) and *The Commonplace Philosopher* (for Drawing!)?

Aren't you relieved you were not among the thirteen boys who played cricket for the First XI during the summer of 1914? Ten of them joined up almost at once, the other three later. One was wounded twice, another four times. Three died, one of them in 1914 – on $22^{nd}$ December.

By the same token, there may be features of your own time at the School – for all your generally fond memories of it – which – if you are honest – you were not sorry to see the back of – the wind, the rain, the famous ice in the wash-basins (for all that you have bored family and friends with it for years, you did not enjoy it at the time...... 'Wake up there, Smithers. Ice in the basins this morning – yippee! And the towels will be like boards – hooray! And with any luck old Ernie will let us have a cold bath if we ask him nicely, after we have begged him for a trot round the rugby field – in our underpants').

Remember the draughts? – in and around windows, doorways, passages, corridors, arches, corners, quadrangles. The runs? – horizontal rain, soaking footwear, thumping chests, blue arms and legs, Arctic ditchwater, and teachers shouting idiotic things at you as you staggered by. School dripping, school porridge..... one old member wrote in his Reminiscences that an enterprising pupil took a leaf out of the book of Oliver Twist one morning, stood up, picked up his bowl of congealing concrete, and walked up to the dais where the Headmaster, Ernie Harries, was about to start his own breakfast. He held forward his plate, and made his complaint. Without uttering a word, Harries took it away from him, gave him his own, and began his meal.

Do you really miss the lack of privacy? Possibly bullying? Transient feelings of inadequacy and bafflement? Moments of loneliness and misery? Fear and dread? Unexpected moods of homesickness?

You have all had one or other of these troubles, because you were victims of new experiences and new emotions which we all need time to learn how to handle. They linger in the darker corners of the memory. The bulk of your recall, however, is usually more pleasant and more positive. If it were not, you would not be here. And this bulk of positive recall could probably go under the heading of gratitude – of differing types.

Gratitude – gleeful gratitude – for having done a lot of less than worthy things – smoking under hedges, smuggling bottles of scrumpy into the dormitory after away matches, passing round dog-eared copies of *Health and Efficiency*, getting thoroughly submerged at the Leavers' Dinner – and getting away with it.

Gratitude – relieved gratitude – for having *escaped* committing other far worse stupidities: smelling of Woodbines instead of Gold Flake in the presence of Sam Howells; in a party of markers for the *Exmoor*, being the one who forgot the matches and the tin-opener; failing to fold your arms in a school rugby photograph; confusing Phoenix Society refreshment with wine; trying to keep up with Keith in conversation. [For over thirty years there was a school servant known to one and all as simply 'Keith', who had a staggering memory for names, but who had also, to an exhausting degree, the capacity to talk the hind legs off a donkey.]

Gratitude – creeping gratitude – for the fixtures and fittings, the sounds and smells. Come across a familiar sound or smell, and you can leap across forty years in a second. We gradually grow gratitude, and respect, for School servants we hardly noticed before – Bill Cockram, who served for over 30 years; Gerald, who retired recently after 51 years; Jim Hobbs and his Dad, Charles Hobbs, who between them notched up 80.

Gratitude – possibly – for having had your mind opened to new knowledge, your body braced by new challenges, your spirit lifted with new insights and inspirations, your spare time enriched by new friends, your horizons raised to embrace visions you never before knew existed, the thought of grasping which made the pulse race.

Some of those new friends are now very old ones – cherished like heirlooms. As with heirlooms, we do not look at the blemishes – the lines, the sags and the wrinkles; we value the gleam in the eye, the grip in the hand, the catch in the laugh. [I was gratified, and touched, at this point, when I saw one member, who had clearly been following me closely, put his arm round the shoulder of the man next to him.]

Finally, the ones who raised those horizons – your teachers – the good ones. You are all the product of your parents, your homes, your families, your genes, your jobs, and your countries, but you are also to a certain extent the product of your teachers. (I said my function was to try and put things in perspective.) I don't need to put the names here; you can do that for yourselves. But you know and I know that the teachers whose memory you treasure are the ones who made you notice, made you think, made you mind, and made you learn (whether you liked it or not is immaterial), so that, when they had finished teaching you, you stayed taught. Something of value remained.

These were great people; anybody who can wrench a adolescent's mind away from self-absorption, sensationalism, and sex for even half an hour has to be a great person. Their faith in the young is both touching and noble. And a glance at our Head of School and Head Girl tonight will show you that their faith is amply justified. [There is a tradition that all old members' social functions are attended by the head boy and head girl. Some years the 'Head Prefect' is a boy; some years it is a girl. They pick the best.]

Stir together all that I have been talking about – the buildings, the teachers, the games, the draughts, wind, rain, worries, fears, moods, stories, rumours, friends, escapades, exaggerations, nearly 150 years of history, well over 100 years of the life of the Association – and you produce the chemical reaction which brings you all here this evening.

Sentiment, yes. But, I hope, realism too. You know it well and you still appreciate it – warts and all. It inspires strong feelings – both ways; there are those, as you are aware, who didn't like it at all, and it was not their fault. That is testimony to the School's positiveness. Like West Buckland or not, there is a definite presence, a personality.

I don't think that you would rush to apply adjectives like 'aesthetic', 'gentle', 'sensitive', or 'demonstrative'. Not until about twenty years ago anyway. You don't think of West Buckland as being particularly well upholstered. There is something a trifle gaunt, unyielding, uncompromising, like a Presbyterian minister; it has craggy cheeks, bushy eyebrows, and bony wrists. But, as a student of its past and of its present, I am constrained to remark that it has always had, and still, apparently, has, a great capacity for inspiring affection – in defiance of a lot of the evidence!

In the New Year 2000 celebrations, Muhammad Ali, as you know, was chosen Sports Personality of the Millennium. In his introduction Harry Carpenter said that a measure of Muhammad Ali's stature was that not only was his name known all over the world, but that, all over the world, wherever you spoke his name, people smiled. Among members of this Association, I sincerely hope that for a long time to come the mention of the School's name will be met with a smile from a great many people.

I beg leave, Mr. President, to propose the health of the partnership of West Buckland School and its Old Members – the Association.

I was particularly chuffed a little later, when I overheard one member remark to another, 'The bugger's got it dead right.'

## 8. Living and Learning

### Where do exams come from?

EVERY PERSON HERE HAS suffered from exams – entrance exams, Key Stage exams, eleven-plus exams, GCSE, A-S level, A level, degree exams, professional exams, music exams, ballet tests, acting auditions, trial games, and so on. Wherever you turn, there they are – lurking like dragons in your path. Every single one of them calculated to spoil your day. Has it ever occurred to you to wonder where they came from?

Because they were not always there; somebody had to invent them. True – believe me. And not all that long ago. Barely 150 years. In fact the very first ancestor of GCSE saw the light of day in the same year as the founding of the School – 1858.

Oxford and Cambridge had started exams for degrees, but you didn't have to pass exams to get in. All you needed was to be born into the right family or be friends with the right people; you didn't need to *know* much, before or after. Latin and Greek and the Bible were usually reckoned to be enough. Most Government ministers got by with very little more.

Well, what about everybody else? How did ordinary people get jobs? How did they beat other people to it? What did they do without a certificate to wave in the air? They fixed things, that's what they did. They wheeled and dealed. They wrote creep letters, they bribed, they did favours, they sucked up to anybody they thought could do them a spot of good. Anything to get a job for their son or their nephew or their cousin. You didn't have to do it much for daughters or nieces; all you had to do for them was find a husband. This was not being callous; it was being practical. There simply were not the openings for girls. A well-off, kind husband was a far better investment for your daughter's security than a chancy job, or life as an overworked chambermaid.

So it was not *what* you knew; it was *whom* you knew, and how you exploited it. One king, George III, reckoned, so it was said, that if you showed enough gumption to get a job, then you were sharp enough to be able to do it.

So why did this situation not continue? Why did it get changed? Quite simply, because there were now so many people; the population was galloping up. The word 'competition' began to creep in. It is no coincidence that the 19th century saw the rise of the three great competitive sports – cricket, football, and rugby. The greatest celebrity in England in the late 19th century was W.G. Grace, a cricketer. It is no coincidence that the most influential book of the mid-19th century was Charles Darwin's great work, *The Origin of Species*, which talked about the survival of the fittest. It is no coincidence that this huge new population needed roads, houses, railways, dockyards, and so on. A new profession was born – engineers. You couldn't have them building all these things knowing only Latin, Greek and the Bible; everything would fall down. They had to become qualified; that meant exams. It is no coincidence that one of the great achievements of the French Revolution was the idea that you should get promotion not because you were rich, or well-connected, or you had blue blood in your veins; it was because you were clever. How did you prove it? Exams.

The Government quite liked the idea of exams. It meant that schools would have to smarten themselves up so that their pupils could pass, so standards would be raised without any taxpayers' money being spent. It meant that anybody who wished could take the exams, so nobody could complain of discrimination. It could be run by the universities, not the Government, so it was no trouble. It was nationwide, it was fair, it was democratic, it was frightfully modern, and it was cheap. It was too good to be true.

There were four men who pioneered these new exams for secondary schools, and, amazingly, all four were closely connected with West Buckland. One was Frederick Temple, who had been Bishop of Exeter. He came here once to present the prizes. The second was Sir Thomas Dyke Acland, a prominent Devon landowner, an early director of the School, and the man, incidentally, who laid out the very first course for the *Exmoor* in 1859. The other two were the Revd. Joseph Lloyd Brereton and Earl Fortescue, the two founders of the School. Temple, Acland, Brereton, and Fortescue – all tied up with us.

Boys sat the very first nationwide secondary exam in the same year that West Buckland began. Within four years, West Buckland boys had done so well that Cambridge University agreed to set up an exam centre *in the School* – the very first. All the other exam centres were in big cities. *The Times* used to publish alphabetical lists of exam centres; they read like this: 'Bath, Birmingham, Cheltenham, Exeter, Leeds, Liverpool, London, Manchester, Oxford, Southampton, and West Buckland.' One mystified reader wrote to *The Times* to ask, 'Where is West Buckland?'

There were league tables too, in the 1860's. West Buckland produced boys who came individual top in the whole country – Stone (1874), Chope (1877), Potbury (1881), Stradling (1895). They are up there on the honours boards. West Buckland gained the highest number of exam passes of any school in England – three years running – top of the league, no less.

So, if you are searching for someone, or something, to blame for starting these accursed exams, you don't have to look very far.

*Nearly off the Record*

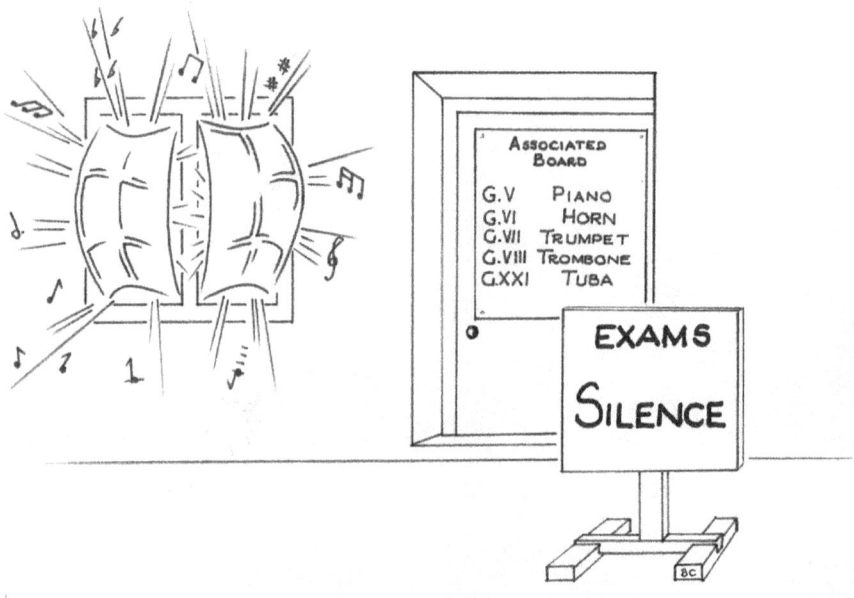

'Oh, for a muse of fire!'

# Nearly off the Record

## What every young person ought to know

HAVE YOU EVER BEEN told that you are, not to put too fine a point on it, ignorant? Worse, have you ever been told that you are even ignorant of how ignorant you are? Have you ever heard old fogeys, or teachers (same thing, really, I suppose), going on about how the youth of today don't have any general knowledge at all? They try to prove it by firing questions at you, and, when you don't know the answer, they say, 'There you are. What did I tell you?'

But that does not get us very far, does it? Because ignorance is a very personal business. You may not know who is the President of Russia, but it does not cause you any loss of sleep because you cannot foresee any circumstances in which you may need to know the name of the President of Russia. You reckon you know enough to get by. Me too. I reckon I know enough to get by, but I have no idea who is the drummer in the Rolling Floyd. I haven't a clue who is the lead guitarist in the Pink Oasis.

Each period of history, too, had its own idea of what constituted a good level of general knowledge. In the 16th century, for instance, a gentleman was not said to be educated unless he could read music and write poetry. In the 18th and 19th centuries, members of Parliament regularly quoted Latin and Greek in their speeches, and expected to be understood by their fellow-members.

The School had its own idea too, because for many years there used to be a General Knowledge Test Paper, and a prize was awarded for the best performer at Speech Day. The questions were set by a man the scope of whose general knowledge was terrifying. His name was Richard Pearse Chope, an Old Boy, and he knew absolutely everything. He inflicted his goodwill on the School for a whole generation, and the place wilted under his gifts and benefactions and bright ideas. There was no stopping him. He set the papers, marked them, and decided on the prizewinner. And no doubt presented the prize itself.

The level of knowledge he demanded was awesome. Try these questions for size:
1. 'Give a plan and description of the Karslake Dining Hall, specifying its dimensions, and the position and size of the windows, doors, and tables.'
2. 'What is the average retail price of wheat, oats, beef, bacon, sugar, tea, butter, and potatoes?'

3. 'Give the names of 10 wild fruits, 10 wild birds, and 10 freshwater fish used for food.'
4. 'Explain the terms Apocalypse, Apocrypha, Pentateuch, Doxology, Synoptic Gospels.'
5. 'Draw a picture of the leaves of the following trees – oak, ash, beech, elm, sycamore, lime, and Spanish chestnut.' [Spanish chestnut!]
6. 'Write down two verses of *Rule Britannia*, the National Anthem, and *Auld Lang Syne.*'

And so it went on, for another 10 questions. The winner richly deserved his prize.

But Mr. Chope had a sense of humour too. Each year he published in the School magazine – the *Register*, as it was then called – a selection of the best wrong answers. Like this:

1. 'Blanc-mange is a powder used for making a desert.'
2. 'Cologne is famous for the odour made there.'
3. 'Caviare is a kind of Indian curry.'
4. 'The armadillo lives chiefly in trees, travelling upside-down.'
5. 'When ladies are [undressed] they are [said to be] *al fresco.*'
6. 'Cheese is a hard, greasy substance, and can be eaten alone, if possible.' [By consenting adults, of course.]
7. 'Australia exports wine to England, made from a bird called the emu.'
8. 'A stockbroker is a man who deals with cattle.' [Which deserves to be right.]
9. 'A refugee is a man who keeps order in a football match.' [Which is still right.]

We don't know how the boys took all this. They certainly went in for the exam, but we have no records of how well they performed, or what percentage the winner achieved.

The Staff privately thought that Chope was a bit of a pain, and that his General Knowledge Test was a bit of a pain too. They reckoned he was right out of touch with what boys actually knew. One year they cooked up their own general knowledge test as a skit on his, and published it in the *Register*, the old name, as I said, for the School magazine. Like this:

1. 'Either give the life-story of a tiddlywink, or describe the growth of a grain of common sense.'
2. 'On a piece of paper 6 inches by 5, describe an imaginary line, using no instruments. Find its area, and make one $2^{7}/_{8}$ as large.'

3. 'Explain these terms: the 12 signs of the Cognac; total eclipse of a moving point.'
4. 'Explain what is meant by the phrases: "One swallow does not make a drink"; "all is not banana that fritters." '

We don't know whether Chope saw the funny side of this or not. He went on setting his General Knowledge Exam, and presenting his prize. Even after he died, it continued right up until 1965. I wonder how well Chope would have done today in *Who Wants to be a Millionaire?* He probably wouldn't have got beyond the first question, because he would have had no idea either who was the lead guitarist in the Pink Oasis.

Poor old Chope – he knew everything, but he didn't seem to know much else – like how young people's minds worked. But then how many of us do?

## Could do better

EVERY SO OFTEN SOMEBODY writes to me in the Archive to say that their father or uncle or whoever it is has recently died and they have discovered in his old cupboards various items relating to his time at West Buckland, and would I be interested in having them. They could be school magazines, or faded photographs taken with an old Brownie camera; sometimes books presented years ago as prizes; occasionally pieces of clothing, like an old blazer or a colours cap.

Anyway, by this method, there came into my possession not long ago a school report, dated 14th December, 1921. There were five subjects reported on. The word 'good' appears twice, the word 'progress' appears twice, the word 'very' appears twice, and the word 'satisfactory' appears three times. The only spark of individualism came from a teacher who was moved to write 'keen, intelligent, and successful'. Add up all the words used in all five reports – the grand total is twenty. The whole report – twenty words. On the basis of this exhaustive summary, the Headmaster wrote at the bottom, 'An excellent report in all ways.' Make of that what you will.

Now, it is easy to criticise a report like this. Shocking. Disgraceful. It's obvious, isn't it? The teachers are a lazy bunch of automatic pilots, dying to get back to their cigarettes, their bridge table, or their *Times* crossword. How much better our school reports are now.

So let's compare them.

I took a random sample of some modern reports, from three pupils at different stages of their education. It would appear that the average report for the early 21st century consists of three single-spaced typewritten pages of A4. At a conservative estimate, about 1,600 words. That's eighty times longer than the one from 90 years ago.

What do we conclude from this? That the report is better because it's longer? That because it's eighty times longer, the teaching is eighty times better than it was in 1921? That the teachers today are eighty times more conscientious than they were in 1921? Difficult to prove. Common sense should tell us that there were good teachers and lazy teachers in 1921, just as there are good teachers and lazy teachers today.

The quality of education should surely not be judged solely by the number of words we write about it. Because a report is short or long, it does not necessarily mean that the teaching and learning are skimpy or overdone. It is the work and the achievement, not the record of them, that counts.

If you can criticise a thin report for using the word 'very', so you can do the same to a fat one which says instead 'hugely' or 'massively'. Why is it bad to have said 'very good' in 1921 and all right to say 'fantastic' now? Why is it bad to use the impersonal surname once in 1921 and good to repeat a pupil's Christian name forty times on the same report today? Why is it bad to have a handwritten scrawl of a teacher's initials in 1921 and good to have a soulless, computerised name today? In 1921 they had words like 'satisfactory', 'keen', 'steady progress'. Now we have words like 'focus', 'commitment', 'motivated', 'engaged'. Who is to decide which are better?

What am I saying? I not 'saying' anything. I am *suggesting* that *perhaps* school reports, like everything else, *might* be subject to the pressures of fashion. They were once short. Now they're long. Perhaps they'll get short again one day. Like skirts and heels going up or down, or trousers going wide or narrow. Maybe they'll be like prices, continually inflating. So if they can go up 80 times in 90 years, in 5 years' time at that rate, they'll be nearly 8,000 words long. Watch out.

But how would it be if teachers were able, or reckless enough, to overturn fashion, and, just for once, say what they *really* think?

So you might have something like this:

'Despite his natural levity, he habitually gravitates to the bottom.'

'The marginal improvement in his handwriting has served only to highlight the deficiencies in his spelling.'

'He has a passion only for apathy, and is loyal only to sedition.'

'Nobody could have a higher opinion of this pupil than I have – and I think he's a lazy little toad.'

**Or** – how about saving time and preparing one report for everybody?: 'I am totally free from any form of prejudice; I find all my pupils equally stupid.'

No. Perhaps not. Pity. Tempting, though, isn't it? But if you do, you'd better have your resignation letter ready as well.

## **What use is education?**

[As I SAY BELOW, this was the first time I had been invited to take a junior assembly – age group about 11-13. All my other assemblies were delivered to an audience upwards of 13. So I took care – or at least tried – to gear it down just a bit.]

I HAVE TAKEN QUITE a lot of senior assemblies, but this is the first junior one. So I thought I would try and find out something about the people I am talking to. It seemed that a good way to do that was to find out what you did all day. So I had printed out a typical Year 8 timetable.

To be honest I didn't find a lot of surprises. True, there are some fairly new subjects like Information Technology and Design Technology, but most of the rest were on the timetable of the schools I taught in years ago. Maths, English, French, Physics. . . . So times haven't changed all that much. History, Chemistry, Geography. . . . I suppose they were *all* new once. Everything has to start somewhere. Did it ever occur to you to wonder how they got there – on the timetable, I mean? More to the point, have you ever wondered why? What *use* are they?

Think about it. Physics – how many of you are going to become professional physicists? Music – how many of you are going to study Music after you leave? Modern Languages – how many of you want to spend all your future holidays in Spain or France? History – how many of you are remotely interested in the fourteenth century? Maths – how many of you want to spend the rest of your lives doing Maths? How many of you want to spend one more *week* doing Maths?

How many of you are going to remember 20% of all this, say, five years after you have left? How many of you are going to remember it even for a few days, for that revision test?

So – what is the point? What is it all *for*? Good question.

Adults are never short of answers, have you noticed? 'Because it does you good.' Like taking your medicine, and going to the dentist, and eating your greens. Doesn't cut much ice, does it? Who wants to be done good to all the time?

Or, again, 'It is good for the character.' You know – discipline, hard work, keeping the rules. Well, OK, but can't they find better ways of developing our characters besides keeping us behind a desk five or six hours every day?

Then there is the common sense argument: 'You will need all that education to get you a good job.' Oh really? How many of you are going to get 'a good job' because you know a lot of dates, or you love blowing up test-tubes, or you are a whiz at netball?

And how much of all this wonderful education is going to be any use to us when we know we shall have forgotten most of it by the time we are twenty-three? Dear God, what are we doing here?

Have no fear, my children. I am here to tell you that all is not lost. Why? Because school is giving you a great deal more than education. And, unlike education, it is all pretty painless. And free.

Look around you, for a start. Hundreds of them, just like you, all shapes and sizes. What am I talking about? Company, that's what I'm talking about. We know they are all peculiar, and that you are the only normal and reasonable person in the whole school. But they're all you've got, so you have to make the best of them. You have to learn to live with them. And if you can live with *them*, you can live with anybody.

Now look at that timetable I started with. You are kept busy – *all the time*. But what is the alternative? Ever tried doing nothing – all day? Ever tried being lazy – all week? Ever tried gazing at telly from dawn to dusk? Ever tried having fun *all the time?* The trouble with fun is that it has to come *after* work. It is no good *instead of work*. And if the work is well organised, by your teachers, it can be quite good fun. In fact, work can be much more fun than fun. Sort that one out.

Company. Fun. Is that it? No. School is very good at surprises too.

The first surprise many of you got when you entered the main school was that it was so big and that so much was going on. How on earth were you going to remember where everything was – the tutor room, the toilets, the labs., the gym.? How were you ever going to get to all those lessons on time? With the right gear. With the right books. With the right homework. Leaving home at crack of dawn to catch the bus. Not getting back till six o'clock, or later. Your nerves were in pieces. You were absolutely whacked.

But you survived, didn't you? You coped, in the end. And that company – all those funny people around you – they helped, didn't they? You soon found out that the next problem, the next surprise, the next crisis, was not the end of the world.

Learning to survive, learning to cope. Now that *is* something that you don't forget. And that *will* be a great deal of use to you for the rest of your life.

Then, after a while, your nerves begin to fade away, and your brains and common sense take over. You learn, for example, that it is better to have two crises on the go than one. When the first crisis starts to get on top of you, you can switch over and start worrying about the other one, and let the first crisis take care of itself.

You discover that Teacher A always demands that his homework be handed in on time, and that he never listens to excuses. But, luckily, Teacher B can always be sidetracked with a sob story or a vague promise to 'hand it in at morning break, sir'. And he doesn't always remember to ask for it anyway. That lesson will get you through no end of trouble in the next sixty years. In the business world, they call it 'juggling deadlines'.

Or again, you notice things, without noticing at the time that you are noticing them, if you see what I mean. You see how a dining hall can be well organised; how a kitchen can produce good meals; how a sports team can be coached successfully; how a choir can produce good performances. In other words, you see how things can be well done, by people who know their business. For the rest of your life, that will give you something to judge by. Out there in the adult world, they call it 'standards'. You will come to know what good standards are. You will know second best when you see it.

So yes – you will forget a lot of things that you are at the moment trying to remember. But there will be a lot of other things that you don't even know you are learning – and you will remember them all right. So take heart – it isn't all a waste of time.

## 9. Records and Records

WITHIN FIVE YEARS OF the school's birth, the powers that be – or that were – decided that it would be a good idea to publish a short, but regular, account of the school's activities, and of course of its successes. The first number of the *Register* appeared in 1863, and in the Archive we have a near-complete run of them, right up to its demise in the 1990's.

It is not the most resounding or evocative of titles. Well, not to us in the 21$^{st}$ century. But perhaps people had a different set of preferences and priorities in 1863. Words and verbal styles change over the years, and we can not possibly, at this distance of time, be aware of all the niceties and implications in meaning of thousands of common words. Even within a generation, words can even reverse their meaning. The most obvious example, maybe, is the word 'gay'. A 'bachelor gay', once, was intensely interested in women; a 'gay bachelor' now is interested in anything but women.

Be that as it may, the word '*Register*' in 1863, at West Buckland at any rate, did not mean a record of attendance but a record of achievement. And '*Register*' it remained till somebody (maybe a new headmaster) decided that it had had a long enough run, and needed to step aside for something a little more lively. (There is an account of this transition below.)

The new title's evolution is also explained below.

It may have been a new title, but the purpose of the magazine was pretty much the same: to records the school's activities and successes. The Archive could by now be said to be one of the school's activities, so it could justifiably claim to have its own 'spot'. And it does, every year. What follows, and in later sections too, is a selection of pieces provided for the '3R's' (again, see below).

## A Hard Cover Story

SKY MASTERSON, THE HERO of the American musical *Guys and Dolls*, had occasion, during the story, to recall the wry advice of his father: 'My Daddy said to me, "No matter who you get married to, you wind up married to somebody else." '

That comment could equally well apply to a lot of jobs. When I agreed to become our School Archivist (its first), I expected lofts and attics, collapsing cardboard boxes and yellowing letters, disintegrating book spines and sepia photographs. And I got them – plenty of them. What I did not expect was a host of other responsibilities and activities, indeed other whole dimensions. They came to account for more of my time than the original duties, and they were to prove more interesting too.

For example, I produce regular pieces for our Press Officer to circulate to the local media – anything of interest which has surfaced in my routine work. I have been interviewed by local radio and TV. The Archive has appeared on Channel 4, in a programme called *Collectors' Lot*. (Half past three on a Friday afternoon – peak viewing, you see.) I have taught lessons about the history of the School. I have taken assemblies. I have spoken at Old Members' and masonic lodge dinners. I have written pieces for the School magazine. I have become the usual reception party for Old Members who visit the School. I have provided research facilities for people outside the School whose investigations have brought them into contact with its history.

There are plenty more examples, but I have mentioned enough to make my point. My point, incidentally, is not to show what a versatile and imaginative archivist I am, but to show that, when you start something like this, you never know what you are letting yourself in for. And quite big things have a tendency to creep up on you.

For instance, about half way through my first term, my Headmaster asked me to dig out something he could use as a talking point for an Old Members' Dinner. I obliged with a menu and programme from the Old Boys' (only boys then) Dinner of 1907. Eight courses, ten toasts and responses, and nine songs – they did things in style in those days, and still had enough breath for *Auld Lang Syne* at the end.

A short while later the Head asked me if I could find anything which he could use for Remembrance Sunday.

A few weeks after that, I was taking to pieces some old photo frames in order to try and bring some order to a host of aged sporting team pictures. I was struck by the fact that the older the pictures, the more robust was the workmanship of the framing. Those of the First World War and just after, for instance, I could practically take to pieces with my bare hands; more glass had cracked; nails had rusted through. Whereas those of the 1890's had been put together using solid screws; glass was thicker; backing was of proper wood, not plywood or cardboard. It struck me that here was material for an article. So I wrote it, not quite knowing what I was going to do with it.

Another strand of activity also emerged (if indeed a 'strand' can 'emerge') – picking the brains of people with long memories of the School. I asked questions; they talked; I wrote it down. When it was over, I put these reminiscences into coherent form – at least coherent enough to be of interest, and, I hoped, enjoyment to anyone who reads it in time to come.

I was forever stumbling over little titbits of news, scandal, and history; curiosities and coincidences; and plain useless information. They were all too good to toss back into the dust.

It was slowly becoming clear that I had a book on my hands. It was not going to be a straight history; somebody had already done that. But there was, it seemed to me, plenty of mileage in putting together a miscellany of sidelong glances at the School's past, which might be of interest to anyone who had had any connection with the place.

I now took pains to maintain editorial consistency, strike a balance between sport and academe, between the serious and the funny, the recent and the deep past, and so on. 'The book' had become a definite 'project', with a definite end – publication.

Luckily, one of our lady members of staff was married to a local publisher. He normally produced books about local villages, but, after he had read some of my material, he agreed to branch out into local schools as well. (He has since done another, on Blundell's.) It was he who insisted on including a lot of photographs – of which there was no shortage – some of them in amazingly good condition. Thanks to the correspondence machinery of the School and the Old Members, we had a potential mailing list of nearly three thousand.

In this short account, I may make it sound all too easy, which it wasn't. There were hiccups, delays and crises, as any writer who has ever produced a book could have prophesied. But the book came out, and, looking back, I enjoyed the process. Any other archivist with half an ego, a decent vocabulary, and a twist of imagination – and a willingness to sit alone at a computer – can try the same.

And it is very gratifying when the book is, as they say, well received. People went out of their way to say some nice things about it.

It wasn't all accolades of course; the world is full of people who will helpfully point out a mistake you made on page 74. But most readers were pretty tolerant, even of my worst *faux pas* – in a photo caption I attributed one lady to the wrong husband.

*The Archives of an Archivist*

## Where did it all come from?

WHERE DID ALL WHAT come from? Let us try and explain by means of three facts. Once upon a time, children, education was supposed to consist of teaching you to read, write, and count. Or – as school kids remembered (wrongly, as usual) – 'Reading, Riting, and Rithmetic'. As people said, 'The three R's.' Fact Number One.

Fact Number Two – the West Buckland School magazine, when it was first published, went under the name of the *Register*. Not the most enlightened of choices, you may think, considering that to most people, in and out of school, the word 'register' describes a mere list of pupils in a class. Well, it does now. Perhaps it didn't then, nearly 150 years ago, when the School began. After all, 'council' schools did not start until about 130 years ago.

Oddly, though, the name proved to be quite apt, because most of the early numbers of the *Register* consisted of boys' names. (No girls then, of course – oh, my goodness me, no.)

The first number of the *Register* saw the light in 1863. We still have it in the Archive. As it modestly said in its very first paragraph, 'The object of this unpretending little publication is to give some information regarding the School and its progress, which may be interesting to its friends.'

And the information certainly followed – a very great deal of it. The School was young – only five years old in 1863 – and was making its way, and its name, in the educational world. It had to tell everybody – or at least its 'friends' – how well it was doing. So, from 1863 onwards, we had lists, as I said – of boys who had been made 'monitors'; of boys who 'deserve mention for excellence in particular subjects'; of boys who 'deserve mention for punctuality'; of boys whose exam papers were 'the neatest'; of boys 'whose conduct and attention to their work are in every respect satisfactory'; of boys who won prizes; and so on and so on. You could half-fill a modern school magazine with gems from these early, yellowing pages.

Now jump fifty years – what do we have? Over twice as many pages on average. A lot of sport reports – football (or, as it originally was, 'foot ball' – note the space); athletics ('Under 14 Consolation Race – 1$^{st}$, J. Vickery'); swimming (before there was a pool, races took place in the 'Pond'); numerous cross-country runs; endless cricket scores, summaries, and averages. The cadets had arrived – or rather the 'Officers' Training

Corps' – nothing so vulgar as 'other ranks'. During the First World War, letters written to the Headmaster by serving soldier Old Boys from the front were regularly published. They could be a douche of cold reality in the face of proud recital of juvenile successes.

A new cover for the magazine appeared in 1906, and continued until 1966. As the twentieth century advanced, various dramas and traumas were recorded – the demise of football, the rise of the Phoenix Society, the end of the famous Gilbert and Sullivan comic opera productions, the growth of rugby, and many others.

Later still, in the 1970's and 1980's, the *Register* got bigger and fatter. The arrival of computers made possible all sorts of pictorial wizardry. More and more activities were reported, till one began to wonder how the pupils managed to find time for anything so mundane as going to lessons, much less doing homework. In the early twentieth century, the Headmaster was the Editor (and, one suspects, almost the sole author). Now, you would have to ask Mrs. Pugsley [the editor of the new-look magazine] to count up a lot of fingers before she could tell you how many people had a hand in the production.

With all this novelty, wizardry, variety, and prolixity, it was only going to be a matter of time before somebody decided to change the very look of the *Register* – as with Doctor Who, to give it a new incarnation. So it got bigger – again; it went into technicolour; it went glossy; it had 'Art' in it. Naturally, it had to have a new name. Now. . . . Something catchy; something snappy; something apt. But something which made a respectful nod in the direction of the past. The word '*Register*' begins with an 'R'. The School motto is 'Read and Reap', with two more 'R's'. And somebody with a grandmother must have remembered that old summary of education. *Eureka!* – 'The Three R's'. Wow!

And that's where it all came from – my Third Fact – just in case you thought I'd forgotten it.

## Something to Shout About

UNLESS YOU HAVE SPENT the last twelve months in a space laboratory preparing for a trip to Mars, or have recently returned from a sabbatical year in a Trappist monastery, you will know that this year – 2002 – has marked the Queen's Golden Jubilee. Or, if you prefer, the Golden Jubilee has been marking the Queen's fiftieth year on the throne.

Since this piece is appearing in the School magazine for 2002, and it is about jubilees, you could be forgiven for thinking that the School is also celebrating some special anniversary at this time. Not so. The only reason it is here is that the Editor approached me with one of her most dazzling smiles (the more dazzling it is, the more wary you are of what is coming next), and asked if I could knock together something 'about the Jubilee'. Could I perhaps 'tie it in with the School somehow'?

A bit of a tall order.

What can we celebrate in this magazine issue? Well, the recent 'A' Level examination results come naturally to mind. The best ever – 99.4% pass rate. But, since they have only just happened, one can hardly put them up against a golden jubilee. There is no type of jubilee that commemorates one year. Fifty, yes. Twenty-five, sixty, a hundred. Fine. There is no species of jubilee that commemorates just one year. Unless you call it a paper jubilee. That's what they call a wedding that is just one year old. (I have no doubt that, in the case of so many of today's fragile relationships, friends and relatives would also call it a surprising achievement.)

Pears *Cyclopaedia* is a mine of information on this topic. For example, the sixth anniversary – wedding, jubilee, or what you will – is the 'sugar' jubilee. The School was founded in 1858. What happened in the year of its sugar jubilee, 1864? A scarlet fever epidemic, which necessitated the evacuation of the entire school while the buildings were fumigated. Hardly an edifying topic.

Let's take another jubilee, or anniversary, at random. Hands up anybody in the class who knows what they call the thirtieth? Yes, Hoskins? Pearl. That's right – well done, Hoskins. How did you know that? It's your mother's middle name. Well, well, well. So – what happened on the occasion of the School's thirtieth anniversary? The first Headmaster, the Revd. J.H. Thompson, retired, after thirty years' service. (Well, it would be, wouldn't it, if he was the first head, and it was the Pearl anniv – let us move on.)

## Nearly off the Record

What happened at the School fifty years ago? The Headmaster died, that's what happened. Sam Howells. The only headmaster to die in office. He had been on the Staff since 1918. Taught English, and, later, Biology. My understanding is that he virtually created Biology as a subject in the School curriculum, and with no degree or anything like that. Just a great interest, and a great skill in the classroom. Sam Howells stands out in the School's history as one of the really great teachers. It is true that he was cordially disliked by some, but they are outnumbered by the many Old Boys (very old boys now) who grow misty-eyed to this day at the mention of his name, and, if not headed off, will launch themselves on to a tidal wave of reminiscence.

1918, incidentally, the year Sam arrived, marked the sixtieth anniversary of the School's founding. So that makes it the Diamond Jubilee. The whole world celebrated that year, never mind the School. The Great War, the War to End Wars, was over. Europe had nearly bled to death. Fifty-six members of the School alone had died in those terrible four years.

The Headmaster, the Revd. E.C. Harries, tried to lift post-war spirits by one of his, by now, traditional productions of Gilbert and Sullivan, this time *The Mikado*. Needless to say, HM ('Ernie') played the leading role.

Long before he had got into his stride with G. and S., Ernie had hit on the technique of marking anniversaries with drama. Only a year after he was appointed, he celebrated the School's own Golden Jubilee in 1908 with a performance of 'Scenes from' *As You Like It*. Not only had he persuaded gangling boys to shed their Eton collars and don 'Shakespearian' dress; he had arranged for the performance to be presented in the open air, in the School grounds. A photograph survives of the cast, striking poses which seem a touching mixture of languor, bafflement, and rustic gawkiness.

In 1928, the seventieth anniversary, Harries maintained the Savoy tradition with *The Pirates of Penzance*. Guess who played Major-General Stanley. Incidentally, here's something I bet you didn't know. The seventieth anniversary – or jubilee – is known as the Iron Jubilee. Yes – iron. My authority is no less than *The New Shorter Oxford Dictionary* – another mine of information. (The lexicographers of that industrial town on the Thames are at odds, however, with the editors of Pear's *Cyclopaedia*, who insist that the seventieth jubilee is known as 'Platinum'. So take your pick.)

Neither authority, unfortunately, comes up with an adjective to describe the hundredth. Which is a pity, because the School really tried to push the boat out in 1958: opening a new playing field; the Duchess of Devonshire as chief guest at Speech Day; an Old Boy who had been an Olympic equestrian medal winner lending his golden spurs for an exhibition of the School's history; a new Physics laboratory inaugurated, the ceremony performed – just – by an Old Boy who had entered the School in 1879; *She Stoops to Conquer* squeezed on to the stage in the Memorial Hall. Oh – and bell-ringing was revived.

That was 44 years ago. In 2002, what is the appropriate name for a jubilee of 144 years? A Gross Jubilee? That could set you thinking, couldn't it?

The School is now – by a simple process of mental arithmetic (I hope I am not going too fast for some of our readers) – only six years away from its 150$^{th}$ anniversary. It might be productive to invite suggestions from our readership as to suitable means of celebration of this auspicious – and, let us be generous, most praiseworthy – achievement.

*The New Shorter Oxford Dictionary* informs us that the word 'jubilee' comes from medieval Church usage, and referred, originally, only to the fiftieth year. It stems from a Latin word meaning 'to celebrate' (think of 'jubilation'), which came from a Greek word, *'iobelaios'*, which in turn came from the Ancient Hebrew *'yobel'*. And the original meaning of that was 'ram'. Yes, 'ram'. Now you must follow me closely. How did early societies make a fuss about something? As often as not, by making a noise. How did they do that? By blowing something hollow. Like a horn. How about a ram's horn? Still with me? So it appears that the ram's horn – the *'yobel'*, was blown to inform everyone in earshot that a special year was about to be inaugurated.

So times don't change much, do they? Here we are, in 2002, with a record crop of 'A' Level results, and our highest-ever position in the League Tables, and we are blowing our trumpet about it. And why shouldn't we?

## West Buckland Writes

INDEED, WEST BUCKLAND HAS always 'wrote', though not consistently. Or at any rate the writing efforts have not been consistently recorded. The *Register*, like any institution with a long history, has gone through 'phases'. (In this, it shares a propensity with light waves, butterflies, teenagers, and the moon.)

There have been periods when the magazine has published the original work of pupils (and, occasionally, teachers), and there have been periods when the well of inspiration seems to have run dry. I say 'seems' because it is unlikely that certain decades of the School's history have produced generations of boys with low creativity, and others have produced those with truly Bardic fluency. The reason has almost certainly to be sought elsewhere. It might be the presence of a gifted or energetic English teacher; it might be the hidden drive of a new Headmaster anxious to make his mark with dynamic new initiatives; it might be a brace of particularly devoted magazine editors; it might be a bigger budget granted by an unusually generous Bursar. (Well, I did say 'might'.)

However that may be, the nineteen-sixties produced just such a crop of 'original work', and the four pieces that follow come from this period.

*From June, 1960 comes this 'Extract from a Letter Home':*

'I've just read a book. I know that may not seem anything much but – well, I don't read many books, as you know, not the stiff-covered ones anyway. I had a look at the notice-board the other day, too, and apparently this G.E.C. or something starts soon so I thought perhaps I'd better read one. You know, it might help. Well, you never know, do you?

'Anyway, I read this book and it wasn't bad either. Quite an old book it was with funny pictures in it and Bill's father's name was in it in the front (where they tell you to put your name and form and the date) and Bill's father was here a long time ago. I don't remember what the date was but – well, it was Bill's *father* after all.

'It was a bit of a funny plot, too. This chap – I've forgotten his name but it was a silly one, like Oliver or Oswald or something – is in love with a silly girl who doesn't love him. I'm a bit hazy about why she won't love him but I think it was because she's lost something or other. Anyway, this girl falls in love with another girl who for some reason is supposed to be dressed as a man but, of course, she can't be in love with her because she's a girl if you see what I mean. Well, this one who's dressed as a man gets in trouble with a drunken old boy who hangs around the place where this first girl lives, and this girl – the second girl, that is – has a fight; but she doesn't *really* have the fight – her brother does. This brother has been shipwrecked and they thought they were dead. I mean, he thought she was and she thought he was. And then when her brother has this fight – with swords – ! That'll show you how old this yarn is – this girl – not the bloke's sister but the other one – asks him to marry her and he says yes, so his sister goes off with the first chap, and, you know, they all live happily ever after.

'I know it doesn't sound much but it wasn't bad. Nothing like that "Caves of Steel" I was telling you about last week but it was fun trying to work out who was which and whether the chap who wrote it got mixed up somewhere.

'Apparently there are two others I ought to read. Bill, the erk, has read all three! Talk about a blackleg. Do you know the others? One's a play called "Toby with the Angels" and the other's a book called 'Big Expectations" or something. Oh, and that other one I read is called "Twelfth Night". Ever heard of it?'

*The second came from December, 1964.* [They used to publish the *Register* twice a year in those days. Much earlier they used to publish once a term.] The piece was called 'The Bird on the Ball':

'Where I live at Instow, a small village in North Devon, between Bideford and Barnstaple, there is a cricket club called the North Devon Cricket Club. In the pavilion there is a small glass box on the wall, in which there is a stuffed Titlark perched on a Cricket Ball. Also in the box there is small card on which is written: –

"This Titlark was killed on the pitch with this ball (the bowler A.J. Tweedie) in the match between the North Devon Cricket Club and West Buckland School on the 4$^{th}$ June, 1890. The umpire was Frank Townsend of the England and Gloucester XI. It was presented by Basil Fanshawe a member of the opposing team."'

*June, 1963 produced the third.* It was entitled 'Trust not the Greeks':
'The average person today is unaware that adventure and romance exist in buying and selling. We consider it a mundane task to be dispensed with in the shortest possible time. This is not always the case. In many countries buying and selling are fine arts and no transaction can take place without a fitting preliminary of bargaining.

'This is especially true in the Levant.

'Market day was always the day on which I replenished my larder and, providing one ignored the flies, shopping was a pleasant pastime. Immediately after the first calling to prayer I would make my way to the Square where I would sit by the fountain with the old men and watch the stalls being erected. As soon as the stalls were set up their owners would begin to advertise their goods.

' "Silks from Norphov," one would shout.

' "Kantara olives," another would bellow.

' "Bellupais chickens," a third would scream. This would continue until a customer distracted the ower's attention.

'Gradually the Square would fill up as buses disgorged countryfolk all anxious to get the first price for their goods: peasants wearing the traditional snake boots and baggy trousers; their wives in black habits and shawls; and, as always, the priest, his high black hat and bun of hair standing out among a sea of heads.

'On one occasion I fell into conversation with a village priest and after we had discussed the grape harvest and the water shortage, he asked if he could help with my shopping. Not wishing to appear impolite, I said I would be delighted, whereupon we embarked on a shopping expedition I was not allowed to forget.

'To my amazement, wherever the priest went his price was accepted without argument. We finished the shopping and I found that I had paid slightly less than usual. I thanked the priest and left him in the crowd.

'When I arrived at the café – all life in the Levant radiates outwards from cafes – I found that I was the joke of the town, but politeness did not allow me to share the joke until I mentioned it. Eventually I plucked up courage and asked Kemel, the Turkish butcher. He explained that the priest had taken me to stalls which only sold the produce from his own village, and that he had therefore made a profit out of me, an unforgivable thing to happen to anyone shopping in the Levant. Between gales of laughter he managed to blurt out, "Trust not the Greek when he comes bearing gifts," and, as an afterthought, he added, "still less a priest." '

*Finally, from the Register of December, 1961, came this.* It was called simply 'The Purchase'.

'I was sitting in the village Gasthaus one evening when a tall man in a black, expensive-looking overcoat walked towards me and asked whether the seat opposite me was taken. I said no, and invited him to sit down. We chatted about the political situation as strangers are apt to do when they first meet, and then he surprised me by asking me a question which bore no relationship either to political or other situations.

' "Would you like to buy a locomotive?" he said.

'Not wanting to appear inexperienced in the field of locomotive purchasing, I regarded him shrewdly, and wondered what attributes a good locomotive should have. I didn't want him to think me a fool in the ways of the world.

' "How many wheels has it got?" I demanded carefully.

' "The usual number," he replied. (Good. I had obviously showed myself the sort of person who knew how many wheels there were on locomotives.) "This engine," he assured me, "is one of the country's very best express models. It is made of best steel and has only done 300,000 miles."

'He continued to impress with facts and figures which sounded very reasonable, so I bought the locomotive from him at what he assured me was a moderate price for the good locomotive in saleroom condition. Then he clinched the deal by offering to deliver it himself free of charge.

'He delivered it next day and we parked what we could of it in the garage. He seemed experienced in garaging locomotives and when he didn't seem to worry overmuch that the front stuck out into the road, I didn't like to mention the fact that neighbours might complain. I paid him by cheque and that was that.

'Some weeks later a distant cousin of mine, a dreadful bore, came to stay with me. He is the sort of person who is never disturbed by any situation, and who invariably displays a calm, which I envy, when things go wrong.

' "Don't you love the delicious aroma of Spring?" I cried, hoping to impress him with my appreciation of Nature.

' "Huh!" he snorted. "Leaf mould."

' "But surely," I coaxed, "you can smell the snowdrops thrusting their way towards the sun?"

' "Huh!" he snorted again. "Leaf mould."

'So I gave up and prayed that he would soon go.

' "I'll go and park my car in the garage," he said, and walked off.

'A few minutes later he returned looking white and haggard. "Th-th-th-there's a locomotive i-i-i-in your g-g-g-garage," he cried.

' "Yes," I replied, looking him boldly in the eyes. "Nice model, don't you think?"

'He shut his eyes tightly and shook his head in disbelief. "Do you use it often?"

' "Not all that much, you know," I replied. "Last week I took a woman to the maternity home, and I sometimes go shopping in it." He turned, looking deadly pale, and rushed down the path to his car. I haven't seen him since.

'Last week I read in the paper that the German Peoples' Railway had lost a locomotive. I called in at the local Lost Property Office and now they've got it back. I've met the chap who sold it to me again since that, too. I was sitting in the same place last night when he came in and asked if I would like to buy a crane. But what on earth would anybody want with a crane?'

Well, there they are. I think they are as good a mixed bag of schoolboy literary composition as you will get in your average school magazine.

Intrigued, I did some detective work, and I have been able to identify three of the authors.

The first, however, signs himself simply 'H.'. We don't know if it refers to his Christian name or surname. It might not refer to his name at all – like 'M.' in the James Bond books. Not even Holmes at his most brilliant – three pipes and all – could have done much with that single initial. The mystery makes him more, in a way, timeless than the other three. The subject-matter reinforces this. 'H.' somehow speaks for all those generations of boys who have been force-fed with Culture – and especially Shakespeare – since – well, almost since that original small boy crept 'like snail unwillingly to school'. It is a fine example of the schoolboy's brilliant knack of expressing his scepticism about the value of education at all, of reducing something to its bare bones, and of getting it wrong and getting it right at one and the same time. His observations came in the *Register* of June, 1960. (It could, of course, be the work of a clever teacher.)

The second, about the bird killed by a cricket ball, is just the sort of academic titbit that would appeal to a bright junior, which is exactly what T.S.H. Hook was in December, 1964, when his contribution was printed. An opportunist too – all he had to do was copy it out. No creative work needed at all. All credit to him, nevertheless, for exploiting a good story when he found it.

The boy who had learnt not to trust the Greeks was Andrew Gould, who attended the School between 1958 and 1966. He wrote his piece for the *Register* of June, 1963. If it seems unusual for an English schoolboy, however clever (and he got an unconditional place at university), to be so fluent and authoritative about the Eastern Mediterranean, the mystery disappears as soon as one reads in his records that his father was a civil servant in the War Department, and had worked abroad for many years. Andrew had spent several years in Cyprus, and at a bad time too – during the terrorist years of the mid-fifties. This is evident from the detailed references to 'silks from Norphov' and 'Kantara olives'. Andrew is no ignorant tourist; he understands the 'edge' between Turk and Greek. And how many package travellers would use the word 'Levant'?

The boy who bought a locomotive was no ignoramus either. His name was Jeremy Barrett, and he attended the School from 1957 to 1964. He was only 15 when he wrote this piece for the December, 1961 *Register*. His father was a Canadian Air Force officer, who had been stationed all over England, and in Germany as well – which explains Jeremy's specialised knowledge. It is quite likely too that the conversation he recalls really did take place in German. One of his university recommendation letters (the forerunner of the UCAS form) speaks of his 'considerable fluency' in the language.

It is interesting that all three of these young writers that we were able to identify had a full and rewarding career at West Buckland. All three became prefects; all three were elected to the Phoenix Society (in those days limited to 25); all three represented the School at one or more of rugby, cricket, tennis, athletics, cross-country, and shooting – with the odd captaincy and school colours thrown in. Barrett won the *Exmoor*, and received a Fortescue Medal. All three went on to university – Hook to Exeter, Gould to Cardiff, Barrett to York.

If there is a moral to this, it is that writing is not some minority hobby or peculiar activity that is resorted to by wimps and failures and frail flowers who can't do anything else. All these boys led busy and active lives, both in and out of the classroom, but they had other ideas too, which they somehow found time to express – and express with some facility.

Of course, it is also possible to say that this is only further evidence of an old truth: if you are good at five or six things, it is more than likely that you will be good at eight or nine things. No matter how hard the educational reformers try to fashion a system that will give opportunity to as wide a range of pupils as possible, there will always be those who seem to be a dab hand at nearly everything. 'To them that hath, it shall be given.' It may not be justice, but it is life.

There is a third moral, which may be slightly more encouraging for those of us who feel we are not especially gifted. All these boys wrote from authority; they knew what they were talking about. Hook had seen for himself that plaque about the bird; Gould knew Cyprus; Barrett spoke good German. The enigmatic 'H.' spoke for himself and for all schoolboys who had suffered from set books. All of us, if we dig deep enough, have a fund of personal experience which we can draw upon to produce something that other people don't know about.

Of course, one has to be able to write coherent English. But that can, to a certain extent, be taught. What can not be taught is the experience. Each writer has to obtain that for himself, and that is what is important; that is what makes him unique. And that is worth communicating; that is what makes him readable.

If he happens to have a natural fluency in language as well, that is a bonus. And, as a tailpiece, it seems that Jeremy Barrett possessed this natural fluency. There is in his file a letter he wrote to the Headmaster, Leslie Stephens, during his first term at York University. It would have been almost worth quoting in its entirety as a contribution to the *Register*.

It is, as you would expect, full of what a young undergraduate might talk about in his first term – hunger, thirst, poverty, the difficulty of getting down to work, the unfamiliarity of city rush and crush after the open air of West Buckland, the full social life, and so on. But there are some touches of sharp observation, and he has a neat line in self-deprecation. For example:-

'My apologies for writing both in biro and on pages from my note book – it is not a measure of my esteem, as I have told you before! To be quite candid, writing paper and fountain pen = approx. 2 meals, and food is primary. You can't eat books! Actually, it is not quite as bad as I make out. Just that the dramatic possibilities of the situation are appealing. They appeal to my parents too, unfortunately, for they can't quite believe that undergraduates are real unless they are poor – when they joke about sending me back with a bag of porridge oats under my arm, I get the feeling they are almost not kidding!'

His rooms were next to the Cadbury's factory, so 'you feel you are breathing cocoa after a while'.

'The [River] Ouse flows stolidly through the city, giving an atmosphere of damp to everything.' (A most evocative adjective – 'stolidly' – which somehow conjures up a whiff of Yorkshire.)

'We are still fraternizing with our teachers, as the constitution seems to demand – my evenings are spent Charlestoning with lecturers' wives in dimly-lit cellars, which is all very well till you feel yourself getting black looks from tutors and seminar lecturers who you never thought had anything to do with that rather forward, gorgeous young thing who you were getting on so well with. That isn't just my propensity for dramatic possibilities either.'

'There is so much Socialist feeling here it is quite overpowering. Somehow it puts you off, as they all spend their time growing beards and raving about coloured bus conductors and Polaris.' (That dates it.)

'I am already a stalwart member of the Apathy Society – and we sit round whenever two or more members meet by chance (there must be no organised meetings – after all, would anyone care?) lamenting immigration and Concorde and wondering whether the Minister of Culture will be a representative of A.E.U. or a shop steward from the Railway Workers.' (This was a time of Labour Government, remember – Old Labour.)

'There is a lot of work to do, if only I can get started, so I had better try.

Best wishes,
Jeremy.'

If Mr. Hook, Mr. Gould, Mr. Barrett, or 'H.' should read this, it would be interesting to hear their recollections, if any, of these lines.

## Going into Relics

WELL, WHY NOT? THE Archive is, after all, concerned with relics of the past; that's what it's there for, among other things. It is also concerned with what are loosely termed 'public relations' – making contact with old pupils, making the world aware of the length, depth, and relevance of the School's history. If people develop enough interest in this, they could become well-disposed towards the School, and this can show dividends in greater willingness to contribute to the School's welfare.

Does that mean that there is a collection box outside the Archive Office? Does the Archivist, at the end of one of his assemblies, pass round the hat in the Memorial Hall? When he comes to a class and takes an occasional lesson on the history of the School, does he ask the resident teacher for a fee? No, no, and no again. Of course not. I trust we are not as clumping and heavy-handed as that.

But it is nevertheless true that one – just one – of the many responsibilities of the Archivist is to be alive to the occasional commercial opportunity. Bit like the Catholic Church, when you think about it.

They were into the relics business in a big way. How many of you have been in a Church in Italy or Spain where the sacristan will tell you in hushed tones that under the altar is a thorn from the original Crown of Thorns, or a piece of straw from the original Manger, or – a regular one, this – a fragment of the True Cross? Yes, I know – the most trifling mental calculation will tell you that, if all these holy relics were put together from all over Christendom, there would be enough thorns to surround the Sleeping Beauty's castle all over again, enough pieces of straw to feed a stableful of racehorses, and enough chunks of the Cross to populate a whole graveyard.

So why is it worth drawing a comparison between the Archive and the Catholic Church? If the majority of the Catholic Church's 'genuine' relics are anything but genuine, how does that do any good to West Buckland's relics? Because there is pretty solid evidence that the relics from the West Buckland Archive are real. And secondly, both organisations, as I said, are alive to the fact that they might be able to turn their respective relics to advantage.

For instance, not long ago, there was an auction on E-bay, in which one of the items on offer was a sweat shirt which had been worn by Jonathan Edwards (the School's, and the world's, most prodigious triple jumper) on the day he heard about England winning the Olympic nomination. We have Mr Edwards' autographed note to prove it. So that raised a bit.

Or again, there has recently come into the School's possession a cricket bat. Ah, but no ordinary cricket bat. This bat belonged to, and was used by, Harold Gimblett, the most celebrated cricketer ever to play for Somerset, and an Old Boy of the School. The ownership of this bat, and the story of its arrival in the School, are both well documented. That could, one day, raise some more – say, a 10p.-a-go competition to estimate the total number of runs scored by Gimblett in a given season.

Of course celebrities, by definition, are pretty few and far between – well, they are in West Buckland. So how about some lateral thinking?

These cricket bats, sweat shirts, and so on are potentially profitable because they belonged to people who were clever or successful. But why should celebrity always be attached to people are clever or successful? If somebody has done something noteworthy, why should he, or she, not be similarly lionised? Surely the celebrity should be attached to the *noteworthiness* of the achievement, not its cleverness or success.

Once you have opened up the argument along these lines, all sorts of opportunities manifest themselves. Why not put up for auction on E-bay the much-thumbed log tables of Gervase Hoskins, late of the West Buckland Fifth Form, who failed his 'O' Level Maths eleven times, and did not leave School till he was twenty-two? (If you think this is outrageous, I can show you evidence of several pupils who were still here after they had passed their twentieth birthday. We had one boy in Year 9 at the age of seventeen.)

What about the long-preserved sticking plaster from the left heel of Theodoric Lumsden-Crawley ('Creepy' to one and all), who came last in the *Exmoor* five years running (to coin a phrase)? Or the expense account of Prince Matthias Pilimathalawa, who regularly treated his whole tutor group to £500 worth of goodies in the tuck shop every week?

This approach throws up endless possibilities. It could send pupil offspring of Old Members scrambling through their parents' lofts and cellars, in the search for physical proof of the wry confession that has punctuated the family conversation for years. Or – the other way round – something could be discovered that revealed for the first time a particularly shy skeleton in Grandpa's cupboard of school memories which he has been keeping quiet about for years.

It is within the reach of all of us, if we stop to think, to lay claim to a unique distinction. I, for instance, am the only person left in the whole human race who has not seen *The Sound of Music*.

If the achievement is unique, why should it not be celebrated? Why should we not be given the chance to feast our eyes on some object which proves it? It could raise a laugh and raise a penny at one and the same time. And what is wrong with that?

# 10. Alphabetical Guide to Emails

This is the result of the Archivist wasting time – doodling on his screen.

**Email** – the common or garden variety
**Amail** – there's only one letter for you, I'm afraid
**Bemail** – used by Hamlet and others incapable of making up their mind
**Demail** – the message has been unsent
**Dreamail** – for messages which tell you you've won the lottery
**Femail** – a facility for ladies, which allows them to change the message after it has been sent
**Fleemail** – run a mile from this stuff; it's chock full of virusesesesesesesesesees==8**33£!!!
**Fremail** – a contradiction in terms – ya don't get nuthin' fer nuthin'
**Glemail** – covered with silver and gold sequins – for glutinous birthday greetings
**Hemail** – for weight-lifters and those who kick sand in the faces of wimps on the beach
**Jemail** – for Americans who are going to get a surprise
**Kemail** – for telling him that you've forgotten the combination on the garage door lock
**Kneemail** – for those who try to operate a laptop in crowded train compartments
**Lemail** – Well, *you* think of something
**Memail** – for lonely hearts, as a last resort
**Pleamail** – begging letters
**Premail** – telling you that a message is on the way
**Remail** – if at first you don't succeed
**Seemail** – you have unread messages
**Screamail** – for Pete's sake don't send any more
**Steamail** – for those who can't make a computer work and who are still stuck with the PO
**Teamail** – a late afternoon message
**Teemail** – a special service for golfers
**Vemail** – for Devon farmers' wives preparing cream for the Pannier Market
**Wemail** – used only by the Queen
**X-mail** – deleted as unsuitable for adult reading

*Nearly off the Record*

**Yemail** – a medieval format, reserved for research students
**Zemail** – some odd Yankee letter or other

## 11. A Spot of History

### A Small World

IT IS A SMALL world. A school world is even smaller. All its events are recorded in a school magazine. Yours is called *The Three R's*. If you are well educated, you will know that the original 'three R's' were Reading, Riting, and 'Rithmetic. If you are well-informed, you will know that, at West Buckland, *The Three R's* stand for 'Read, Reap, and Register'. 'Read and Reap' because it is the School motto – take a look at your blazer badge, if you can bend your necks that far. The third 'R' stands for 'Register', because that was the name of the original school magazine, which began in 1863, and came to an end only in 1997.

Up in the Archive we have an almost complete run of these magazines, over 300. If your mental arithmetic is good, you should be asking yourselves why there were 300 of them, when they began only 139 years ago. The answer is that, for most of its history, the *Register* used to come out every term, not every year. They can make interesting reading.

Take the *Register* for exactly a hundred years ago – for the Autumn Term, 1902. It consisted of 27 pages. Very few of the contents would get past an editor today.

Would Mrs. Pugsley [a new young teacher who was immediately given the chore of editing the magazine – which she performed with skill and devotion] allow an account of a French language course in Normandy attended by the School Chaplain, running to four pages? I doubt it. Would she print a three-page essay on Cecil Rhodes, one of the great British heroes of 1902? Hardly. Would she even allow a three-page biography of a modern hero like David Beckham? I doubt that too.

So far we have accounted for seven pages out of a total of twenty-seven. If you are particularly quick on the uptake, you will be wondering what they put in the other twenty. I can tell you in one word – cricket. And I don't suppose Mrs. Pugsley would have allowed that either.

Cricket. The whole school, it seems, was nuts about cricket. Well, the editors were anyway. Accounts and scorecards of every match played by the School teams – both boys and masters. Two and half pages of statistics and averages alone.

Top of the boys' averages was T.H. Watts. He took nearly three times as many wickets as anybody else, and his batting average was four times greater than that of his nearest rival. He was quite an athlete. He held the School record for throwing the cricket ball – 105 yards. Next summer go out on to the field and try that one for yourself. 105 yards. After he left, he went on to play football for Notts County. He was killed in the First World War.

Bottom of the teachers' batting averages was Mr. R.H. Spear. Innings – 3; highest score – 7; total runs for the season – 7. He had come to the School in 1900 – the first teacher to be appointed specifically to teach Science. They didn't build any laboratories for him till 1904, by which time he had left. Given up waiting, I suppose.

Fifth in the batting averages was the Head Boy. His name was Wheeler. When the School was in danger of being closed because its numbers had dropped so low – 31 (that's the total – 31), in a school designed to accommodate over 150 – he went in person to Earl Fortescue and begged him to change his mind. And succeeded. A few years later, the School was in danger of closure again – no money. Wheeler, now a young governor, did his second rescue act. This time he said he knew just the man to save the School – a new headmaster. The Revd. E.C. Harries. Harries arrived in 1907 and stayed till 1934 – and saved the School.

Also in the masters' cricket team was the School Chaplain, the one who went to Normandy, the Revd. E.C. Harries. Yes, the same Harries. He left in 1904 to work at Blundell's, then came back again in 1907 at Wheeler's suggestion. Wheeler himself became Headmaster in 1952. The current Headmaster in 1902, Mr. Knight, was also a keen cricketer. Top of the teachers' averages. So that teachers' team of 1902 contained three West Buckland Heads.

Second in the batting and fourth in the bowling was Mr. Taylor, who wore a moustache as big as Wyatt Earp's – if you know who he was. He taught Drawing, Music, Shorthand, Book-keeping, and Geography, and ran the School Choir. His nickname was 'Judy' because, apparently, he had a voice like that of Mr. Punch. He also played the organ at East Buckland Church, and is buried in the churchyard. Harries is buried there too. Beside him lies his wife, who lived to be ninety-nine. She died only 17 years ago. She was the sister of the Head Boy of 1907. How many headmasters have married the sister of an ex-Head Boy – of his own school?

Also in that cricket team – quite a team, this – was a boy called G.E.L. Carter, one of four Carter brothers. He was the one who wrote the article about Cecil Rhodes. He was also the first president of the School Debating Society, founded 99 years ago. The teacher in charge of the present Debating Society is Mr. Richard Carter. G.E.L. Carter is his grandfather.

It is indeed a small world.

## Tablets of Stone

THE MOTION BEFORE THE House this morning, ladies and gentlemen, is stones. That's right – stones. And not just any old stones. Nor do I refer to gem stones, tombstones, prune stones, gallstones, or paving stones. I mean the sort of stones you stick up or lay down somewhere – memorial stones and foundation stones.

I wonder how many you have noticed around the place. Two? Three? Four? In fact, it could be as many as ten – maybe even more. I don't have time to talk about all of them – you will be relieved to know. Just a sample. Let us begin with an old one – one you have to look at quite hard to read.

It's dated 1880, and it was laid, unusually, by two people, not one. They were very clever boys who had once come top in their public exams in the whole of the country, so they were invited to lay this one in the wall of a Fives Court. What are Fives? Ask Mr Ponder. And where was the Fives Court? The court itself is not there, but the building still is. Look around. And one of the boys who laid the stone was called Chope – Richard Pearse Chope. A most remarkable boy, and an even more remarkable Old Boy – he deserves a whole assembly to himself. And he'll get one one of these days. You will find his name over a door too – somewhere.

What was remarkable about this stone? What was remarkable was that he – Chope – was invited to lay it *while he was still a pupil at the School*. Beat that.

The oldest stone, of course, is the Foundation Stone of the whole School, dated 1860. You should know where that is. It was laid by the second Earl Fortescue, who had provided the land for the School in the first place. Sadly he died just days before the building was completed and opened, so his son, the third Earl, did it.

Outside the Dining Hall, you will find another, very wordy stone set into the wall. It tells you why the Hall was called the Karslake. In fact there is a wealth of information on that wall. A lot of detail about the Reverend William Karslake, naturally, and, next to it, a stern warning: *No bags/instruments to be left here*.

To read the next stone, you have to be student of Braille. All the ink or stain has been worn away from the lettering, and you have get the sun in exactly the right position in order to discover that it was laid in 1962 by Sir Bernard Waley-Cohen, that the Chairman of Governors was Brigadier Michael Roberts, D.S.O., and that the Headmaster was Mr. Leslie Stephens. Have a look for that.

In 1930 there was a big fire in the School. To replace the lost buildings, they built the Memorial Hall. Of course a stone was laid for that too. But they went and laid the wrong stone. We have in the Archive a photograph of Earl Fortescue – the fourth Earl this time – doing the honours with the trowel and the mallet. And I also found a picture of the stone, complete with inscription. It said: 'This foundation stone was laid by Hugh, fifth Earl Fortescue, K.C.B., on 12$^{th}$ October, 1932.'

Did you catch that? I said the fourth Earl laid the stone, but the inscription said it was the fifth Earl. I rang up Lady Margaret Fortescue herself at Castle Hill, and she confirmed it was her grandfather, the fourth Earl, who did it. She should know; she was there. 75 years ago. And the photograph of course proved it.

So why did they get the inscription on the stone wrong? And why did nobody notice it? Or did everybody notice it, and did nobody have the courage to tell the old Earl, or the masons, or the Headmaster, or all the assembled VIP's, that there had been a mistake? Was everybody *that* well-mannered?

However, if you go now to the foot of the wall of the Memorial Hall – outside here – you will see that the inscription says 'Hugh, *fourth* Earl Fortescue', the old man. Well, actually, because the lettering has been damaged by the weather, it doesn't say 'Hugh, fourth Earl'; it says 'H-gi, fourth Earl'. What had happened? Apparently, an eagle-eyed headmaster near the end of the 1930's at last noticed, but still nobody did anything about it until 1944, in the middle of the Second World War. A gang of workmen arrived, pulled out the wrong foundation stone (without bringing down the wall of the Memorial Hall), and put in a new one. I have a letter from an Old Boy who remembers watching them do it.

So that's the saga of the wrong foundation stone. In his speech in 1932, the fourth Earl said that he remembered, as a very small boy, watching *his* grandfather, the second Earl, lay the first stone in 1860. Lady Margaret Fortescue, who lives still at Castle Hill up the road, knew the fourth Earl. So a lady who is alive now – 2007 – once sat on the knee of a man who had witnessed the laying of the first stone in 1860 – 147 years ago.

Now – isn't that interesting! Or perhaps it leaves you stone cold. Stone? Foundation stone? Stone cold? Never mind.

And do you know the very latest memorial stone? Laid this year? You should do; you probably walked across it to get to this assembly.

## Yet Another Centenary

THERE IS SOMETHING SPECIAL about the number 100, have you noticed? Nobody claps when a batsman reaches 99, but they don't half clap when he reaches 100, and it's only 1 per cent more. Your family don't make a fuss when you reach your 99th birthday (well, they didn't for me), but they really push the boat out when you make it to 100. Even the Queen sends you a telegram. So I'm looking forward.

Why a hundred? Is it the third digit? I shouldn't think so. Nobody does much for the figure 101, or any of the others. Is it the two noughts? Maybe. If anybody reached his thousandth birthday, the celebrations would be world-shaking, wouldn't they? I'm looking forward to that too.

What is this figure 100 to do with us today? Well, I'll tell you. West Buckland is 100 years old this year, in fact this month. In ten days' time – 24th May.

Rubbish, you say; you're right out of touch – been up in the Archive too long. West Buckland had its *150th* anniversary four years ago. Well, yes – but only in a way. Because *I've* got news for *you*. A hundred and one years ago, West Buckland School did not exist.

Oh, there was a school here all right, but it wasn't called West Buckland. It was called the Devon County School. It was all the work of that man there – Revd. Joseph Lloyd Brereton. [I made a dramatic gesture towards his portrait on the wall of the Memorial Hall.]

He had the bright idea of setting up a system of secondary schools for the whole country. Why? Because there weren't any. Believe it or not, 150 years ago, secondary education in England, as a system, simply did not exist. Oh, yes, there were the posh, expensive public schools, like Eton and Harrow and Winchester. And some old town grammar schools. But no national system. There were millions of boys and girls whose education just stopped at eleven – if indeed it had even started.

Brereton wanted to set up a secondary school in every county for what he called the 'middle class' – with moderate fees and modern subjects like Science and practical Maths. No endless Latin and Greek and Bible-bashing. The first one was here – that's why he called it the Devon County School. As the years went by, he had a hand in setting up county schools in Somerset, Hampshire, Gloucestershire, Bedfordshire, Surrey, Suffolk, Norfolk, Durham, and so on. But we were the first. Many of these schools failed, but the DCS – the Devon County School – survived.

It became something of a celebrity. It was a pioneer. Journalists wrote articles about it. Celebrities came and had a look – cabinet ministers, peers of the realm, famous writers, a couple of archbishops of Canterbury. Headmasters of other schools came to pick up a few ideas. The DCS came top of the league for public exam results in the whole country – three times running.

But it had a weak spot – its finance. It ran as a limited company, with shareholders, directors, and all. When times were bad – as all times are – from time to time – the share value fell, and the dividends could not be paid. The school came close to being shut down – twice. At the end of the 19$^{th}$ century, we were down to 31 pupils, in a school built to take 180.

There was another crisis in 1907, and we came within a whisker of closing yet again. This clearly could not go on. Directors, benefactors, wealthy old boys, members of the county authority, and local celebrities put their heads together. They agreed that there was no future in trying to make the creaky old Devon County School Company keep struggling. They went right back to square one.

They decided that the company would go into voluntary liquidation – if you like that it would commit suicide. This took time, because they had to persuade all the shareholders to give up their shares and so lose most of their money. When they had enough agreement, they set up a new school, with a board of governors. But no more shares and no more dividends. The school's income was to be raised entirely by fees. All the money was to be spent on the school. The local education committee agreed to pay an annual grant as well, provided that the school gave some places to bright scholarship boys from local primary schools. That was the deal.

A new headmaster was appointed who was going to make the deal work. Luckily, he did. And on Friday, 24$^{th}$ May, 1912, the ultimate, really, absolutely final meeting of the Devon County School Company took place in Bridge Buildings, Barnstaple. The very last papers were signed, and West Buckland School was born. A hundred years ago. So – for the birthday you didn't know you had – many happy returns.

## The *Exmoor*

THERE WAS ONCE AN English actor, who enjoyed a long career in British films – way before your time – called Wilfrid Hyde-White. Always the polished English gentleman, well groomed, frightfully well spoken. A familiar face for years. Couldn't act for toffee, but he was just a delightful man. He had been to drama school though. He said he had learned two things from drama school: 1. He could not act. 2. It did not matter. For which he was always grateful.

I have been a history teacher for most of my working life. Do I expect my pupils to remember the facts I taught them? Of course not. But that, as Mr. Hyde-White would have said, does not matter. What matters is that History makes you grateful – grateful that you live in the twenty-first century, and not in any of the others that came before.

Later on this week, you will be engaged in something the thought of which may not make you clap your hands with excitement. If any of you have been living on the moon recently, I refer to the *Exmoor*. But take heart and be grateful, ladies and gentlemen; if you had been a pupil of the School in bygone years, you would have had to face much more than that. Adding up all the Senior and Junior cross-country runs, you would have had to face no fewer than fifteen. Imagine – fifteen cross-country runs.

Like the *Exmoor*, they all had names – the *Bray*, the *Beeches*, the *Tuck*, the *Leary*, the *Westacott*, the *Stoodleigh*, and so on. One or two had less romantic names – the *Railway*, the *North-West*, and there was one with the sinister title, the *Long* – which, according to Mr. Robert Clarke, was even worse than the *Exmoor*.

Only the *Exmoor* survives. Thank God, you may say. And with good reason – a six-mile walk to the Poltimore Arms for the start, and a nine-mile run back from Five Barrows to the School (if you are a senior boy, that is – if you are merely a junior or a girl, you do rather less). The oldest, longest, regular, compulsory school cross-country run in the length and breadth of England. Well, that's what we have been saying since 1859, and nobody has come up with anything to disprove it yet.

It has been cancelled only twice in 157 years – once in the arctic winter of 1947, when the River Taw froze; and once in 2001, because of the foot-and-mouth epidemic.

In that time, the *Exmoor* has built up its fair share of legends and tall stories. For the first forty-nine years of its existence, it was a Hare-and-Hounds paper chase; sometimes even the Headmaster joined in the laying of the trail. The modern course was laid out in 1908, by another Headmaster, and one of his staff. There have been a few chops and changes since, but it is substantially what those two men set out 96 years ago.

There have been star performers over the years. Arthur Pearce, who left in 1908, won thirteen out of fourteen races. A boy called Farmer – C.S.R. Farmer – during the First World War, won nineteen out of twenty, and would have won the twentieth but for an accident. He also won eight events out of nine in the School sports in 1917 – in one afternoon. But records get beaten; Herbert Tully, between 1930 and 1936, won the under-13 *Exmoor* twice, the under-15 *Exmoor* twice, and the Exmoor *Exmoor* twice. Thirty years later, his son won the *Exmoor*. And even that has been beaten; J.R. Jones, in the 1950s, won four straight *Exmoors*.

The markers built their own traditions too. Talk to any Old Boy from over thirty years ago, and you will hear the tallest of stories about cooking sausages and baked beans, building fires which nearly brought down a barn, and the mysterious Case of the Disappearing Chicken.

Any old *Exmoor* hand will tell you, naturally, that things are not what they used to be. In the Archive is the piece of paper which set out the entire arrangements for the 100$^{th}$ *Exmoor* in 1959. This is what it says: '9 – Breakfast. 10 – Assembly. 10.30 – Markers collect food. 12.15 – Lunch. 2.30 – START. 3.45 – Soup and baths. 5.30 – Tea and optional bed. [Bed! At half-past five.] 7.30 – Supper. 7.45 – Obligatory bed.' That's it – the entire arrangements. Twenty words. A few years ago, Mr. Clarke needed, for the same purpose, 83 sheets of closely-typed A4.

Because it *was* the centenary, the School tried to push the boat out a bit. They invited television news teams to West Buckland to film the hundredth *Exmoor*. The BBC crew made the runners start twice because they needed time to get somewhere else. The ITV crew got tangled up with a flock of sheep, and missed the finish, and made the first seven or eight runners finish again. The whole School crowded round the telly in the evening to watch. The BBC provided sixty seconds. ITV forgot about it altogether. But that, as they say, is show business. Mr. Hyde-White would surely have understood.

## 12. The Shock of the New

### Building for the Future

THE ROMAN EMPEROR AUGUSTUS, so it was said, boasted that he found Rome a city of brick, and left it a city of marble. The unmistakable implication of this statement is that the city was enhanced, and that he was proud of it. This seems to be a pretty general trend: kings, emperors, presidents, headmasters, governors, councillors, and bosses in general are fond of referring to the constructions they have initiated, driven along, and opened, by way of offering a measure of their success during their tenure of office.

The latest building on the West Buckland campus is, of course, the Sports Hall. We have, for the last year or so, watched it grow, contemplated its several incarnations – from single sod to Martian war machine, to Dutch barn, to aircraft hangar, and so through all its forms to its final manifestation as the new home of athletic aspiration and social gathering, and a luxurious haven for the PE staff.

There has of course been no chief executive or single governing unit during the whole of West Buckland's existence, so it would not be possible or fair to pose a possible parallel between them and Augustus. Nevertheless, the situation provokes contemplation on the idea of using this edifice as a means of judging the progress the school has made during its 150 years of existence? How does the Sports Hall compare? How does it fit? Where does it stand?

Clearly it dwarfs the original farmhouse at Middle Stoodleigh, where three fourteen-year-old boys from Bishop's Tawton came together to form the West Buckland Farm and County School in November, 1858. Ditto the farmhouses at Tideport and Middle Hill, whither they migrated as numbers grew. Ditto the wooden dormitory that was opened on Queen Victoria's birthday on Tuesday, 24$^{th}$ May, 1859.

The first permanent building – the 'proper' school if you like – is a different matter. The School fathers wanted something solid and definite, and that is what they got. When the first railway stations were constructed in the nineteenth century, nobody had any idea of what a railway station was supposed to look like, because stations had never been built before. But people reckoned that they knew what a school should look like, for all that West Buckland was the first of its kind – a school for 'the middle class'.

A school was a home of learning, a sign of serious intent, and a vessel of the Truth of God. So what did we get? Some massive masonry, pointy arches, and a foundation plaque which expressed the hope that 'that the Great Architect of the Universe. . . . will bless and prosper the work this day commenced. . . . the promotion of God's glory in the extension of sound and practical education. . . . the diffusion of useful knowledge, upon the imperishable foundation of God's truth'.

These stern features outside, and some hard wooden benches and cold passages inside, have survived nearly 150 years of constant usage, and have, somewhat surprisingly, inspired a great deal of affection and loyalty in generations of pupils.

The additions which soon followed, to form the Quadrangle and the Karslake Hall, were in the same style and intent. The only oddity was the isolation 'hospital', now in use as the miniature range. Do any cadets, as they ease springs, ever wonder how many ghosts of bedbound boys with funny spots may be gazing down on their efforts?

The twentieth century presented a whole housing estate-ful of buildings – a small forest of prefab and pebble-dash, breeze block and brick, fibre-glass and fireproofing, timber and concrete, plastic and glass, which has catered for the needs of swimmers, sleepers, scholars, scientists, sixth-formers, small children, sweaty games players, and seekers after artistic, dramatic, and electronic truth.

How does the new temple of Muscle and Sinew compare with all that? Does it fit that tradition, grace it, or depart from it? How will it fare in the next 150 years?

Ironically, the main material visible in the new Sports Hall is brick. The most striking feature of the entrance passage of the original building is the foundation stone, with its humble and inspiring inscription. And what is it made of? Marble.

What, I wonder, would the Emperor Augustus have made of that?

But the irony, if irony it is, need not worry us. 150 years from now, the argument will be academic. Everything will be done by computer, simulation, and virtualisation. Teachers will not exist; students will choose which lessons, which subjects, which examinations, to download, and they will simply phone in their contribution, if any. The School will be a website on a screen. There won't be a need for any buildings at all.

## Are We All Talking About the Same Thing?

ANY NEW BUILDING BIG enough to attract notice will soon attract comment. The '150' Building is no exception.

Perhaps the first crop of remarks may spring from its very name. It seems an unusual strategy to rely on numbers rather than on words, though it does open an intriguing vista, which would offer simplicity and universality. Why not extend the principle to the whole campus? So the Sports Centre, which opened two years ago, becomes the '148' Building; the Science Block reappears as '134'; the Sixth Form Centre is identified as '120', the Karslake as '20', and the main front building as a mere '2'.

Precisionists will then hasten to point out that the Sports Centre, which was opened in 2008, should really be the '150' Building, and that therefore the Arts Block should be '152'.

Then consider this: all the classrooms are already known by numbers. Form names have disappeared, and are identified by year groups – Year 2, Year 5, and so on. There are scores of further numbers for the countless telephone extensions, unavoidably. If you added building numbers to the mix, perhaps that would be asking for trouble. . . . 'Year 10 French set 2, madam? – ring up 574 to tell them you're coming, and then go to to 17B in 39.' And suppose you numbered the corridors and staircases as well. No – perhaps we had better stick to names.

But that still leaves the possible debate over putting a name to the '150' Building. How about a charity competition, similar to the one instituted a few years ago to find a name for the Headmaster's new kitten? The Titian Position? The Goya Foyer? The Turner Learner? The Nouvre Louvre?

When we move from consideration of names to consideration of the building itself, we come up against personality. Put another way, your judgment and opinion will depend upon who you are.

Founders are naturally proud of their pet project, and will extol its style, its modernity, its daring experimentation, and its relevance. Well, they would, wouldn't they?

Designers will be relieved that a modest part of their original conception has survived the attentions of the planners, the local authority, the accountants, the environmental lobby, and English Heritage. But they can have the satisfaction of being able to gaze modestly at their toes while the opening speeches heap praise on their vision and creativity.

The builders will heave a collective, and heartfelt, sigh of of relief that the whole thing is over, that the weather didn't ruin everything, that they didn't puncture an oil well, that it was all finished on time, that the bills have been paid, and that they are not burdened with the tiresome application of penalty clauses.

Parents invited to the opening party will gaze and wonder at the style, marvel at all the goodies inside (comparing them grumpily with the paucity – or total absence – of facilities available when *they* were children), and speculate darkly on the extent to which the overall cost will be reflected in the coming years' fees.

And so the list could go on. A few moments' thought, and you could make a fair stab at the likely reaction of, say, teachers, pupils, inspectors, advisers, governors, or professional visitors from other schools. It all depends, as I said, on your point of view.

After all, you couldn't expect a very appreciative reaction from the charladies in the Parthenon, who had to get up on ladders every day with their feather flicks and dust off the marble friezes. It is easy to imagine and sympathise with the remarks of gladiators who might complain bitterly about the appalling sanitary arrangements provided for performers in the Colosseum.

But time is the great healer; the sharpest critical emotions are eroded by the years into acceptance. It's a bit like being married.

Look at the great medieval cathedrals. Most of us haven't a clue about the host of different styles which were the fruit of centuries of addition and modification. They don't jar on us. Everything has coalesced, and we now simply gaze in admiration.

We may not gaze in admiration at the '150' Building in 300 years' time, but we shall come to live with it. Its very sins and weaknesses (if there are any) will become wryly, almost fondly, accepted as quirks and oddities that, far from detracting from the whole, will come to enhance it, like wrinkles in a grandfather's face. It will all merge, in survivors' minds, into a seamless unity which 'is' West Buckland.

## A Fiery Chariot

IF YOU ARE FAMILIAR with the Old Testament, you will know that the prophet Elijah, at the end of his life, was 'translated' – not from Hebrew into English, but from earth to Heaven – in a fiery chariot, to be precise. Well, actually, not precisely. I looked it up, and it just shows you that you can carry a memory round for years and believe it to be true, only to find, when you check, that it isn't. There was a fiery chariot all right, and some fiery horses too, but they were doing the duty of separating Elijah from his disciple – and successor – Elisha, at the crucial moment. Elijah went up into Heaven sure enough, but apparently it was in a whirlwind. Bit safer than a fiery chariot, I suppose, when you think about it.

Well, the Archive has been translated. Not into Heaven, it must be admitted, but a significant distance in that direction, right up under the main gable at the front of the old building. No chariot and horses of fire either – pity, really; it would have made quite a spectacle. Perhaps they didn't dare, because the main school fire alarm is right outside the new Archive Office window.

But certainly a sort of whirlwind was involved. On Tuesday morning it was business as usual; by two o'clock in the afternoon, the Archivist was knee-deep in boxes and cases, in a brand-new office up in 'the gods'. Everything had been moved – files, cabinets, desk, drawers, clothes (oh, yes, we have some 'Archive' clothes too), pictures, computer kit, phone. . . . the only thing left behind was the carpet.

Why? Because we have a new carpet. We have new paint too, new sort of double glazing (they keep telling me what it's really called, but I keep forgetting), new shelves, even a new light and a new radiator, all gleam and chrome. Beside the new desk site is a fearsome array of sockets and switches – enough to start a radio station. Which could set off a train of thought, couldn't it?

Whichever way you look at it, that is some translation.

But, like all translations – the good ones anyway – it has to make sense. It has to be readily accessible. It has to be useful.

It certainly makes sense to the powers that be. After all, they decided to do it, and it is not for a mere Archivist to question the actions of the Almighty, any more than it would have crossed the mind of Elijah to do so. Now that it has happened, it is up to the Archivist also to make sense of it.

Is it readily accessible? Certainly – if you are sound in wind and limb and have done your apprenticeship on the Matterhorn. But then we can turn that to advantage. If you want to make something attractive, make it just a little bit difficult. As the Pope once said to a young author, 'If you wish to get a wide readership for your new book, I could always get it put on the Index for you.' It is to be hoped, therefore, that curiosity, and perversity, will draw the customers.

Is it going to be useful? Well, it was useful before; we shall have the same gear and the same contents; so we should be able to offer the same service. As a matter of fact, the technical bits and pieces may be somewhat better. Certainly that array of switches and plugs promises well. Who knows? A radio station may turn out to be rather more than a mischievous gleam in the eye. . . . 'Your friendly Archivist, full of chat and gossip – the latest news on who said what to whom at the back of the changing rooms last Friday – make a date with a dinner lady – the top ten from the Music Director's recording out-takes – searching interviews with rejects from the First XV – a sneak preview of the Headmaster's memoirs. Tuesdays and Thursdays every week – same spot on the dial. Available on I-pods, E-pods, A-pods, pea-pods, pod-casts, broadcasts, out-casts, compatible with PDF's, BF's, BBQ's and IQ's.'

As with every other similar situation, there will be snags and there will be opportunities. An obstacle may block your path, but in stepping on it you gain a vantage point from which to view the way ahead. Who knows what will show up? One thing you can be sure of: there will be some surprises.

Elijah must have been curious, at the very least, to know what was going to happen after the whirlwind, after the translation. Similarly, we wonder in the Archive what the future will hold after our translation. Just how good will the new version be?

Like Mr. Asquith, we shall have to 'wait and see'.

## Bed and Board

[WE ARE INFORMED THAT the new boarding block at the back of the school will provide accommodation for seventy sixth-formers, and that each inmate will enjoy en-suite facilities.]

Under the heading of Useless Information, did you know that the word 'Board' in the title does not refer to the primitive bed you might have slept on, but to the table at which you would eat? Well, it does. The earliest tables were planks laid on trestles.

I do not suggest that the early accommodation at West Buckland (originally the West Buckland Farm and County School) was as primitive as this, but, at the kindest estimate, it was not by any stretch of the imagination enviable.

The first three pupils, fourteen years old, all from Bishop's Tawton, all boarded (that word again) in a farmhouse just up the road. There is a plaque on the wall still in place. Farmhouses in the nineteenth century were not the cosy nooks with blushing pink hollyhocks round the edge, as displayed today on greetings cards. Chilly stone, grubby whitewash, iron beds, rush matting, mice (or worse), jugs and china bowls, and outside toilets. Nor did the food boast three Michelin stars.

The boys, despite growing numbers, had to put up with two more farmhouses in the first three years, till at last the governors got round to building the stone edifice you see today facing the road. So dormitories appeared for the first time. A dining-hall came along in the 1870's. Nobody thought of putting toilets inside the building. In fact, for quite a long time, they were generally opposed everywhere as unhygienic: who ever heard of putting such a smelly, germy place *inside* the house? Disgusting.

And, while we're about it, it would be well to remember that there was no mains water. The school was on septic tank drainage. (It still is.) Electricity did not make its appearance till the 1920's. In fact, one school servant was retained whose sole duty was to trim all the lamps in the place. There was of course, no mains gas. (And there still isn't.)

So there was no question of central heating. That did not reach the dormitories till the *nineteen*-eighties, never mind the eighteen-eighties. By coal or oil. Boys not only slept without heating; they slept with the windows open. Healthy, you see. Plenty of fresh air.

The wonder was how robust they all were. A small isolation facility was built to accommodate patients with infectious diseases, but it was so little needed that it was turned into a miniature shooting range. One government medical report after another stressed the boys' rude health. When cadet groups went to summer camps, they dealt with the discomfort far better than the more pampered contingents from the fashionable public schools. Old boys have told me that, when they were captured in the War, they found a German prison camp, after West Buckland, a doddle.

And so it went on. Prospectuses from 1907 show dormitories with beds lined up like 'rijiments o' sawjers', as one Devonian put it. You could at least have extra blankets, apparently. Very good blankets they were too. More than one old boy has told me that forty, fifty, sixty years on, his school blanket was in good nick, even still used.

So the school was no place for weeds. Indeed, one prospectus from as late as the mid-twentieth century drew would-be parents' attention to the fact that 'boys suffering from weakness of bladder or sleepwalking, and delicate boys needing constant care and attention or special diets cannot be accepted'.

The Second World War produced a further refinement to dormitory comfort. Every night, the boarders (in other words, nearly everybody) had to put great sheets of grey cardboard up against the windows, for fear lest the thousands of German bombers that flew nightly over Exmoor might be guided by the dormitories of West Buckland to drop their high explosives on vitally strategic targets like Challacombe or Heasley Mill.

The authorities were not satisfied even with that. However efficient the grey screens were, they said, some light would still escape round the edges. But that would be dealt with, because some Government boffin had discovered that, if you painted your window-panes blue and your light bulbs orange, it would baffle the most fiendishly perceptive German pilots, who would presumably fly off to seek other targets in unmilitary, sparsely-populated sites in the back of beyond like Plymouth or Bristol.

It is to be hoped that the palatial new facilities promised by the new sixth-form accommodation will be an advance on rows of iron beds, wash-basins with ice in them, freezing floors, dark screens, blue windows, and startled, pyjama-ed boys with orange faces.

'They say Prince Charles disapproves of it already.'

'If she's here, who have they sent to open Parliament?'

## 13. Music and Monarchs

THE SCHOOL'S DIRECTOR OF Music, Emma Kent, got the bright idea of giving a concert the theme of which was well-known music pieces taken from the reigns of a selection of English kings. Hence the title: *Music and Monarchs*. The selection was to include William the Conqueror, Henry III, Henry VIII, George II, Queen Victoria, and Queen Elizabeth II – which would clearly offer a wide range of musical styles and sounds.

The concert was a great success, as Emma's concerts usually were.

In order to raise the interest, and to enable the audience to find its historical and musical feet, as it were, I was invited to produce short recitations, in order to offer a simple introduction to each composition, and to put it in some kind of perspective.

## Another Norman Conquest

IF YOU TOOK A hundred people off the street, and demanded that they quote a memorable date from English history, it is ten to one that they would say '1066'.

And with good reason. The Battle of Hastings was the greatest battle ever fought on British soil. We all think we know about the Norman Conquest.

What was the Norman Conquest? Oh, yes, that was all about William the Conqueror, and chain mail, and those ghastly helmets with the bits down the nose, and great charging horses, and castles and keeps and dungeons and all the rest.

True, by and large. But the Conquest was a great deal more than that. It was the greatest shift of land ownership in the history of England. Much of the Saxon nobility had been wiped out at Hastings. The whole country was in effect taken over by a military elite of about 180 new owners. It was a military occupation. That changed only when the Normans looked for wives and began to settle down with local girls. And you know what the hand that rocked the cradle did.

But the Conquest was more than that too. It was not a conquest of the English language, but it was the biggest foreign transfusion the English language ever received. It was to take three hundred years for a sort of 'joint' language to be born out of the blending of Old English and Norman French.

The Normans still weren't finished. They decided that the entire English Church needed a complete overhaul. A flood of foreign priests, chaplains, abbots, and bishops came in to take the best jobs, and change everything. Not only that. A colossal programme of cathedral renewal was begun, and those vast buildings are still visible all over England.

Even that wasn't enough for the Normans. They wanted to change the whole organisation and ritual of the Church, and that included singing.

All this did not come about without a great deal of opposition among the Saxons. One particular Norman abbot was so disliked that the monks staged a mutiny. But Abbot Thurstan of Glastonbury was ready for them. He had his own private troops herd the worst offenders into the abbey church, where they proceeded to fire arrows at the mutineers till they gave in. That's how determined the Normans were to enforce their rule.

So the Normans conquered us in music too. Try this little taste of Norman plainsong, and see if you would have agreed with those Saxon monks in Glastonbury.

## 'Sumer is icumen in.'

IF YOU PAID ANY attention to your music lessons when you were at school – those of you who had any music lessons – you would have come across a particularly useless piece of information, to the effect that our very earliest well-known song was a little something known by its first line – 'summer is on its way'. Or, to be strictly accurate, 'sumer is icumen in'. I hope you all appreciate my Middle English accent.

Perhaps you had a music teacher who was a bit of a wag, and who informed you that 'sumer is icumen in' was top of the pops round about the year 1240. Which is another useless piece of information. This little essay is bristling with useless information.

If the date 1240 didn't stick, you will certainly recall that it was written a very long time ago, because it talks about summer coming in, and who can remember when that last happened?

Third piece of useless information – Henry III was on the throne at the time. One of those totally faceless monarchs in our history. Nobody remembers anything about him, and yet he was on the throne for 56 years. 56 years! You would think *something* would have come down to us about him, wouldn't you? So it looks as if all that we are left with for the years between 1216 and 1272 is this quaint little song, written probably by some monk with a bit of spare time on his hands in between the various services laid down by the blessed Saint Benedict for the regulation of properly-run monasteries.. Very few laymen at that time would have had the education, or the time, to do it.

Whether you will like it remains to be seen, or rather heard. As I said, it is very old. It has no electronic backing. If it is sung in proper dialect and with the right accent, it will be totally incomprehensible. But do not let that worry you. As the great British conductor Sir Thomas Beecham once observed, 'The English may not like music, but they absolutely love the noise it makes.'

Or take heart from the admission of one of our greatest dramatists, Sir William Gilbert (of Gilbert and Sullivan fame). He once said, 'I only know two tunes. One of them is "God Save the Queen"; the other one isn't.'

And you may actually have heard it without knowing. It was whistled, apparently, by Little John just before he met Robin Hood in the 1938 Hollywood film *The Adventures of Robin Hood*.

And you can't get information much more useless than that.

## Greensleeves

LEGENDS DIE HARD IN music, just as they die hard everywhere else. Alfred did not burn any cakes; King Harold almost certainly did not get an arrow in the eye; and King John did not sign Magna Carta. By the same token, King Henry VIII did not compose the song *Greensleeves* because he was keen on Anne Boleyn.

He was keen on Anne Boleyn all right, and it is quite likely that he wrote music. He could certainly play it. He was also an accomplished linguist, a knowledgeable theologian, and had an above average command of mathematics and astronomy. Moreover, the period in which he lived was a time when a gentleman's education was not considered complete unless he could play a musical instrument and write poetry.

But, for all that, Henry VIII did not compose *Greensleeves*. The scholars tell us that the style in which it was written was Italian, and that that style did not reach England until after Henry had died.

As a sort of consolation prize, Henry has been credited with writing the words, to his beloved Anne. Even this presents something of a problem, because the very title refers to a lady whose dress contains the colour green. Green was considered to be a somewhat flippant colour, and the suggestion was that any female who had acquired green marks on her dress must have been somewhere very close to grass, and what lady would admit to having been close to grass? Certainly not Anne, who kept her virtue impregnable despite nearly six years of ardent courtship by the eager Henry.

But what does all this matter? Why should we allow our enjoyment of *Greensleeves* to be skewed by speculation about Henry in the throes of composition (or not, as the case may be), or by contemplation of a most uninspiring relationship which began with Henry losing his head at the start and ended with Anne losing her head at the finish?

*Greensleeves* is just a very English and totally bewitching melody, and, to the average listener, there is nothing quite like it in the repertoire. So let us simply enjoy it.

## Zadok the Priest

I DON'T KNOW ABOUT you, but I find certain names exciting. I don't mean the people they refer to, though they may indeed be exciting. No. I mean the very sound of those names.

I have never thoroughly analysed the components of this excitement. The best way to explain, I suppose, is to give some examples.

We once had a prime minister called Sir Henry Campbell-Bannerman. I think that has a splendid 'rumble factor' to it. Campbell-Bannerman. Anyone with a name like that *ought* to be Prime Minister.

Here's one I bet you don't know – the national hero of the Ukraine. Wait for it. Bogdan Chmielnitski. How about that? Bogdan Chmielnitski. Any Ukranian with a name like that *deserves* to be the national hero.

The one we are coming to tonight is straight out of fantasy – Zadok. I think that is a terrific name. Zadok. He is straight out of the Old Testament too, which is a marvellous repository of evocative names – Ezekiel, Zephaniah, Jezebel, Judas Maccabeus.

But the best of them all is Zadok. Well, it's the best in my book. Now put that name into the context of what he did. He anointed one of the great ancient Israelites as King. He was assisted by another pretty fearsome figure – remember a prophet called Nathan, who told King David where he got off?

Any coronation is an impressive business. It is supposed to be. The British coronation service goes right back to the tenth century. Every monarch since King Edgar has been crowned according to the same ritual. Now that is a colossal weight of tradition. Anyone who sets out to write music for such an event must rise to the heights.

When George Frederic Handel was commissioned by George II to write the music for his coronation in 1727, that is what he did; he rose to the heights. And to help the music to rise even higher, he took the words from the Old Testament service. With the choir and full orchestra in overdrive, he opened his anthem with these words: 'Zadok the priest, and Nathan the prophet, anointed Solomon King.'

I think that is one of the most exciting sentences in the whole English language. Set to a shattering score, it must have blown them right out of the Abbey.

'Zadok the priest, and Nathan the prophet, anointed Solomon King.' Listen, and see if you agree.

## Salut d'Amour

IF YOU ASKED ORDINARY people to name four great composers, the chances are that most of them would come up with 'Mozart, Haydn, Beethoven, and Schubert'. And of course Bach. Ask them to name four more, and you would probably get something like 'Brahms, Tchaikovsky, Mendelssohn', and perhaps 'Verdi'. As you sit here now and listen to those two lists, many of you will take issue with me and be saying to yourselves, 'Why didn't he mention Liszt, Grieg, Dvorak, Gounod, Puccini, Rossini, Bizet, Strauss?'

Why indeed? But, whichever of those composers you choose to put in your top flight, have you noticed that not one of them is English?

It is a (perhaps sad) fact that there are only two or three English composers who, in any period, can claim a place among the giants. One is Henry Purcell, who is by common consent of the musical world our very greatest. The second is Handel, who doesn't really count because he was born German. The third is Edward Elgar.

What do we know about Edward Elgar? Yes, of course, he wrote *Land of Hope and Glory*. Well, he didn't actually; he wrote the music. It was a march called *Pomp and Circumstance*. Somebody else wrote the words.

A fair number of us also know that he wrote the *Enigma Variations*. Now that is getting into long-hair country and promenade concerts. If you add to that his Violin Concerto, his Cello Concerto, and his oratorio *The Dream of Gerontius*, you are moving out of most people's range. Elgar becomes grand and classical, and a mite obscure.

But, like many great composers, he could also be 'small' and accessible and charming.

When he was courting his future wife, Caroline Alice Roberts, she wrote him a poem called *Love's Grace*. He responded by writing a short piece of music for her, which he called *Love's Greeting*. He dedicated it to 'Carice', which is a contraction of his fiancée's two names Caroline and Alice. The publisher he submitted it to changed the title to *Salut d'Amour*, because he thought it would sell better. This was in 1889. It was Elgar's first published work.

It has never been out of the repertoire ever since. It is the staple diet of teatime trios, palm court orchestras, and ocean line serenaders. Audiences never tire of its gentleness and fondness and – yes – again its charm (I can't think of a better word). To this day they speak to us across the years.

## The Beatles

I AM GOING TO give you three names: Muhammad Ali, Mozart, and Mickey Mouse. Now what have they got in common? I put it to you that they are familiar names to *billions* of people. Those billions may not know much about them, but they have all heard of them.

And up there with Muhammad Ali, Mozart, and Mickey Mouse are four young men from Liverpool. – the Beatles. Indeed, it is said that one of those Beatles, John Lennon, once claimed that they had become more famous than Jesus.

Why?

Ah, there you take a lot of us into deep waters. Their seismic effect on the world of pop music, or rock, or whatever you want to call it, is explained by the enthusiasm of the young, and a lot of us are not young – well, not any more.

When the Beatles, originally the Quarrymen (the Quarrymen!), first exploded into the public consciousness, anybody over thirty recoiled in surprise, bafflement, in many cases shock, and frankly distaste. Good God – these chaps let their hair grow right down to their collars! Whatever next? Hardly a musical appreciation.

To the young they had the perfect qualifications – they were young themselves, they were new, fresh, a bit loud, and they shocked their elders. So they must be good.

The amazing thing about the Beatles is that, fifty years later, they are still world-famous, and still revered. And they still capture fans who were not born even when they broke up in 1970.

So there must be something about them. They clearly did not stay so famous by being simply the flavour of the month. They worked hard. They travelled; they performed; both on stage and in the recording studio – their output was enormous. They were never content to stand still. All of them composed as well as played, and three of them at least were constantly trying to push back the frontiers, to venture into unknown musical territory.

Do many of us understand what they were up to? I doubt it. If you don't grab them, you don't grab them, and that is that. As Louis Armstrong said about jazz, 'If you has to ask what it is, you ain't got it, and you ain't never goin' ta get it.'

Is this piece, *Blackbird*, going to convert you, or make you understand? One composition in hundreds? I doubt that too. But we can't play them all. Just this one.

Even so, try it; you may get a surprise.

## The Twenty-First Century

YOU HAVE ALL HEARD somebody say, at one time or another, 'I don't understand modern art, but I know what I like.' Perhaps you have said it yourselves. Perhaps you did not have the courage, or the cruel honesty, to say it, but you may have thought it.

Has it ever occurred to you that the same remark could be applied to modern music? By 'modern music' I do not mean the pop music industry, with its Martian war-machines armoury of electronic thunder and lightning, and its gyrating, microphone-eating performers of incomprehensible lyrics. That is a land of total mystery to anybody over the age of forty, and it is not for me – or possibly for many of you – to venture to pass comment.

No – I mean the world of 'serious' modern music. You know – full orchestral scores, the complete range of instruments that people actually play instead of just plug in, and so on. And God knows – that generates enough mysteries and puzzles to keep any listener going. Any listener, that is, who attempts to make sense of it, much less derive some old-fashioned enjoyment from it.

Now this may be simply a reflection on the listener. On us. We may be too limited in our taste, too unmusical, too – frankly – ignorant. Perhaps there really is something in it, but we have to be content with the fact that its merit escapes us. It is something we shall never understand.

However, whatever the average listener's musical education and knowledge and taste – or lack of it – he must surely accept that we cannot go on listening to the same music for ever – and nothing else. There must be change, innovation, development. And the people most likely to search for this change are the young. This is all very right and proper.

So if they write music, they deserve to be at least listened to – if only once. They are new; they are keen; they are often knowledgeable; and they do try. And an occasion like this is the perfect forum for them to be given an opportunity.

You are here because you are willing to support a charity. You are being offered some entertainment as thanks for your attendance and your generosity. We cannot guarantee that you will relish that entertainment – well, not all of it. But it is well meant, and it is sincere. All we ask is that you give it the benefit of the doubt, and listen. Who knows? You might catch yourself enjoying it.

## 14. The *Exmoor* – first verse

THE EXMOOR IS A cross-country run. A very long cross-country run. West Buckland School does it every year, towards the end of the Easter Term. By tradition every pupil takes part. (And, now that the school is co-educational, that means girls as well.)

Its origins go right back to the very foundation, and the peculiar circumstances in which the school, and its masters and boys, found themselves. As everyone who ever comes here knows, it is the back of beyond, the end of the line, miles from anywhere, Injun country.

In the early days, it was extremely difficult to get to. In the middle of the nineteenth century, there were of course no motor cars. Not much in the way of roads either, if it comes to that. The railways did not reach Devon till the mid-1860's. So, once you were here, you tended to stay. Indeed, pupils from distant homes did not even get home for the holidays – well, not every holiday anyway.

Keeping them occupied in the classroom was no great problem; they had lessons for that. Keeping them occupied out of it was another matter. There was football and cricket of course, of a sort. The school made up its own rules for football. Cricket facilities did not stretch very far – no pavilion, no sight screens, no boundaries. Up there on the edge of Exmoor at 650 feet above sea level, the wickets and outfield must have been beyond modern imagination.

So – how to work off the steam of boys'surplus energy. As one weary headmaster wryly remarked, 'Healthy, vigorous boys do not do nothing.'

And there, of course, under their noses as you might say, was the solution – the moor. The fields, valleys, hills, heather, combes, lanes – the delights of the North Devon countryside. It was all tailor-made for cross-country runs. The staff fell on to the idea with alacrity. By the twentieth century, they had evolved, or inflicted (dependent on your point of view), no fewer than fifteen different runs, of varying length and pain.

The earliest, and nearly the longest (the actual longest one was called, predictably, 'the Long') became known as the *Exmoor*. It was first run in 1859. It proved to be such a splendid absorber of male adolescent energy that it continues to this day. It has been cancelled only twice in over 150 years – once in the arctic winter of 1947, when the River Taw froze, and once because of the foot-and-mouth outbreak in 2001.

As the years have gone by, all the other runs have evaporated – largely because of too much competition from other sports, and new roads cutting across running routes. Only the *Exmoor* remains. Thanks to force of habit, the passage of time, and general sentiment, it has become the oldest tradition in school life, and is now regarded as something as awful and as unavoidable as the puberty rites in a primitive tribe. There is also the smug feeling that comes from the belief that it is the longest, roughest, toughest cross-country run in the length and breadth of the realm, and all the other namby-pamby schools couldn't manage it.

In theory everybody has to do it – girls too – but no doubt there have been, over the years, plenty of slackers, skivers, wimps, drop-outs, cowards, cissies, rogues, mavericks, and general undesirables who have spent as much energy thinking of ways to avoid it as they would have spent running it.

Be that as it may, it is still a big event in the school year. The whole school shuts down for it. Little traditions of procedure have evolved, like the rest of the school clapping as each section leaves the assembly hall to get changed – Senior Boys, Senior Girls, Junior Boys, Junior Girls (well, there are still the staff left to clap *them* out).

Another habit which has grown is due to the work of a long-serving teacher who started regaling the assembly with some verses about the *Exmoor*, laced thickly of course with topical references to school personalities and notorious features of the race's course.

He did this for many years, and, when he retired, another teacher took on the mantle of *Exmoor* bard. And when *he* retired, the School Archivist got a bright idea: suppose *he* were to produce yet another *Exmoor* song?

And this is it.

*West Buckland, West Buckland, West Buckland are best.*
*I wouldn't give tuppence for all of the rest.*

Each year, in the Easter Term's ultimate week,
West Buckland can demonstrate that it's unique.
It shuts down its lessons and stages a race
That no other school in the country would face.

*West Buckland are daring, tenacious, and strong,*
*And no-one can live with West Buckland for long.*

The wimps out at Shebbear have nothing like this,
And softies at Blundell's all give it a miss.
The College at Grenville have turned a blind eye,
And Kingsley are too scared to give it a try.

*West Buckland are up for it, eager to run,*
*And only feel sad when the racing is done.*

And all around England, wherever one goes,
They shudder with horror and turn up their nose.
Harrow play cricket at Lords, if at all,
And Eton confine all their sport to a wall.

*West Buckland are sportsmen, West Buckland are game,
And wonder why everyone isn't the same.*

We're dying to start in the hail and the sleet,
And like nothing more than two soaking wet feet.
We revel in cowpats, we welcome the mud,
And cheer when we come across rivers in flood.

*West Buckland, West Buckland, West Buckland are best,
So up with West Buckland and down with the rest.*

We want to be so far ahead at the end
We vanish from sight, we're so far round the bend.
For the Headmasters' Conference says we should be
In a class on our own, and I'm sure – yes, I'm sure –
That you all – that you all – will agree.

## 15. Should do well

### Acid in the inkwell

ONE OF THE EARLIEST tasks that confronted me in the Archive was the discovery of two or three enormous cardboard boxes, which had lain for goodness knows how long in a cupboard the door of which was half-way up a staircase. It is difficult to deduce why they put a door in such an inaccessible position. You needed a set of steps to get to it. As I said, when we finally got into this cupboard, we found, among the dust-stifled rubbish, two or three boxes full to bursting with buff files containing personal information about previous generations of pupils, dating back to the fifties and sixties. They were of the thin, 'folder' variety, not the 'envelope' variety, so it was up to me to try and produce some kind of permanent protection for them. That meant metal filing cabinets and envelope files for every single one.

It is all very well for someone to say, 'Why not digitise them and have done with it?' But it is not as simple as that. Nearly all the old reports were carbon copies, and may not have shown up on a scanner. Secondly, I didn't at the time have a scanner, which, you will understand, put something of an obstacle in the way of that strategy. Nor did I have the budget big enough to buy one. (At that time, I didn't have a budget at all.)

Even if I had had the money and the gadgets, it would not have been practical. I was working on my own, and my working contract specified only four hours a week; at that rate, with other duties to attend to, I could reckon on getting them scanned, filed, and stowed, with luck, by about 2020.

In any case, the point of an archive is to preserve records, of whatever type. They are interesting in themselves, and add character to any collection. You can't beat holding an original in your hands. There is nothing romantic about an entry on a computer screen. Which would you rather have? An engraved tombstone or a scanned photograph in a database?

The short answer is, of course, is that you should, ideally, have both. But if you can't afford the time or the money, you have to make do. So I made do, and transferred all these records to envelope files and stowed them in filing cabinets. It took quite a while.

Inevitably, as you handled these documents, you would find yourself reading some of them. The vast majority of the entries, of course, were what one would have expected, but now and again you would come across a teacher or a headmaster who combined perception with humour, who could wrap up an unwelcome piece of news in a wry joke. I thought some of these were worth preserving, so long, of course, as I kept them separate from the names of the boys in question. (Remember this was, then, an all-boys' school.)

*Nearly off the Record*

Here, then, is a random selection of the some of the remarks that teachers saw fit to make about their charges. It makes you wonder how these boys went on to earn a decent living.

1. 'His general attitude may be summed up as half-hearted and late.'

2. 'He has never played a prominent part in the life of the School, academic or otherwise. He is not a hard worker, though he deludes himself that he is. . . He is in many ways a "dark horse" and a "lone wolf", if it is possible for this biological freak to be perpetrated.'

3. 'He does a lot of fishing, which speaks well for his patience and self-control.'

4. 'No great success academically. Thinks slowly but clearly... outstanding skill at rugby.'

5. 'Sense of humour strong and not always under control.'

6. This boy failed all his 'O' Levels, bar one, three times – he got a 3 in Geography at the third attempt. On the summary page in his file, someone wrote, 'Very keen on motor cycles. Polite and helpful.'

7. 'There are few people in authority he has not offended at some time or other during this term.'

8. 'He has all the qualities that make a good undergraduate, except high academic ability.'

9. 'He is hardworking and thorough with no sign of brilliance.'

10. 'He is looked upon as an automatic choice as Stage Manger [sic] for the annual school play.' [Should come in very useful for the Nativity.]

11. 'He has been for most of his life in a variety of "scrapes", not of a very serious kind taken separately, but collectively adding up to an unsatisfactory record. Earlier this year he was given a final warning. . .

'In spite of his past I find -------- fundamentally a likeable boy. . . I hope he will be given the opportunity to emigrate.'

## All in a Good Caws

EVER SINCE ROBERT LOUIS Stevenson wrote *Treasure Island*, we have all been vulnerable to the attraction of an old map, a faded document, a faint pencil-written letter – with their glimpses into a past culture, their promise of intrigue, adventure, detective work, even (one hopes) of financial gain. And even if they do not lead us to the crock of gold at the end of the rainbow, the trip has usually been absorbing, interesting, and often very satisfying. The quest can become more important than the discovery; the journey richer than the arriving.

One is lucky in being an archivist, because, obviously, and by definition, the chances of coming across such an item are that much greater than average. I mean, you wouldn't be very likely to have a treasure map turn up in a sheaf of old income-tax returns or a batch of out-of-date grocery invoices, would you?

But, if you work in an archive, people send you things. Sometimes they genuinely want to find out what they are. Sometimes they are interested in sharing your quest to find out. Or, up in the loft, they have opened an old chest that belonged to great-uncle George, and some papers and books have 'West Buckland School' printed on them. Even within the school itself, a head of biology decides that a clutch of documents is taking up valuable space in his specimen cupboard. He can't identify them; they don't excite him; the only obvious feature of them is that they are 'old'. So they finish up in the Archive.

Not long ago, I had a telephone message from a gentleman who had nothing to do with the school at all. We spent several days trying, and failing, to contact each other by phone, till, at last (in desperation, I suspect) he decided to write to me, with some enclosures.

What made it more potentially interesting than usual was that the very story of his acquisition of them was in itself a little saga.

This gentleman, a Mr. Woodhead, had an uncle who had been an antique dealer. One of the things he left behind when he died was a drawer full of letters. No doubt many of these letters had themselves been found in old drawers and cabinets handled by Mr. Woodhead's uncle in the course of his work. It is just the sort of job you would give yourself, isn't it: One day, when I retire, I'll go through them and see if there is anything interesting tucked away. Apparently, Mr. Woodhead's uncle never got around to it.

*The Archives of an Archivist*

But Mr. Woodhead did. When *he* retired. Among them was a pair of letters written by two pupils of West Buckland School in 1918. How do we know? Because each letter had the address of the school and the date at the top. So far so good.

They meant nothing to Mr. Woodhead, because he had no idea who the writers were, and I don't suppose he had ever heard of West Buckland School. But these letters proved to have great intrinsic interest. For all sorts of reasons. They gave the flavour of a past era, naturally; the sort of things boys mentioned when they wrote home, and the sort of things they did not mention. Glimpses of boarding school life nearly a hundred years ago – food, the timetable, the standards of dress, the quality of handwriting, the formal modes of address, sport, the prevalence of church. And so on.

Mr. Woodhead was able to deduce the rough age of the boys, and hazard the guess that they were brothers, perhaps twins. He could go no further, because no surname was mentioned.

That was how the letters reached me. Could I take the inquiry any further?

Well, it was an interesting prospect, wasn't it? In order to squeeze the maximum value out of them, I reckoned it would be necessary to put on three hats – historian, psychologist, and detective.

The history bit was pretty straightforward. West Buckland then, in 1918, was almost entirely a boarding school, so matters of dress and dormitory regulations figured – for example, one of the boys – 'Jack' – says that Saturday evening was when 'best suits' were put out, along with pyjamas, shirt, towel, collar (separate collar – the junior boys wore Eton collars, though the practice died out in the 1920's), stockings (presumably, being in a lowly class, they still wore knickerbockers), a handkerchief, and 'a clean pair of combinations every fortnight [every fortnight!]'.

The other brother – 'Dick' – referred to being taught by three 'mistresses' – which shows that the bastion of male domination in a boys' boarding school was already, in the First World War (perhaps *because* of the First World War), being breached. It must have been quite an intrusion; right up to the 1960's, the only females the boarders normally saw, from beginning to end of term, were chambermaids, cooks, and the school nurse. So lady teachers must have been quite a novelty. This might also give a clue to the age of the boys; knowing what I know of the school, I think it unlikely that 'mistresses' would have been given charge of senior classes. At any rate for a while. West Buckland did not change easily or quickly.

Regular religious attendance was another 'give-away'. It helped, of course, that the Headmaster was a clergyman, who, besides being Head, was the incumbent at East Buckland church just up the road. Everyone knows about the decline of religious observance since the Second World War. Boarding schools hung on to it longer than the lay population, but they too have gone with the times. It does not seem to be an overstatement to say now that 'religion', and its formal public expression, have ceased to be a regular part of everyday life for the majority of the population.

Well, it was very much there in 1918. Maybe the War had something to do with it. They say that you can't beat a war for raising church attendance. At any rate, the boys – Jack and Dick – seem to have accepted it as easily as they did the sun coming up. Jack went so far as to say that he liked it, and, moreover, that he regretted that he had not gone as often as his parents when he was at home with them. He even declared his intention to remedy the situation when he came home.

Another immovable, and unavoidable, part of West Buckland life was cross-country running, and it is no coincidence that both boys mention it. It must have been quite a shock, both physical and cultural, to come up against this phenomenon. It went right back to the school's very earliest days. Imagine – a school full of vigorous boys, brimming with testosterone, miles from anywhere; no buses, no cars, no trains. Only Exmoor for company. How then to absorb all that surplus, and demanding, energy? The Moor – there was nothing else. By the time of the First World War, there must have been over ten or a dozen separate runs, each with its own name.

These two boys were pitched into a five-mile run within a fortnight of arriving. Dick referred to 'mud *over* your ankles' and 'water *up to* your ankles' [my italics]; Jack related that the Headmaster said 'we could borrow a pair of stinkers (gym shoes) for the term' [how kind of him]. Mud over your ankles in plimsoles! Jack admitted that the 'sea breezes' made it 'cold', but added nobly that one got used to it, and it became merely 'very bracing and not cold'. After only a fortnight, the West Buckland ethos was beginning to have an effect.

So much for the history. What about the psychology – at any rate the personal element?

One of the first things anyone would notice today would be the quality of the handwriting. Careful, clear, regular, and not a single word difficult to read. Spelling a bit 'iffy', but that makes them boys and human. The capital letters were beautifully crafted.

A feature which would strike us as odd today was the fact that both boys referred to their natural surroundings: 'when the sun is out, it is glorious'; 'snapdragons grow wild in the hedges'; 'daises growing in the fields'. Dick even mentioned that there were 'a few daisies still in the ground in October'. Jack referred to the fact that the corn stooks have been out so long (because of the wet weather) that weeds are growing on them. How often would a remark like that get into a boy's letter home today? Well, of course, it wouldn't, because he would have written an email or phoned up, but I bet he still wouldn't have mentioned anything like this.

We don't know if the Headmaster insisted that the boys write home regularly, and stood over them to make sure they did so. But, reading these two letters, one does not get the feeling that there was anything of the press gang about them. There was none of the 'Hallo-how-are-you-I'm fine-love-Jack' about them.

They are full of news and observations. One runs to nearly two pages of closely-written A4. There are no complaints. Criticisms, perhaps, but no complaints. And they had been at the school less than three weeks (proof of this comes later).

Another striking feature would be the mode of address: 'Dear Father and Mother'. Not 'Dear Mum and Dad'. And notice how the mother-and-father word order has been reversed. Now how, when, and why did *that* happen?

There are endearing little personal touches too. Both end of course with 'with love from'. Well, you would expect that. What is heartwarming though is the concern for other members of the family – clearly quite a big one. There are references to 'Donald' and 'Beatrice' (from the context an elder sister who is about to be married; at any rate Jack wants to buy a jam dish for her). Both refer to 'Baby', presumably a youngest sister. Dick sends her a picture and three kisses.

All of which does not tell us who these boys were and where they came from. Time to put on the detective hat.

I thought I had only one lead – the date 1918. It was a daunting prospect, to have to go through every school magazine from about 1916 to 1920, in the search for a couple of identical surnames. Then, reading

Dick's letter again, I realised that I had another clue: he mentioned that he and Jack had worked themselves into (or had been told to volunteer for) the cast of a Gilbert and Sullivan opera.

The Headmaster, the Revd. Harries, was crackers about G. and S., and from 1915 till the mid-thirties, every year, staged a complete production of one or other of the comic operas. (Of course he had the starring part in each one.) They were regularly recorded in the school magazine. All I had to do was look up to find out which of them had been staged in 1918. There it was – *The Mikado*. Dick charmingly confirmed it with true schoolboy approximate spelling – '*a Macardo*'.

There was the review, and there, sure enough, was the cast list. And there, sure enough again, were two identical surnames – Caws. Both in the female chorus – which also conveniently placed them in regard to age. Not even West Buckland, short as it was of good voices, were prepared to have baritone ladies. So they had to be under thirteen or fourteen at the very most.

The rest was plain sailing. I looked up our database of past pupils. It is far from complete, but I knew that it was pretty full for 1918 and thereabouts. There they were; arrived in September, 1918, left in July, 1923. Which fitted. It also confirmed that the boys had been at the school only two or three weeks when they had been sent on that run. Term usually began in mid-September, the letters are dated 6$^{th}$ October, Jack refers to a run 'yesterday', and the school magazine records that there was a run on 5$^{th}$ October. QED.

Back to the magazine for September, 1918. 'The following boys entered this term': John Powell Caws, and Richard Allen Caws. Jack and Dick. One was in Form III, one in Form II. So, brothers, not twins.

The magazine also used to record where these new boys came from. The Caws Bros came from Sheffield. Now, why on earth would a father of a largish family in Sheffield choose to send two of his sons all the way down to Devon for their education? Alas, we have no idea.

A final look at the date of the 'leaving' number of the magazine, July, 1923. Leavers usually had a miniature biography attached to their names. So we know that Jack got his running colours, won the school General Knowledge prize (quite a feat; the GK prize was a saga in itself), and made Sergeant in the Cadet Corps. Dick, the younger, won his colours for Shooting, and got up to Corporal in the cadets. So they didn't do too badly.

And that would have been that. An interesting, but not rare, investigation into the school careers of two worthy lads doing their best. But, besides the letters the two brothers sent home were two other documents, which Mr. Woodhead presumably found in the same drawer at the same time, and sent on to me. And this is a good example of the fact that you never know what you are going to get in the Archive.

They are dated 1915, and they were written by a Professor John Williams Taylor. What was Professor Taylor? He was a phrenologist.

What is phrenology? The word is derived from the Ancient Greek word 'phren', which means 'mind'. It would appear, then, that it is a concept of mental, as opposed to physical, medicine. And anything ending in 'ology' must be pretty intellectual. So we have a word which initially looks unfamiliar (which it is) but whose derivation is designed to make an impression.

The proposition which it sets out to convey is that the future of a young person's life can be, if not clearly foreshadowed, at any rate hinted at, by the study of the lumps and bumps on the skull (the thing which covers and protects the mind, and so which must be connected with it). Perhaps, from the way I have presented it, this makes it look little removed from crystal-gazing.

Well, that looks to me far and away the most likely verdict on it. But I am no scientist, and I know nothing *about* phrenology. The trouble was that nobody else knew much about it either, so the public was at the mercy of any know-all who set himself up as a 'professor' and offered (for a fee) to examine a child's head and make interesting prognostications. It would appear that, for a select few of resourceful, and imaginative, practitioners, it was a nice little earner.

Apparently phrenology had a vogue in the mid-nineteenth century, fell out of favour, and made a sort of come-back early in the twentieth. At any rate, the boys' father had thought it worthwhile to arrange for his sons' heads to be examined by 'Professor' Taylor. And included in the little folio of papers Mr. Woodhead sent me were his reports on both Jack and Dick.

They were handwritten in pencil, and dated May, 1915. At the top it says, in a bracket, 'as remembered'. So maybe this was a copy made by Mr. Caws himself. Even so, it seems odd that, if Mr. Caws had taken the trouble to get his boys examined by so eminent an academic, he did not keep a copy of the report, which should have been typewritten.

Unless, of course, the Professor did *not* submit a written report, and Mr. Caws relied solely on what the Professor told him in his consulting room (wherever that was). If there really was no formal written report, it makes the Professor's activities (and motives) rather more questionable.

Even more alarm bells start to ring when one actually reads these 'reports'. They are chock full of compliments. Jack's head measurements are 'very good'. He has 'tremendous driving power'. He is 'always questioning'. 'There is no end to his plans.' His brain is 'wonderfully developed' and he has a 'most analytical mind'. He possesses 'a most marked sense of justice'. Oh – and he is 'a born leader'.

One is curious to know how long this examination actually lasted. In addition to the psychological observations recorded above, the Professor found time to discover the medical 'facts' that his 'driving power of brain gives him a tendency to internal inflammation especially of the kidneys'. He also 'has a weakness of the throat and a tendency to deafness'.

Dick is a similar prodigy. He shows 'judgment equal to that of a man'. He is 'ambitious and most doggedly persevering'. He 'speaks little but observes much'. (Now how did the Professor work *that* out if the boy was so taciturn?)

If Jack's 'sense of justice' was remarkable, how about this for Dick? 'His great sense of self-respect and dignity would prevent his ever doing anything that a gentleman would not do.'

Very cannily the Professor ventures the suggestion that both boys will continue to develop as they go along, and he says he would like to examine them when they are about fifteen. (Of course he would; there would be another fee available.)

As I put together the foregoing paragraphs, naturally I had to refer constantly to the text of the reports, and the more I read these words of the Professor (as recalled by Mr. Caws), the more I wondered why Mr. Caws was prepared to part with good money to receive them, and why he thought it worthwhile to record them – unless of course he was an exceptionally fond father, and wanted to believe them.

So here is another loose end. There is a lot we still do not know about these boys. But I submit that we *have* found out is interesting. I fancy we would like to know how they turned out. Did Jack become a great leader? Did they fulfil the distinct scientific aptitude that they both apparently exhibited to the Professor? And what happened to Jack's 'tendency to internal inflammation'?

'Friends of the Earth say all that sweat will increase global warming.'

'No, Roderick, despite popular rumour, Mr. Blobby will not be arriving with a kissogram girl.'

# The Archives of an Archivist

'What can I put you down for, sir?'
'Nothing.'

'Who's celebrating?
Us or them?'

'Just like ordinary lessons then.'

## 16. Well, how would you describe it?

### What was it really like?

WELL, WHAT *WAS* IT really like – in 1858? What were the tiny stitches of schoolboys' lives all those years ago? How long did their shoes last? How often did they use toothbrushes? How prickly were their thick woollen socks? We don't know.

What sort of underclothes did they wear in 1858? Wool or cotton, yes, but we don't know what an 1858 vest or a pair of pants *looked* like. No School tie survives, no shirt, no pair of trousers, no headgear (well, not so far as I am aware).

Again, we don't know what an 1858 bar of soap looked like (not that 1858 schoolboys would have been very well acquainted with it). We don't know how often they changed their socks. (Anybody who has stood in a boys' changing room, when scores of sweaty feet are donning or shedding trainers, will know that this is something that simply cannot escape notice.) We don't know how their athletic footwear coped with mud on the *Exmoor*. And there were more cross-country runs in the old days than there are now.

It goes on. What was it like to sleep on a nineteenth-century mattress? What did porridge look like in 1858? Nobody ever saw fit to describe it. (We do, however, get a glimmering of what school food was like generally from the recollection of an Old Boy who attended in the middle of the 20$^{th}$ century – 'in my memory it was universally grey'.) We know that the boys were once regularly served with beer, but we have no idea what it tasted like.

Things like these are the nuts and bolts, the bits and pieces, of life. These are what boys from a bygone age had to deal with. They were not concerned with what takes up the mental energies of historians now, like the principle of religious toleration, or the validity of girls' schools, or cognitive learning, or the decline of Classics, or the history of dyslexia.

So what was life like for a schoolboy in the 1850's (or the 1890's or the 1920's)? How would he have seen it? Hard to say. Ask any boy or girl now, 'How was school today?' What will you get? 'Oh, all right.' Things are so ordinary that it doesn't occur to anybody to write them down. A boy from the past would no more think of putting down facts about pants or socks or porridge than a boy today would think of recording in a diary how many strokes of the brush he gave his teeth in the morning.

The nearest we can get is a glimpse of what boys from the past actually looked like, thanks to the invention of photography. The earliest school photograph dates from about 1874.

Take a look at it. Perhaps the first thing that will strike you is the informality of it. It is simply a large, a very large, group, who have ambled along and obligingly stood around while somebody took a picture. Little attempt has been made to arrange any kind of order. Compare that with the regimentation that goes on now for a School photograph, with the loud-hailers and the ramparts of scaffolding and benches and five hundred human beings perched on what looks like a gigantic piece of Meccano.

Then, suddenly, it seemed, things went formal. Was it the development of new photographic processes? Was it the growing need of people to 'look good', now that they were waking up to the possibilities of this new medium? Whatever it was, compare the 1874 picture with the two pictures of Masters and Monitors in the 1880's. Look at the studied poses. Look at the waistcoats, watch chains, and bowler hats – among the boys too. Look at the universal moustaches among the staff. And none of your little slimline pencils either – full-bodied soup-strainers.

Look at the widespread presence of boots among the staff of the early 20th century. Was this a general fashion, or was it yet another concession to the stern surroundings of West Buckland?

Anybody sufficiently interested can make his or her own interpretations, and spot his or her own favourite oddities – Eton collars before 1914, or baggy, creaseless flannel trousers between the two wars. And look for the negative evidence. You won't find many ties at half-mast, for instance. You see a lot more partings in the hair then than you do now. And so on and so on.

But you can look at these photos till you're blue in the face, and the full picture of life then remains so incomplete. What a pity we don't know more about those bars of soap or those mattresses or those pairs of pants – or those glasses of beer.

## Getting Somebody Famous

THE TROUBLE WITH WEST Buckland is that nobody knows where it is.

It's a bit like the 'where-are-you-going-for-your-holiday' conversation. If you are honest and say 'Nanyuki' or 'Culler Coats' or even a bigger place like 'Corsica', a glaze often settles on the questioner's face. And, if *they* are honest, they will grimace and say, 'I'm not quite sure where that is.'

It's the same with West Buckland. In the early days of public exams, it was customary to send candidates to the big cities. Because the School was so far out, it was given the unique privilege of being allowed to organise its exams on the premises. *The Times* used to print the list of exam centres each year. So it looked like this: 'Bath, Birmingham, Cheltenham, Exeter, Leeds, Liverpool, London, Manchester, Oxford, Southampton, and West Buckland.' One mystified reader wrote to the Editor: 'Where is West Buckland?'

What I'm getting at in a laborious sort of way is the fact that West Buckland's obscurity may account for the fact that it doesn't seem to attract a particularly large number of celebrities; they've never heard of the place.

Oh, yes, we got Princess Anne not long ago, and she shot to the top of the list partly because she didn't have a great deal of opposition. And she did happen to know the place because she had done a great deal of horse practice in the area – just up the road, in fact.

But the rest of the 150 years does not throw up an exactly glittering list – though we did manage a couple of archbishops of Canterbury, in 1863 and 1873. Oh – and a chancellor of the Exchequer and a (retired) first lord of the Admiralty. That was Lord Fortescue's work. Fortescue was the co-founder of the School, with Revd. J.L. Brereton. Brereton had the ideas and the drive; Fortescue had the clout. He knew absolutely everybody.

We inveigled the Bishop of Exeter a few times, but you would expect that, wouldn't you? And a veritable horde of clergymen attended regularly – what you might call a Heavenly Host. They came in droves – 10 in 1880, 12 in 1882, 14 in 1883, and a full rugby team of them in 1884. One is tempted by the uncharitable thought that they regarded the Speech Day lunch as a great improvement on the cooking in their lonely rural rectories.

And that really is about that. There was the usual collection of successful businessmen, prominent members of the Armed Forces, the inevitable MP's, headmasters of other schools, and high-ranking civil servants. But very few with a name you could really get your teeth into.

That means no disrespect to any of these worthy gentlemen (the list, apart from HRH, contains very, very few women – another reason perhaps why she went straight to the top). They were all obviously highly successful in their chosen careers. Some were remarkable men in their own right, as it were. Take the case of Sir Westcott Stile Abell, KBE.

He was an Old Boy, as it happened. (So at least *he* knew where it was.) After leaving school, he entered the Royal Naval Engineering College. One day, on a picnic, he was burning some coloured lights when a sudden explosion shattered his right hand and damaged his thighs and throat. He was saved from severe damage to his face by the rim of his hat, which was sheared completely off.

He had to walk half a mile to reach a doctor, who duly despatched him to the nearest hospital, which necessitated an eleven-mile cab drive. He was still conscious when he arrived. He learnt to write with his left hand, took his exams less than three months later, and came out top of the list. He later won a knighthood – 'KBE', remember? His name would cut no ice among today's young, but he was clearly, as I said, a remarkable man.

Which brings one to the matter of what constitutes a 'celebrity' by modern terms. We have been visited by no film stars, World Cup soccer players, or disgraced politicians. The nearest we have come is the (then) World Snooker Champion, Steve Davis, and of course our own Jonathan Edwards.

If we follow the criteria of the gossip magazines and the chat shows, the pickings are nil. There exist no pictures (well, not to my knowledge) of mini-skirted bimbos tumbling out of the Karslake at three in the morning, and no soap actress has come here to tell an assembly all about her televised Caesarean operation while her boy-friend held her hand and said it was a 'fantastic experience'.

So it looks as if we shall have to be content with bishops and MP's, businessmen and headmasters. Oh – and HRH of course. But look at it another way. *We* have had her; look at all those puny places that haven't.

*Nearly off the Record*

## The Pyramids are still there

IF AN ANCIENT EGYPTIAN could be brought back to have a look at his country today, he would of course be baffled, amazed, and overwhelmed by the changes he would see. But he might take comfort from the sight of one thing – the pyramids. He would be glad to find out that some things do not change – even in 4,000 years.

Mr. Ponder [a recently-retired member of staff] did not serve the school for 4,000 years – only 40 – and he wouldn't have seen as many changes as that Ancient Egyptian. Even so, forty years gives you quite a broad view of the passage of time. With that in mind, I asked him, as well as two other long-serving members of staff, and an old pupil, to give me their impressions of what has changed at West Buckland and what hasn't. This is a distillation of what they said.

If you pluck the sleeve of any old boy who left forty or more years ago, I guarantee that, before twenty minutes of the conversation have elapsed, the business of The Ice in the Washbasins will arise. Let us therefore have it engraved in stone: **THE DORMITORIES WERE COLD.** Central heating did not reach them till 1987, and then, apparently, not for the sake of the pupils. No – the dormitories got central hearing because of the *parents*. Work that one out.

The school was so out of the loop that it had not been until 1963 that it even went on mains water.

The swimming pool was unroofed. Any boy who wished could take a dawn dip, so long as he was prepared to share the water with rotten leaves and dead newts. It was so muddy that you couldn't see the bottom.

A school servant regularly tended the sewerage plant (there was, and still is, no mains sewerage); then, when he had finished, he would repair to the Karslake to assist with serving tea – in a white overall, to be sure, but still wearing his wellington boots.

What other regular features of school life have gone? In no particular order: in the Karslake, the serving of meals *at the table*; grace being said before anybody so much as touched a knife and fork; Saturday morning school; the handbell being rung in the morning by Gerald (a universally-treasured servant who gave fifty-one years of his life to the school); and the much-talked-of but rarely-seen school glider.

Corporal punishment too. It had once been permissible even for prefects to inflict it. Why did it go? A mixture of reasons probably, the real truth obscured in a haze of gossip, speculation, and legend. One head boy-to-be was said to have told the headmaster that, if appointed, he would stop it. If it were to continue, he did not want to be head boy. He was appointed. When girls arrived on the campus, clearly they could not be given six of the best; and if you couldn't cane girls, you couldn't cane boys. And, more generally, the climate of opinion: beating was 'going out', like turn-ups in trousers and trolleybuses and steam trains and smoking in public places.

By contrast, what pioneering features of school life came to be accepted without thought? Probably the biggest is – in a word – girls. It may take an effort of imagination now to conjure up a vision of a single-sex school here. But before 1978, not only did the boys not see a female pupil; apart from an occasional visit to see the nurse about a verruca, they hardly ever spoke to a female at all.

At about the same time as the arrival of girls, the school was overrun by day pupils. In fact it was overrun by all sorts of invasions – the Prep for one. Then the 'Pre-Prep'. Then the Nursery section. Then more foreign pupils (the total of nationalities who have studied here approaches sixty). With all these immigrations, you would think the school was bursting at the seams.

But a rash of new buildings helped to cope with that – a Sixth-Form centre; a set of science laboratories; extra boarding houses; a suite of rooms for computers; a sports centre; a (nearly brand-new) arts and drama complex; and, most recently, a new library, study centre, and boarding block. A complete metamorphosis. As one correspondent put it, from 'rough around the edges to polished and professional', from 'basic provisioning to high-quality facilities'.

So much for the changes. What has stayed constant?

The stories, for a start. Apocryphal or otherwise, they are bred in every decade: the mini on the lab. roof; the girl – *girl* – who came fourth in the boys' *Exmoor*; and the notorious chicken-stranglers of Heasley Mill.

The companionship stays the same, the approachability of the teachers (well, most of them anyway), and the front façade – which looks like our fantasies of what every traditional country school should look like.

And finally – of course – the weather. Like the pyramids, still there, and still unchanged in its changeability. It was there long before the pyramids, and my guess is that it will still be there long after.

## Make a Date

ANNIVERSARIES ARE HYPNOTIC. WITNESS the current fixation on the outbreak of the 'Great' War in 1914. [This was written in 2014.] We cannot move for programmes, articles, books, websites, Sunday supplements, 'special editions', diaries, memoirs, newsreel compilations, and I don't know what, dedicated to the conflict that was 'declared' by Great Britain on 4th August, 1914.

Yet the fact that we make a fuss about it now does not necessarily mean that we made a fuss about it then. By 'we' I mean West Buckland, the school. Take 1914. Take the event which set the awful train of disaster in motion – the assassination of Archduke Franz Ferdinand in Sarajevo on 28th June of that year. The school had its speech day on 2nd July, only four days later. Nobody said a word about it.

It was the same in 1939. In the *Register* of October, 1939, there are 27 pages. Nearly half are devoted to cricket matches. There is not one reference to the outbreak of war. The nearest they came was to announce that 60 members of the school were in uniform.

It all depends on your point of view. For example, on 14th July, 1789, the French mob in Paris stormed the Bastille, and so split the proletarian atom of the French Revolution. King Louis wrote in his diary for that day '*Rien*' – 'nothing'. Well, he had been hunting.

Schools too can be, and often are, very inward-looking. What the country regards as important is not necessarily the same as what the school regards as important.

All right, so both wars were to have a tragic effect on the school in time, as witnessed by the fact that between 1914 and 1918, 58 members of the school died. The average number of boys on the roll in the five years before the War was just under 120. Terrible.

But there was no doubt about the school's *survival*. There was no threat to the school's existence. It wasn't like that in 1899, when the current Headmaster, John Challen, resigned. There had been a mighty 'incident', the nature of which is not recorded in the Governors' minutes. But the upshot was that he had been asked for his resignation. He had given it, had left, and had taken over half the school with him to set up another one in Barnstaple. The next headmaster took over a school reduced to 31 pupils, in a building designed for over 150. It was touch and go.

It was touch and go six years later, when the school was faced with a second possible closure. The new headmaster, Revd. E.C Harries, pulled it round, stayed for 27 years, and left it well established.

That was not the last of the crises. There was another one at the end of the 1960's. Once again, they pulled round. To look at the school now, you would never think that it came close to closure three times.

So those are, arguably, the really important 'dates' in the school's history. But we don't commemorate our narrow escapes from oblivion.

True, we marked the school's foundation in 1858, but we don't make any fuss about 1860, when Lord Fortescue laid the foundation stone of a permanent building. (The school had made do for two years with farmhouses and wooden outside dormitories.) The building was completed only twelve months after the stone had been laid. Not bad going. The *Illustrated London News* informed an enraptured public that the entire project had cost all of £2,000. We don't say anything about that either.

And incidentally, the school was born in the very same year as the Oxford and Cambridge Local Examinations, the ancestor of GCSE. Within less than a decade of its foundation, the school came top of the league of exam successes in the whole country, three times – surely another anniversary worth marking. (Though it is unlikely that any pupil would think the birth of examinations worth celebrating.)

Again, nobody now would see anything very special in the year 2012. But that was the hundredth anniversary of the School's name. Before that it had been the Devon County School.

Will we celebrate, when it comes, the fiftieth anniversary of the arrival of girls in the school? (The first head girl appeared in 1980.) But it was an event regarded with dismay by some people. It all depends on your point of view.

Nobody noticed that last year was the hundredth anniversary of a remarkable sporting feat. In the summer of that year – 1913 – the Brereton junior cricket team dismissed the Courtenay junior cricket team for 0 – that is nought, nothing, zero, all of them. (Extras didn't score either.) The Brereton may like to celebrate it. I bet the Courtenay won't.

As I said, it all depends on your point of view.

## 17. Becoming an archive

ONE OF THE FEATURES of a historian's work (and an archivist's for that matter) is that his business is largely with people who are not there. They have decamped, disappeared, departed, or died. What the archivist has to deal with, in developing their acquaintance, is merely records – aural, visual, or documentary. Even if a man, or woman, talks about their past for the sake of the record, what you get is not what actually happened, but what they *think* happened, albeit to the best of their honest recall. Moreover, what they are talking about is not themselves, but themselves however many years ago. We change, often more than we realise, and in ways that had never occurred to us. And we all know that our memory is never as good as we like to think it is.

It might therefore be a fruitful task, or at least an interesting one, to catch a person while he is still there, but just before he goes. On the brink, on the very dividing line between being a live entity and becoming an item in the record. At the birth, if you like, of an archive.

In July of 2016, John Vick retires after nineteen years' service to West Buckland School as Headmaster. I caught him just four months before that date – on the brink, as I said. He was happy to answer questions, consider others, pass on some more, and muse generally on the business of being a headmaster. This record of our conversation is by no means an exhaustive or definitive analysis, and was not intended to be. It is simply a summary of the answers he gave to my questions, in the time that an average working day allowed.

At best it will provide a feature, a facet, a mere thread in the tapestry of the full record.

My very first question produced an answer which I should have seen coming. I said, 'When you were first appointed, how long did you envisage that you would stay?' Back came the immediate reply: 'That is the only consistent question I have been asked.' Which is sense when you think about it.

But then the interviewer has to be content with what he has been able to devise within the time on offer. No doubt, if I had given more thought to the problem, I could have come up with a completely different set of questions, and no doubt I would have thought some of *them* were inadequate the moment I had put them. It is unlikely that the most brilliant of interviewers can concoct a set of inquiries which are all searching and original enough to keep the subject constantly on his toes, and which produce a full and fair picture..

However, John Vick did suggest that his impression was that the Governors were not keen on the idea of a headmaster 'being around for long' (whatever that means). On the other hand, when a new chairman was appointed, he asked him whether the Governors wanted a change, and was assured that they had 'no wish for him to leave'.

So the ball was in his court. The school was coming up to an interesting period of development (thanks to sound management, the funds were now available), and he thought he would like to be part of it and preside over it. Which he did – sports hall, arts and drama block, library, study centre, new boarding facilities. It must have been very satisfying. So he stayed. (That may not be the full story, but, as I said, my record is incomplete, and unavoidably so.)

Now that he is going, what will he miss about West Buckland? The answer was pretty pat about that too. Everybody says it: the environment, the fields, the moor, the vastness and openness, the sheer breathability of it. On a good day, it is so content-making. (We don't talk about the weather on all the other days.) But of course – and everybody says this too – it is cut off. Never mind not being in a city or a town; it is not even in a village.

Nevertheless, it does force the school community back on its own resources. It makes do with what it's got; members learn to live together; it makes for a tighter, almost a family, bond. (As the archivist, I have noticed evidence of this, going right back to the earliest days. West Buckland has a remarkable gift for generating not only loyalty but affection. I have looked at venerable lists of old boys who came back – often a very long way – for reunion dinners, and the records show that many of them had attended here for only two or three years, some barely eighteen months.)

I asked him about the things he had seen coming and going during his term of office – what he most welcomed and most deplored. He took up the point about 'arrivals' (which is fair enough; we had barely half an hour and we could not discuss everything). He interpreted the question to mean staff, and discussed the appointments he had made in nineteen years.

'I gave been able to appoint some terrific people, who have changed the culture and direction of the school.' Yes, one did learn to become a good picker. (The verdict of history backs this up; successful leaders usually appoint excellent subordinates.) Obviously, there had been some unfortunate choices, but he did not think the 'error rate' was high.

It is a familiar feature of life in an independent school that any sentient member of staff thinks now and again how lucky he is to be in a privileged institution. John Vick said that this occurred to him 'almost daily'. Of course the 'system' was 'significantly imperfect'. But West Buckland (like every other independent school of my acquaintance) exerts every muscle to raise funds for bursaries on behalf of deserving pupils in straightened circumstances. Just like archivists, headmasters, no matter how acutely aware they are of a frustrating situation, can only do their best with the facilities and resources at their disposal.

Did he believe in a 'West Buckland' tradition? The answer was again very ready. Yes, there was something definable about West Buckland, and it was mainly to do with its location. If the school had been in, say, Exeter, it would have had access to so many convenient places – academic, sporting, cultural, and more. Everything one does outside West Buckland is a long way away. Even a normal academic day, with its after-school activities, its need to catch buses very early from distant parts (the catchment area is huge), can mean absence from home for anything up to eleven hours – a big strain on an eleven-year-old. Travel, and a lot of it, becomes an indispensable part of the school's calculations.

But this remoteness can produce a society more self-sufficing than average, and a sense of being a community apart can produce strong bonds of pride, affection, loyalty, team spirit, what you will.

I asked whether he felt he had a sense of vocation. After all, it is not everybody who wants to become a teacher or a doctor or a missionary. No, he said, not like that. He got impatient with those who, with hand on heart, said they wanted to change the world. No, he was not dewy-eyed about it.

'But it is a job that I think has a real purpose, and I don't feel I have been mainly motivated by money.' And it has certainly had its moments: 'I can think of some whose direction in life has been changed for the good, and I have been part of that.'

He was firm that the job 'gives pleasure every day, both as teacher and as headmaster. I can't think what I could have enjoyed more.'

Would he be pleased to be going? 'I'm not pleased in that I'm counting the days, but nineteen years is enough.' The school had reached a definite stage in its development, and it was time for someone else to take it further. In a word, it was fitting.

West Buckland, he affirmed, was a most unusual place in all sorts of ways, and it fulfilled an important role in the life of North Devon. It was a great blessing that it sustained the interest and loyalty of so many very creative people, who made a significant contribution to both school and county.

At the end he let slip the admission that, when the moment finally did come, he expected that it would make considerable demands upon his emotional resilience.

We ran out of time on the first day, and, because I know that headmasters are busy people, I gave him the rest of the questions I had prepared, asking him to knock out a few answers when he had the opportunity.

Instead, he offered to come to my office again, to complete the project. Now that was both generous and imaginative. He appreciated that, when one talks in the presence of another, the comments had a very good chance of being more interesting than when one simply sits, alone, at a keyboard, and taps out a few formal sentences. As he put it, it could produce more interesting answers, and 'take us on other paths which might be fruitful'.

Whether or not the rest of this account turns out to be 'more interesting', or to take us on 'fruitful' paths is for the reader to decide. Our conversation ranged pretty widely, and it does not follow that everything he said has been included in this account. I may have left out the most 'interesting' or 'fruitful' bits, I don't know. Discretion will have played a part in this, because he talked freely, and relied on me not to tell any tales out of school. A headmaster is privy to a thousand secrets, and secrets they should remain. Nor should every outspoken comment necessarily deserve to be fitted into the record, and that too is how it should be. But, take it from me, there was both humanity and humour in what he said.

He felt that he had, during his stewardship, attended to the mundane matters of keeping the school a viable entity, according necessary attention to the daily details of administration, recruitment, and general overseeing of the school's academic progress. A school, after all, is primarily an academic institution, and (despite its being a truism), learning counts.

He set great store by the pastoral dimension, and must have been proud of an inspector's comment that West Buckland was ahead of its peers in the respect which its pupils showed *for each other*. He believed strongly in developing the cultural side of school life. He had devoted attention and energy to the increase of West Buckland's profile in North Devon, and in the enhancement of its distinctive contribution to local life.

He was keen to record the fact that his tenure of office was not 'on its own'; he fitted into a process, an evolution. (As a historian, he would naturally have appreciated that.) Put another way, he was sharply aware that he owed a great deal to the legacy which had been left by George Ridding, in saving the school from closure, and by Michael Downward, in building the school's academic reputation. For example, it was the latter who had won West Buckland's re-entry to the Headmasters' Conference. Simply compare the public exam results of, say, 1968 with those of 1998.

Any job like a headship is a collaborative business, both with the past and with the present. He paid tribute not only to his predecessors but to the colleagues — at all levels — who had surrounded him throughout his term of office. He gave especial thanks to the governors. Which is timely, because most people have a pretty good idea of what teachers do, and pupils, and gardeners, and cooks, and so on, but not many understand the governor's role. Perhaps because it does not get played out in public view.

Another agency which had played its part was a rather mysterious ingredient — luck. Nobody quite knows how luck works, but most people know when it is working. John Vick was sure he had been lucky.

Every one of us takes pleasure in feeling that he has been useful, and John Vick was gratified by recalling how he had been able to facilitate the entry and successful career of many children whose personal circumstances would not otherwise have allowed them to do so.

In his term of office, he had witnessed a broadening of the school's sense of itself. By that he meant going 'outwards' more. For example, in a more adventurous policy regarding physical development — new buildings. To put it another way, the school was now 'thinking bigger' than it had once done, and he felt he had played a part in that.

There were of course some projects which he wished had come nearer to fruition — which is inevitable. Nobody polishes off his entire agenda. But he had done his bit, and, after nineteen years, it was time to make way for someone else. That someone else will be, he hoped, different, and that was a good thing.

My parting shot was: were there any questions he wished I had asked and didn't?

His parting shot was 'No'.

So there.

## 18. Exmoor encores

### The *Exmoor* – second verse (2013)

The Archivist began to get the habit of versifying about it.

It's the month, and the week, and the day, and the hour
Of the greatest event of the year.
It's the pearl, it's the treasure, the gem, and the flower
Of all that West Buckland holds dear.
Who would have thought that a cross-country run
Would gather a school-ful of fans?
But to them it's right up there; it's second to none,
Though nobody else understands.
When it's time for the Exmoor we say,
'Let's all forget work and let's play.'
We shout to the world that we don't mind the pain.
The world says, 'West Buckland are at it again.'
It's time for the *Exmoor* – hooray!
If you're ill, there's the Devil to pay.
It's filthy, it's wet, and you run out of puff.
It's also the longest in England – and rough.
But, we assure you, we can't get enough.
So join us on Exmoor today.

Forget all your worries and doubts and alarms.
It's only six miles to the start.
And as teachers go past to the Poltimore Arms,
They wave (from their cars), so take heart.
Up on Five Barrows the rain or the snow
Will bring such a glow to your cheeks.
Feel grateful it's only about ten below.
And we haven't had floods now for weeks.
So what if the weather is grey?
Once more to the breach, and the fray.
And if you get lost in the mist and the murk,
There's one chance in ten that your mobile might work.
Let's cast off; let's get under way.
Who's afraid of a mere River Bray?
So wipe your wet nose on the edge of your sleeve.
Don't forget to say grace when you come to the Cleave:
'We thank you for what we're about to receive –
The very best part of the day.'

## Nearly off the Record

Just think, as you run, or you trot, or you walk,
As you stumble, and stagger, and roll,
It's all so much better than blackboard and chalk –
Such wonderful food for the soul.
Face up to the challenge, and rise to the dare,
Plunge into it, right to the hilt.
Like Everest, it must be done, 'cos it's there.
That's how our great Empire was built.
So mind over matter today.
Don't look at the mud on the way.
Who cares if the weather is not very calm?
They say that fresh air never did you much harm.
So stiff upper lip, come what may.
For honour and house, we obey.
Ignore all the cowpats; imagine the sun.
And think how you'll feel what it's over and done.
You'll tell the whole world, 'Well, *we* thought it was fun!
We've run on the *Exmoor* today.'
If you so much as finish, you feel you have won it –
'The hairiest run of them all, *and we've done it.*
We've run on the *Exmoor* today.'

# The *Exmoor* – third verse (2014)

**The day before**
 Tomorrow's the day of the *Exmoor*; it can't come too soon for me.
  My performance last year was an all-time low.
  But now I've been training – I'm raring to go.
  I'm determined to put up a jolly good show.
  I shall leave them all standing – you'll see.

**The day**
 'Three cheers for the jolly old *Exmoor*,' I say to my friends on the morning.
  I'm blind to the black looks and deaf to the curses.
  I listen to Mr. Price as he rehearses.
  I laugh at the jokes in Mr. Coates' verses.
  I'm not worried or nervous or yawning.

**Just before the start**
 We're getting close now to the *Exmoor*. Six miles was the ideal warm-up.
  There's a glow in the cheeks and a spring in the feet.
  That beer in the Polti went down a treat.
  Bit breezy, it's true, but you don't want much heat.
  And that cloud doesn't mean there's a storm up.

**Thirty minutes later**
 God's got it in for the *Exmoor*. He's up there, lying in wait.
  He's turned that light breeze to a spiteful gale.
  He's dropped enough rain to wash out every trail.
  And – just for good measure – He's thrown in some hail.
  And the mud has stuck up every gate.

### Forty minutes later

How *did* I get here in the *Exmoor*? How did I get mud *in my hair*?
It's splashed up each leg, along every sleeve.
It's crept into places you wouldn't believe.
And you can't get your hand down to grope and relieve.
Dear God – it just isn't fair.

### Fifty minutes later

I hate the bloody *Exmoor*; it's the pits, it's the very worst.
Six pounds of cow-pat are stuck to your shoes.
The whole of the Moor is a desert of ooze.
And you wouldn't have thought you'd be cursing booze,
But your bladder is fit to burst.

### A month later

The *Exmoor*? Oh, yes, it was great. It's the thing that we hold most dear.
It's our proudest tradition, you know, and so old.
No – we don't mind the wind and the rain and the cold.
Don't you believe all the stories you're told.
We simply can't wait for next year.

## The *Exmoor* – fourth verse (2015)

At West Buckland in the Moor, the time is fast approaching for the *Exmoor*.
At West Buckland in the Moor, it's *the* event where everyone expects more.
Now how could we dream up a wheeze to add to all the fun?
I know: we'd ask celebrities to come and join the run.
We thought it would produce a lovely day for everyone
At West Buckland in the Moor.


So, first, to catch the world's attention, we advertised on Facebook and on Twitter.
And there, of course, we had to mention, that *Exmoor* running isn't for the quitter.
It's rough and long and hard and breaks the very strongest heart.
The guts and grit required to finish take you off the chart.
You have to walk six miles before you even reach the start
From West Buckland in the Moor.


To prove the brotherhood of man, we sent a challenge to each hostile nation.
It was our harmless little plan for international co-operation.
Mr. Putin said the competition was too hot.
North Korea said it was a wicked western plot.
The President of Syria declared war on the spot
On West Buckland in the Moor.

We flung open wide the door – the guest list couldn't possibly be bigger.
From each and every distant shore, we invited every group and public figure.
The American Marines said they could never stand the strain.
The SAS said they'd prefer an Afghan war again.
The whole New Zealand rugby team rushed off to board their plane.
Not *one* of them could face the Moor.

The French Foreign Legion wrote, and said they hadn't had that type of
training.
The Scots Guards sent us a note, and said they might come if it wasn't
raining.
The card from Lewis Hamilton said he would like to know
How many circuits were there and how fast he'd have to go.
And if he broke down in the Cleave would boys give him a tow
To West Buckland in the Moor.
George Clooney was afraid his wife would never understand.
Wayne Rooney asked us, if he fell and swore, would he be banned?
Richard Branson said 'Yes' – if his aeroplane could land
By West Buckland in the Moor.

So to Hell with their excuses. Let the wimps all stay away.
We don't mind being on our own. We'll have a smashing day.
The *Exmoor* is all ours and let us keep it just that way
At West Buckland in the Moor.

## Exmoor – fifth verse (2016)

It becomes progressively more difficult with each passing year to think up something different. After all, how many things can you say about a cross-country run? However, an old idea occurred to me – that we do not see ourselves as other see us. So how would the *Exmoor*, and its sufferers, perhaps appear to chance walkers on the Moor. This, coupled with a flight of fancy about the hard life of WB pupils out there in the middle of nowhere, produced the following:

>The world is full of mysteries and horrors, Heaven knows.
>The Abominable Snowman comes to mind.
>The Loch Ness Monster, Pharaoh's curse, Vesuvius overflows.
>If you want fear, then search, and you will find.
>
>But oh, beware, and have a care, when you come down to Devon,
>For there, if you're unlucky, will befall
>The most accursed, the very worst, on earth, in Hell, or Heaven,
>The ghastliest apparition of them all.
>
>For you can be as free as me, just walking on the Moor,
>When suddenly, in brightest bloom of day,
>You'll get a view which very few have ever seen before,
>And lived to tell the tale another day.
>
>It's dread, it's dark, it's fell, it's stark, but, thank God, we're told
>It comes to human view just once a year.
>But all declare it raises hair, and makes the blood run cold,
>And paralyses witnesses with fear.

Monsters like the Beast of Exmoor simply don't compare.
　　The Hound of Baskerville is but a pup.
But when West Buckland's boys and girls all break out from their lair,
　　Men flee and shout, 'West Buckland's blood is up!'

Crouched in sedge, behind a hedge, I watched in mortal dread
　　As all four ghastly tribes of them went by –
Bloodthirsty Brereton, cruel Courtenay, Grenville's eyes blood red,
　　The Fortescue in fury and full cry.

The puff, the sigh, the staring eye, the oath and imprecation,
　　Bad language fit to scorch a soldier's ears.
Jaw set tight, all main and might, and fierce determination.
　　Sweat and sores and blisters, toil and tears.

The wheezing gasps, the breath that rasps, the lungs near torn asunder;
　　Blinding perspiration in the eyes;
The aches and pains, the cramps and sprains, the stumble and the blunder;
　　Fatigue that conquers, crushes, stupefies.

The mud-soaked trail, the rain, the hail, the ice-wind like a knife;
　　More hellish than what God poured on Gomorrah.
Put together all the worst things you've seen in your life –
　　They won't add up to match this dreadful horror.

Like Northern Lights, there are great sights, that some men strive to see.
　　Not me. I've stayed away from trouble – then
I saw that race, the *Exmoor* chase. And take it true from me:
　　I'll never be the man I was again.

'It's high time they came up with a better way to develop our characters.'

'What I always say is, it's not the winning; it's the taking part.'

*The Archives of an Archivist*

'But it's quicker this way.'

'When the Duke gives me my medal, d'you know what I'm going to do with it?'

## 19. We are all human

### The latest word

HAVE YOU EVER BEEN told that you are 'going through a phase'? A 'phase'. Of paramount importance right now, but it won't last. Even you know it won't last. It could be anything – long hair, short hair, green hair; wide trousers, narrow trousers; pigtails, rats' tails; black eye-shadow that makes you look like a dead Egyptian pharaoh, bare navels that threaten frostbite, rings in unmentionable places. It could be warts, spots, verrucas, boils, greasy skin, dry skin, and a host of other physical ailments that conspire, along with school rules, parents, and small brothers, to make adolescent life a misery.

But do not despair, my children. The wisdom of the world tells us that these things do not last; they are only a 'phase'. Words operate in phases too – have you noticed? They come and they go. They are hauled out of the dictionary, given a new twist, and sent out into the world to describe a whole host of situations that they were not originally designed for. Then they go out of fashion, they get shoved back into the dictionary, and they resume their original meaning.

Words which any pupil would have instantly recognised a generation or two ago would need a translator now. Even if you knew them, you would certainly not use them. If you were pleased about something today, would you say 'I think that's ripping'? Or 'How topping'? I don't suppose you'd even say 'smashing'. No – you would say 'brilliant'. 'Brilliant!' Or, alternatively, 'fantastic'. 'Brilliant' actually means 'shining brightly'; 'fantastic' actually means 'so unbelievable that it borders on the edge of fable'. But who cares? Whatever you like is 'brilliant' or it is 'fantastic'. Words like this are born very quickly.

The system operates like this. A new term starts. Suddenly the 'in' word – the 'cool' word – would be something like – 'smear'. Anyone who appeared stupid would be a 'smear'. Anyone who had no friends would be a 'smear'. Anyone who did anything out of the ordinary would be 'a complete smear'. Cheats, cry-babies, cissies, bullies, nerds, creeps, weeds, wimps – they would all be 'smears'. Then over the holidays the word would go out of fashion by some mysterious alchemy of linguistics, and the next term the word would be – let's say – 'blot'. Every ignoramus, oddball, and outsider would be a 'total blot'. I worked in a school once where the 'cool' word for a term or two was – believe it nor not – 'spastic'. *Everything* was 'spastic'.

So too with the adjective 'brilliant'. Something looks nice? It is 'brilliant'. Something tastes nice? It is 'brilliant'. It is a pleasant surprise? 'Brilliant'. Somebody does you a favour? 'Brilliant'. Your friend is wearing something new? 'Brilliant.' Somebody passes you the tomato sauce? 'Brilliant.' Never mind what the dictionary says; what is important is that you are up to date – using the 'in' word – in short, 'cool'.

The very word 'cool', besides meaning – whatever it means – is itself a cool word. I repeat – the whole point of a word like this is that it is modern, with it, up to date, hip, freshly-minted, cool. It could be of course that, by repeating this word 'cool' all the time, I am being distinctly un-cool and betraying my ignorance. If this is the case, I apologise. But I want to put it to you that you too are un-cool – just a bit.

If I said that you don't have 'swipes' these days, you would probably not have the faintest idea what I was talking about. 'Swipes.' Swiping – beating – corporal punishment? Not bad – six out of ten. Or stealing. People 'swipe' things off shop counters. A good try – eight out of ten. But wrong again. I shall put you out of your misery.

It is to do with – drinking. 'Swipes' was beer. Beer. In the nineteenth century, the water supply of a lot of boarding schools was a trifle suspect, to say the least. A lot of schools supplied their pupils with beer instead. Yes. Weak beer, admittedly, but beer. Some schools brewed their own. There's an idea! This school's founder, the Revd. J.L. Brereton, in his book about setting up schools like this, goes into tremendous details about costs and expenses, and one of the items in his sums refers to 'beer'.

Now, I would bet that, if you had regular supplies of beer these days, you would not be content with a measly old nineteenth-century word for it. 'Swipes' – a hundred and eighty years old – how un-cool could you get? Surely you would have worked out your own new word by now.

And yet you use another word in school, every day, many of you, which is just as ancient (and I don't mean swearwords), and you don't stop to think about it. Where do you go to buy your wagon wheels and your diet coke? Exactly – the 'tuck' shop. But the word 'tuck' – the word you are all happy to use – is nearly two hundred years old. It's not cool at all. Can it be that you're slipping? Or can it be that, like the rest of us, you like a spot of tradition?

## What do governors do?

WHAT DO YOU KNOW about school governors? Apart, of course, from knowing that we have some. And that they sit on a board. Quite probably, not much.

The trouble is that you can't see them at work. Watch a teacher, a doctor, a shop assistant, a navvy digging a hole in the road, and you get a pretty good idea. But governors are not like that; you don't see them actually doing their governing. They do what they do far away from prying eyes. In that sense, governors are like judges in chambers, poets, party chairmen, secret agents, and hired assassins.

About the only time you see them is on Speech Day, when they step very carefully up on to the stage in front of the assembled School, and sit in attitudes of congealed humanity for about an hour and a half while the prizes are handed out and the Chief Guest tells you all how to make a success of your lives. Then they step even more carefully down again, and that is that for another year.

I don't know about you, but when I was a boy, my overwhelming general impression of governors was that they were old. Very old. At my school, the governors secretly took their places up on the stage behind a closed curtain. At a given signal, the curtains were wound back, and there they were, like some kind of exhibit from Madame Tussaud's. Since they never moved, apart from the Chairman, and they were, as I said, old, you began to wonder by the time the proceedings were over whether they were still alive.

At the back of our School hall was a huge clock. When zero hour struck, the Chairman, an enormous man, lumbered to his feet. He was a retired Army officer, with a crop of white hair and a bristling white moustache. Very impressive. Probably a veteran of the Crimean War. But he knew little about public speaking. What he had to say came out in a series of growls. He would screw up his eyes, and talk straight at the clock. From time to time he would turn to make vague gestures with a ham-like hand, and his voice would trail off, then suddenly come on wavelength again. We only knew when he had finished because he sat down, and the Headmaster came to the rescue with something we could understand.

So you see? Experiences like that make it difficult for pupils to take governors seriously. But that's not fair, is it? Common sense should tell you that they must do something. After all, you don't advertise for a clutch of pensioners just to come and sit on a stage once a year, do you?

Which brings me to the question of just how you do become a governor.

I once asked a group of Year 7 pupils how they thought it was done. One said that governors were elected by the parents. Another said that a governor must have a university degree. A third said that you had to be in the House of Lords. A fourth said that candidates should 'go through a course and see what the Headmaster thinks of you'. There was one cynic. In answer to the question 'What qualifications do governors need?' he replied 'None'.

There was one quiet, shrewd voice. Its owner said that he thought you became a governor by 'being a good person for the School'. I reckon that takes a bit of beating.

Think about it. Governors are not paid. Most of them have done a lifetime's work already. So – yes – they may not be young any more. But they still feel that they have something to offer – chiefly energy and experience. And they want to do something worthwhile.

Yet there is nothing especially exciting about what they have to deal with. Look at the Minutes of the Governors' Meetings. Not much drama there. Mostly things like bank balances, cleaners' wages, water in the dormitories, corrosion in the pipes, dry rot, chlorination plants, and septic tanks. Once in a while they have to do something more interesting like buy some fresh land or appoint a new headmaster. But for the most part it's pretty bread-and-butter stuff – all of which is still very necessary.

As a way of summarising what governors do, I offer the comparison with parents. Neither parents nor governors have a recognised way of becoming parents or governors. There are no exams to pass. A governor can't shove his way through a crowd and say, 'Make way; I am a trained governor.' There are no perks or privileges or bonuses associated with the work. Both parents and governors are unpaid, unsung, and unpublicised. Nobody ever gets voted the 'Parent of the Year' or the 'Governor of the Year'.

Both get accused, at various times, of being quaint, infuriating, stuffy, unfair, short-sighted, inefficient, negligent, pompous, old-fashioned spoilsports. Yet both would get noticed most easily if they were not there. Neither set out to become what they became; it just sort of happened. And both no doubt must have wondered at times what they had let themselves in for.

But nobody forced them to do it – whatever it is that they do. Parents are not teachers, doctors, dentists, therapists, or games coaches; they just do everything else. Governors do not run the accounts, the classes, the exams, the playing fields, the dormitories, the kitchens, or the drains; they just do everything else. And they do it, presumably, because, like parents, they want to.

And they do it because, as that perceptive young analyst in Year 7 observed, they are each 'a good person for the School'.

## Play up and play the game

You could divide the pupils of West Buckland into three. How? By saying to them the words 'Games' or 'P.E.', and listening to the reaction. The first group will say 'Oh, wow!' The second will say, 'Oh, yes?' The third will say, 'Oh, Lord!' I am not concerned with the 'Oh wow-ers' or the 'Oh yes-ers.' This is a plea for the 'Oh Lord-ers'.

It is difficult for those who are good at games to understand what it is like to be bad at them. Flicking a hockey ball, delivering a leg spinner, pasting an overhead smash – it is all so easy. All you have to do is – well, just do it. For those who can't, these routine games skills are only slightly less complicated than piloting a space ship through a cosmic storm while simultaneously solving Fermat's last theorem on the back of an envelope.

Non-benders simply have to reconcile themselves to the fact that there will always be certain things that are beyond them. My grandson has long since reached this happy stage of what is known as 'CAI' – Contented Athletic Incompetence. He has three left feet, seventeen thumbs on each hand, and the physical co-ordination of your average alcoholic. Luckily, it doesn't bother him.

But it might bother some when they see how much attention is focussed on those who *are* good at games – the school teams, the colours, the coach trips, the foreign tours, the blazer badges, the mentions in the magazine, the celebrity, the admiration of small boys and girls. All because, it seems, God put them together in a slightly different way.

Look at the School's history, as recorded in the 150-odd years of magazines. I could tell you of a boy called William Stradling, who in the mid-1890's won every prize, cup and medal going. Every scholarship too. Absolutely sickening.

I could tell you of Cecil Farmer, who, on a bleak, rain-swept Whit Monday in 1917, won the mile, the half-mile, the quarter-mile, the 100 yards, the hurdles, the long jump, the steeplechase, and throwing the cricket ball. He had to make do with second place in the high jump; otherwise it would have been a clean sweep. The conditions were so bad that it was touch and go, after a night of storms, whether they called the sports off altogether. He beat one of his own records, equalled another, and set up a new record in a third. Oh, yes – and he did all this in a single afternoon.

We even had a sporting celebrity headmaster – John Challen. He was a soccer international, and a superb cricketer. In 1898, he scored seven centuries in an aggregate of 1,285 runs, in only 15 innings. In that year, his average was more than double that of the greatest of all English cricketers, Dr. W.G. Grace. And so on and so on. Today we are constantly being reminded of the exploits of Jonathan Edwards and Steve Ojomoh and Victor Ubogu. So sportsmen get a pretty good press.

Yet, if you think about it, players in school teams are, by definition, in a minority. So are they truly representative of the School? Would it not be a good idea to find a way of celebrating also the non-athletic prowess of the majority?

What about a competition to find the greatest non-bender on the whole campus? Mirror, mirror on the wall, who is the weediest, wimpiest, limpiest, lumpiest, dumpiest, chumpiest of us all? I don't mean disabled; that would of course be unfair and criminally unkind. I mean simply inept, totally lacking in athletic talent – the one with the most thumbs on each hand, the one who is slowest off the mark, the best dolly-dropper in the business. Invite candidates to submit their CV of Fumble, Stumble, and Tumble. Who can claim to have come last in more cross-country races than anybody else? Who, because of his, or her, total inability to make an impression on anything remotely spherical, has driven his, or her, games teacher the furthest up the wall? Who, when he slides off the wall bars, bears the strongest resemblance to a wet autumn leaf?

And mind – there must be no cheating about this. The candidate must have made honest effort, with no hope of reward at the time. The result must have come about through really trying, not through laziness, calculated inertia, or plain sleep.

There must of course be a jury. I would suggest one that consists of those with a pride-worthy history of consistent failure, because only they will know the difference between not succeeding and not bothering. We might persuade some benefactor or other (say, an Old Boy or Old Girl whose athletic record is distinguished only by its total lack of distinction) to donate a cup, to be presented to the Duffer of the Year, the Most Hopeless Case of the Year, the creator of the most teacher nervous breakdowns of the year. What about a House Bumble Competition Shield, to be presented immediately after the Southcomb Shield, if only to recognise the work of the majority?

Make it of strong metal, in case the recipient drops it.

## Something in the air

THIS YEAR, OVER AND over again [this was 2008], you are being told that West Buckland is 150 years old. You are having it poured into you till it is trickling out of the top of your head. Well, I've got news for you. It is not 150 years old; it is nearly four hundred million years old. Not the building, obviously. Nor the staff. But the land. The land.

We had an Old Boy years ago, a Mr. R. P. Chope, who did research on this, and he wrote a quite unreadable article in the School magazine about it. It was full of references to things like plutonic rocks, brown micaceous sandstone, and silicious ooze chert. How do you feel about running round the rugby field on 'silicious ooze chert'?

He also put in some alarming information about some of the creatures who once lived here. If you had been around all those millions of years ago, you could have met, behind the cricket nets, things called 'trilobites', which apparently were 'three-lobed animals with a head-shield and compound eyes'. Ghastly! But again, not members of staff.

Technically, the rock on which we stand is called 'Devonian', which is nice, isn't it? Then, it seems, another layer was deposited on top, from something called the 'Carboniferous Age'. This isn't here now, says Mr. Chope, because it has been 'worn away by the combined action of rain, frost, and wind'. Rain, frost, and wind. Sound familiar? So nothing much has changed about West Buckland weather for over three hundred million years.

Rain, frost, and wind. If you can survive that – for three hundred million years – I reckon you can survive anything. I have talked to many Old Boys who served in the Second World War. Some of them spent time in German prisoner-of-war camps. After years of boarding-school at West Buckland, they said, it was a doddle. A piece of cake.

This capacity for survival goes a long way to explain, I think, why so many people associated with West Buckland live for a long time. However, what is surprising is that so many people, given a choice, *choose* to stay here for a long time. The old School magazines are full of names and statistics about this.

Take David Clark, the Deputy Head who retired in 2003. He and his wife Helen, the Headmaster's Secretary, who retired with him, served over 50 years between them. This term, Mr. and Mrs. Whittal-Williams will retire with a total of 66 years' service to the School. We had a gardener who retired in 1916 – George Balment – who had been working at the School ever since it was founded in 1858. One man – 58 years. And he didn't want to go.

Look round the School, and you will find plenty of staff who have twenty years' service to their credit, some with over thirty. Don't rush up to them and ask how old they are, but they might be willing to tell you how many years they have been here.

And they don't all totter away and die as soon as they have left either. The first Headmaster, Joseph Thompson (you can see a marble plaque about him on the wall at the foot of the Memorial Hall stairs) – Joseph Thompson was here for thirty years, left, got married, had a family, served locally as a priest, and lived to be 85. Possibly the School's greatest headmaster, the Revd. Harries, was Head for 27 years, also got married when he was past fifty, had a family, and lived to be 86. Mr. Wheeler, who was an Old Boy, a teacher at the School, a governor, a president of the Old Boys' Association, and, later, a caretaker headmaster, lived to be 88, and was associated with the School for 77 years. A headmaster from the 1950's, Leslie Stephens, died only a few years ago at nearly 90. And during the Second World War, we had another caretaker headmaster, who had retired owing to a health breakdown and come to live in Devon. He worked here for a year, retired again, and lived to be 95, and was playing bridge the evening before he died.

So there is something about this place. A few years ago, I met an old lady whose father – whose *father* – had left the School in 1896. Those of you who are in Fortescue House will know about Lady Margaret Fortescue. Her ancestor helped to set the School up in the first place. Every head of the Fortescue family since has served as a governor. Lady Margaret did it for 38 years, and now her daughter, Lady Arran, continues the tradition. The Fortescue family have been benefactors to the School for six generations.

And how's this for a link with the past? There was a fire here in 1930, and they built the Memorial Hall to replace the losses. It was opened in 1932. Lady Margaret was present – in 1932 – 76 years ago. It was opened by her grandfather, the fourth Earl Fortescue. He, the fourth Earl, said he could remember watching *his* grandfather, the second Earl, lay the foundation stone of the School in 1860. So Lady Margaret, who is very much alive, once sat on the knee of a man who saw the first foundation stone of the School laid 148 years ago.

I repeat, there seems to be something about this place. It must be all that Devonian Rock from all those millions of years ago, all that 'micaceous sandstone', all that 'silicious ooze chert', and that 'combined action of rain, frost, and wind'. So next time you are getting soaked on the games field, or shivering on an *Exmoor* run, or simply hunched against the bitter wind in an exposed corridor, take heart; just think how long you are going to live when it is all over.

## You got problems?

I ONCE HAD A colleague who was Jewish – proper orthodox Jew. And he was fond of telling stories *against* the Jews. For example:

Two Jewish businessmen met in the street. They said good morning to each other. Then they just stood there for a minute, in total silence. At last one of them said, 'Well, Jacob, aren't you going to ask me how I am?'

Jacob said, 'All right, Isaac. How are you?'

Isaac shook his head and said, 'Don't ask me.'

Jacob was not impressed. He said, 'You got problems? I got problems. We all got problems.'

We have indeed. Some are easier to see than others.

Take me. Some of my problems are obvious, aren't they? Well, they are from your point of view anyway. I'm old. I'm bald. I'm overweight. I'm left-handed. Then there are the problems you notice after talking to me. I'm ignorant: I don't know anything about important things like Facebook, I-pads, being cool, text messages, the 'X' Factor, Twitter, and Justin Bieber. Thirdly, there are the problems you can't see easily – like how many pills I may take; how hard of hearing I may be; how many stairs I can climb without getting puffed.

Finally, there are the things you know about all old people, because everybody knows them: they are old-fashioned; they are out of touch; they are grumpy; they suffer from complaints with peculiar names like Alzheimer's, Parkinson's, Hodgkinson's, osteoporosis, rheumatoid arthritis, hypothermia. In fact, with all those things wrong with them, you wonder why they think it's worth going on. But they do. Very brave actually. As the man said, old age is not for cissies.

What you may miss is that they still think, and they still feel, and they still know a thing or two. Don't be fooled by appearances. Many old people are not really old; they are young people who have just been around a long time.

And they are not the only people with problems. Remember what Jacob said? 'You got problems; I got problems; we all got problems.'

Take middle age. You may have wished now and then that you were grown up. Able to do all the things that those infuriating adults can do. Be careful before you wish away your youth. What do you have to look forward to? I'll tell you what you have to look forward to: Maintaining a mortgage; raising a family; paying all the household bills; sudden illness; losing your job; looking after ageing or sick relatives; setting up and servicing a pension; coping with bereavement; dealing with crises like divorce, accident, delinquency, sheer bad luck.

And that's not all; while all that is going on, you have to face up to, and deal with, fallen arches, pulled muscles, torn cartileges, fatty secretion, cellulite, weak ankles, irritable bowel syndrome, nervous tension, haemorrhoids, slipped discs, hiatus hernias, ordinary hernias, frozen shoulders, high blood pressure, low blood pressure, anaemia, clinical depression, vitamin deficiency, hot flushes, menopauses (they've invented one now for men as well), sags, scrags, bags, paunches – put simply, everything has dropped. What a prospect lies before you.

So you had better enjoy what you've got before it all gets you. And watch out; *you've* got problems too. What problems? I'll tell you. Your health for a start – spots, measles, warts, chicken pox, verrucas, allergies, teeth braces, mumps, ingrowing toenails, eczema, asthma, obesity, anorexia, dyslexia, dyspraxia, and all the other exia's and axia's that the psychologists keep inventing. That's just the physical things; what about the mental ones? Complexes, phobias, syndromes, crushes, rages, crazes, phases. More exia's and axia's. Then there is the small matter of the human race all around you. How many times have you been teased, tormented, enraged, embarrassed, driven to despair by parents, older brothers and sisters, younger brothers and sisters, grandparents, boy friends, girl friends? How often do you feel that old age begins at 23?

So – to repeat our friend Jacob, 'I got problems; you got problems; we all got problems.'

Is there no hope? Yes, a bit. All those elderly dodderers over the age of 23 have been through what you are going through, and they survived. If they hadn't, you wouldn't be here. Some of them are even prepared, now and then, to help you with their experience. So try listening.

And you can always try relying on yourself. Ever thought of that? It's quite a good idea to have two crises on the go at the same time. So that when you are sick of being driven up the wall by one, you can switch over to the other. Try that. You can also try putting all your crises together, as if they were a box of chocolates, and, in the morning, choose one to worry about. Or again – and this is maybe the best one – just do the next thing. Whether it is your Maths homework, or taking the dog for a walk, or cleaning your teeth, or listening to Justin Bieber – just do the next thing.

There was a bishop (admittedly a wealthy one) who used to fall behind with answering his letters. Whenever he began to worry about his huge pile of unanswered correspondence, he used to open a bottle of Champagne. He said that, by the time he had finished drinking it, he didn't give a damn whether he answered the wretched letters or not.

You may not be able to afford a bottle of Champagne, but you should be able to think of something that needs doing. Well, that's it; do it. Do the next thing. Never forget that we are all in it together. Remember what Jacob said to his friend Isaac: 'You got problems? I got problems; we all got problems.'

## Beat That

[I WENT UP ON the stage carrying an old-fashioned cane – allegedly a cane which had belonged to Sam Howells, a teacher of between-the-wars vintage, later a wartime headmaster, and a noted disciplinarian.]

SEE THAT? NO PRIZES for guessing that it is a cane. For beating boys. In fact, not *a* cane but *the* cane. This is the actual cane used by a previous Headmaster of this school. A very observant caretaker rescued it when its owner retired, and he gave it to me in the Archive over forty years later.

That headmaster used it for quite a long time too; he was Head for eleven years. . . . Doesn't look very dangerous, does it? It seems to have had a good deal of wear and tear. But it can still make a noise. . . . and it could still sting.

The victims of it naturally took what steps they could to soften the effects. One way was to turn up at the Headmaster's study fifteen minutes early. You would of course be told to wait outside. Outside you sat on one of the stone steps of the old staircase. Fifteen minutes on cold stone provided a sort of frozen insulation which deadened the pain when it came.

Another way was to go to one's dormitory beforehand (don't forget that the school then was almost a hundred per cent boarding), and put on as many pairs of pants as possible – more insulation. One spoilsport headmaster got round this by issuing a decree that in future all boys who were up for caning were to wear pyjamas – and nothing else.

And so it went on – round after round in the eternal undeclared war that exists between teachers and pupils. You won some; you lost some. Everybody accepted it.

You mean they accepted corporal punishment? By and large, on the whole, for the most part, generally speaking – yes, they did.

How cruel. How awful. How shocking. How degrading. There ought to be a law. Well, there is now, I believe.

But what about then? How they must have suffered. Poor creatures. And what sadistic adults they must have been to inflict such brutal treatment on young people in their charge.

Now here I think you have to be careful. Consider for a moment what the situation was. It may surprise you to be told that universal education in this country is barely more than a century old. True, there were schools before that, but it was all very random, patchy, a typical British bumble.

How did you run a national education system? Nobody knew.

When the first schools came along, nobody had ever had so many young people in one room, together, before. Five, six, seven, in a family, yes. Maybe a few more in a nursery. But never before twenty, thirty, forty, fifty – even more – in one room – with one teacher. Don't forget that if there was a shortage, to start with, of schools, there was also a shortage of teachers.

So – fifty of them, one teacher. How did you keep order? You hit them. There was no other way. It was what everybody did. Masters thrashed their apprentices; officers in the Army had their soldiers flogged; fathers took the strap to their children. Nannies smacked their toddlers. Dammit, husbands sometimes beat their wives.

That was the way society was. Indeed, some fathers who said they would not beat their children were considered weak, or soft, or cranky. Rather like parents today who boast that they never say 'No' to their children.

I suppose it came down in the end to fear. There was one of you; there was a lot of them. Fear of numbers, fear of disorder, fear of chaos if all authority was overturned. In many of the famous old public schools, the great fear was not of sex and drugs; it was fear of violence, mutiny. So you had to maintain order. It took a long time for society to work out that there were other ways to keep order besides the belt, the birch, the lash, the cat, or the cane – or, at the extreme end, the rope.

There are still those to this day, aren't there, who maintain that the cure for the ills of society is to bring back the stick and the rope. Bring back fear.

And it is also true that the teacher you least respect is not the one who keeps too much order but the one who does not keep enough.

All right, so we have moved forward. We are more sensitive, more enlightened. School, and society altogether, are better places than they were. Now that we are in the comforting shelter of the twenty-first century, we can look back with pity and scorn on those benighted souls of the twentieth and the nineteenth who did all those nasty things because they didn't know any better. How stupid they were; how backward, how ignorant; how uncivilised.

We don't do things like that now – dear me, no. Nowadays we stalk people; we make abusive telephone calls; we put obscene material in the post to our victim; we send texts which are explicitly designed to create misery, we indulge in binge drinking. And most of this, have you noticed, is done, not by teachers, but by pupils.

That is sad, isn't it? But there is always hope. The cane has gone, along with the dunce's cap, along with bear-baiting and freak shows. Can we look forward to a society where nasty texts and emails and stalking and postal dirt become a thing of the past? I wonder.

Are we in danger of the 22$^{nd}$ century looking back at us and thinking *we* are backward and ignorant and uncivilised? If so, I suggest that we still have quite a bit to do.

## Harold be thy name

WE ALL MAKE MISTAKES. Well, there'a nothing very wrong with that. You know the saying: 'The man who never made any mistakes never made anything.' It is a sign of our humanity, isn't it? A sign of our fallibility. Anyway, who wants to be perfect? To get every sum right? To solve every problem? To turn over the winning card every time? To carry off every single prize? It sounds nice, but we all know that, in actual practice, it would turn out to be pretty terrible. We would yearn, we would pray, 'Dear God, let me, just once, get something wrong.'

So let us not be ashamed of our mistakes. Moreover, let us not be too unkind when we see other people making mistakes. That is sometimes difficult. If an elderly lady in the street stumbles over her shopping bag and falls, we don't usually double up in hysterics, but if a teacher were to slip on a banana skin, it would be very hard to keep a straight face.

It is all to do with circumstances, isn't it? If some arrogant teenager says she thinks Joan of Arc is the daughter of Noah, we can all have a jolly good laugh, because she ought to know better. But if a small child comes out with a wrong word, we mix our amusement with kind smiles, because that small child does *not* know better. Moreover, he is saying what he says because he is quite sure he has heard it before. It shows that he has been paying attention. It was just that he didn't quite hit the nail on the head.

For instance, like all families, we have our collection of things a young member of it once said. My son used to call a butterfly a 'buttonflower'. A bumblebee was a 'bimbombee'. It gets to the stage when the wrong version is often much more attractive than the correct one. 'Buttonflower' sounds much more fun, almost more romantic, than 'butterfly', don't you think?

Then again, some errors become such good jokes that they pass into family folklore. My son (again) for quite a while referred to 'trousers' as 'trajels'. Heaven knows why. 'Buttonflower' does sound a bit like 'butterfly', but by no stretch of imagination does 'trajels' sound like 'trousers'. But there; 'trajels' it was. In the end, we all became so used to it that, to this day, we still use the word with a completely straight face. 'Put your best trajels on today.' Like that. Dead straight, without thinking.

There are errors and errors, aren't there? You come across lots of them in the teaching trade, obviously. And I don't mean the ones that come about from laziness, or not paying attention, or total ignorance. We always have to live with those; we are all human, as I said at the start.

No. The mistakes I treasure are like the ones my son used to make. The pupil has listened; he has remembered; and he has used his common sense. He has just missed a trick along the way.

Take the Roman Empire. One boy knew you could get into trouble in the early days if you were a Christian and set up an altar to Christ. Or, as he put it, St. Alban was killed because 'he burnt incense under the Emperor'. You can't wonder they killed him, can you?

Of what about this from the Stone Age? This pupil was *not* ignorant; he understood how primitive life was. 'Question: What did men use to build the prehistoric huts on Dartmoor? Answer: Their hands.' Well?

Let's go back even further, to Adam and Eve and the Garden of Eden. As you know, they didn't bother much with clothes, until they took a bite out of an apple, which mysteriously improved their eyesight. When God came along, they hid themselves. This candidate got it so nearly right; he was only one letter out: 'They knew that they were naked so they got a leaf covered themselves a bit and then ran off into the buses.' Must have caused a bit of a stir on the lower deck.

Then there is the answer that starts out as logical, then looks silly, until you wonder whether the candidate is being very stupid or very crafty. 'Q. What was Lenin's real name? A. Something else.'

Now and again, you come across genuine creativity. 'Question: How would you improve the defences of a castle? Answer: Have dragons.' What a good idea.

Very occasionally, you find an answer which almost deserves to go into an anthology. 'Question: Who searched for a cure for malaria in 19th century Africa? Answer: Dr. Livingstone, I presume.'

But – I repeat – when we laugh, we must always remember that we too make mistakes. Worse, that we have blind spots, and that we can continue to make the same mistake for years. I was turned thirty before I discovered that that show you went to see just after Christmas was called a 'pantomime'. I had always called it a 'pantomine'. God knows why. Blind spot, you see.

When I was in infants' school, I was always comforted by the end of the Lord's Prayer, because it said 'for ever and ever are men'. God was clearly a chauvinist who didn't care much for the future welfare of women. But the men were all right – 'for ever and ever are men'. I found that very reassuring.

I knew a man who told me that, when he was six, he found out what God's Christian name was. It wasn't anything biblical, like Josiah or Ezekiel or Nicodemus. It was Harold. It suddenly dawned on him one day when he listened to the beginning of the Lord's Prayer; 'Our Father, which art in Heaven, Harold be thy name.'

So – laugh, yes. But, when you do, keep a little bit of mercy and kindness in reserve, because you never know: the next mistake could be yours. Your next awful clanger is just round the corner. Like the pupil who was asked in an RE question, 'What does the name "Christ" mean?' He wrote, ' "Christ" means when something goes wrong.'

'Now come on – somebody must have some news somewhere.'

*The Archives of an Archivist*

'Out of the frying pan.'

*Nearly off the Record*

'We don't let him out till he's done those reports.'

## 20. Songs of Praise

DAFFODILS, SUNSETS, MOUNTAINS, LOVERS, nightingales, and Grecian urns get their fair share of poems or songs written about them. But remote country boarding schools don't. To my knowledge, West Buckland has had only four.

The first was written by the Revd. J.L. Brereton. Well, you would expect that, wouldn't you? After all, he founded the school. He was proud of it. He wanted, like any fond parent, to talk about it, extol its virtues, hold out high hopes for its future, put it on the map, and induce parents to send their sons to it. He was also a man of cauldronic energy (if there is such a word). He wrote about nearly everything – schools, education, farming, year books for his village (West Buckland), Christian teaching, the organisation of a boarding school, the establishment of a Cambridge college, the building of a railway to serve his new school, memos, articles, pamphlets, prospectuses, and so on and so on, almost *ad infinitum*. There was no stopping him. He must have been a bit of a trial to live with. (And sixteen children!)

As this is the middle of the nineteenth century, the song was shot through with respectability, hope, Christian virtue, verbosity, and quaint, rather touchingly optimistic pride in his county, and in the virtues of his country at the time. As if Bible, Book, Bat, and Pen were the best inspirers of boys and shapers of character yet devised by the human brain, or ever likely to be devised.

One may smile now, but there was no question about Brereton's sincerity, or his confidence. It would be hard for anybody to deny that these two qualities are rather necessary prerequisites for success in any long-term project. He was sure, and he meant it, and he laid his cards plainly on the table. You may not agree with a man like that, but you could respect him.

Oddly, too, one sees tiny shafts of plain practicality in the verses. Healthy plants need deep, strong roots. 'When it was wanted' – there was no question that Brereton had put his finger on a vital truth: that the sons of 'middle-class men' had, then, no national system of secondary education provided for them. Finally, anyone looking at an aerial photograph of West Buckland would sooner or later wonder how a school came to be founded here at all. 'On these wild hills, apart from all learning and art.' It is a tribute to Brereton's honesty that he knew, deep down, that it was all a mighty long shot.

The tune, incidentally, was written by Hubert Bath, a young Devon composer. He became a prolific and popular composer of waltzes, marches, overtures, cantatas, and orchestral suites, including one called *Devonia*. The second movement was entitled *Lorna of Exmoor*. He later turned his hand to writing film scores. He is best known for the score to the film *Cornish Rhapsody*. One of his marches, *Out of the Blue*, was used for years as the signature tune of BBC Radio's Sports Report.

## The Song of the Devon County School

There are seeds that will grow under ice and snow;
There are roots that hold fast through the wild mountain blast,
Through the wild mountain blast.

*Chorus* [The score reminds us that this should be delivered 'slowly and majestically'.]

Then Hail to the School that by good grace of Heav'n,
Took root and bore fruit on the Hills of North Devon.

The score decrees a repetition of the chorus – 'ff' too. [Never waste a good tune or a good idea.]

The seed that's well grown in due time is well known;
And the plant that strikes root shall be famed for its fruit,
Shall be famed for its fruit.

*Chorus*

Men will ask how it came to take root and win fame
On these wild hills, apart from all learning and art,
From all learning and art.

*Chorus*

The truth is 'twas planted just when it was wanted;
And of Schools in the West we account it the best,
We account it the best.

*Chorus*

May it still teach to youth, men's arts and God's truth,
And with Book, Bat, and Pen, fit its boys to be men!
Fit its boys to be men.

Oddly, Brereton didn't put the exclamation mark after the second 'men'. A mistake? An oversight? Don't be too quick to decide. Never underestimate Brereton.

I have been told that this song was sung at the end of term right up to the early 1960's.

## The School Hymn

I DON'T KNOW HOW or why the school came to adopt as its own a hymn by Sir Arthur Sullivan of all people. I very much doubt whether Sir Arthur wrote it on the invitation of West Buckland. (Although, to his credit, the Revd. Brereton did know a great many people, and Lord Fortescue knew everybody.)

Nor can I find any information on the author of the words. Nor, again, have I been able to find out when the hymn was last sung by the school as a whole. The sheet just popped up in the records, and there it was, at the top of the page: The School Hymn. So the information, I'm afraid, is a bit thin on the ground for this subject.

It's a good tune though. Well, it would be, wouldn't it? Arthur Sullivan.

**70** BISHOPGARTH 8 7 8 7 D  
A. Sullivan (1842-1900)

THE SCHOOL HYMN

1 Great Lord of wisdom, life and light,
  Before the hills were founded,
  Thy quickening breath dissolved the night
  And stirred through deeps unsounded.
  Beneath thy hand the formless earth
  And ocean rolled asunder,
  And in thy likeness man had birth,
  Thy crowning work and wonder.

2 Through that grey dawn thou callest him,
  Untaught but not unheeding,
  His feet were faint, his lamp was dim,
  Yet faith discerned thy leading.
  Age after age and line on line
  Thy book unfolded clearer,
  Till, like a flush of morn divine
  Thy Son proclaimed thee nearer.

3 His work from east to slumbering west
  Went out through all creation;
  Our far-off island woke and blest
  Thy name with adoration.
  We kneel where our forefathers knelt,
  They trod these courts before us,
  Unseen, though near, our hearts have felt
  Their blessings hover o'er us.

4 We praise thy name for one and all
  Who founded for thy glory
  Each ancient School, each Minster tall,
  To teach their sons thy story.
  May we, like them, our lamp display
  Of love and wisdom burning,
  Till twilight melt in golden day
  At our dear Lord's returning.

*Augustus Lawrence Francis (1848-1925)*

**71**

1 To you, O Lord, our hearts we raise
  In hymns of adoration;
  Accept our sacrifice of praise,
  Our shouts of exultation;
  For by your hand our souls are fed –
  What joys your love has given!
  You give to us our daily bread,
  So give us bread from heaven!

2 And now on this our festal day,
  Your love to us expressing
  Our gifts before you, Lord, we lay,
  The firstfruits of your blessing:
  Bright robes of gold the fields adorn,
  The hills with joy are ringing;
  The valleys stand so thick with corn
  That even they are singing.

3 Yet in your presence we confess,
  O Lord of earth and heaven,
  Our pride, our greed and selfishness –
  We ask to be forgiven:
  And where the hungry suffer still
  Because of our ambition,
  There let our riches serve your will
  Your love be our commission.

4 There is a country bright as day
  Beyond the crystal river,
  Where hunger will be done away
  And thirst be gone for ever;
  Where praises ring out loud and strong
  That now with ours are blending;
  Where we shall sing the harvest-song
  That never has an ending.

*after W. C. Dix (1837-98)*

Words © In this version Word & Music/Jubilate Hymns

*Nearly off the Record*

## Ode to West Buckland

I CANNOT VOUCH FOR the genuineness of this title to the third one, but it fits the tone and intent of the piece, and, from one's knowledge of the author, one can easily imagine his writing it.

It is attributed to R.F. Delderfield ('Ronnie' to his friends, 'Dido' to his schoolmates, after a part he performed in a school play). RFD came to the school in 1926, after a string of unsuccessful and unhappy (and brief) stays in five or six previous ones. But he loved WB, and wrote a long novel about it, as everyone who has any acquaintance with the school finds out sooner or later. (Like Hubert Bath with his music, RFD was a prolific writer – plays, novels, straight history books, and much else.)

I am not qualified to pass judgment on the quality of this poetry. And good or bad, it is not a vindication either of the transcendent virtue of West Buckland. What is important is that West Buckland inspired him to write it. He didn't write poems about his previous schools.

It is an illustration (yet another illustration) of the capacity of this school to inspire affection in its pupils. As archivist, I have noticed it in scores of contexts. What is more remarkable is that this affection is generated after surprisingly brief stays here. RFD was at the school for only two years. Scores of old boys, some with only two or three years, a few with barely eighteen months, to their credit (I know, because I have seen their attendance records), used to turn up regularly at the annual dinners – cigars, white tie, and all. And, according to the magazine reports, they laughed, cheered, and sang most lustily. Something must have put that goodwill there.

RFD did not forget when he left. He maintained regular contact with the school, assisted in this by old school friend Harold Boyer (a member of staff – who, incidentally, enjoyed the nickname 'Romeo'). Boyer produced RFD's most famous play *Worm's Eye View* in the Memorial Hall, and RFD wrote to say that it was one of the most enjoyable productions of it he had seen. And he had seen a few; the play ran for five years at the Whitehall Theatre in London, and became staple diet for local amateur companies up and down the country for years.

Delderfield also took a great interest in the Phoenix Society, and often visited its debates. It was at one of these debates that another old boy, Nicky Armstrong, met him. This was when Nicky was a sixth-former. RFD said that he had just completed his latest novel, but was stuck for a title. He explained a little about it, and Nicky – well, so he says – offered one. He had just been studying the poetry of Yeats, and had come across the verse about

'Cast a cold eye on life, on death! Horseman, pass by!'

Delderfield used it, but gave it a twist, as all artists do – *A Horseman Riding By*. He sent

*The Archives of an Archivist*

Nicky a copy of the first edition.
   Well, here it is – at last.

   Gold in the beeches at school year's beginning,
    First fleeting glimpse of a girdle of stone.
   Old jokes exchanged by the gay and familiar,
    Newcomers standing uncertain, alone.

     There goes the bell!
     On its notes we remember
  How we stood mute and how sharp were our fears;
   Yet with the seasons came sense of belonging,
   Down went the roots that outlasted the years.

   White figures running down from the skyline,
    Chasing the end of the short winter's day,
   Mud-spattered footsteps, tired but triumphant,
    Home from the *Exmoor,* home from the *Bray*.

     There goes the bell!
    And the mem'ries are surging,
   Names are forgotten by faces recalled,
  Laughter remembered but errant achievements
   Lost on the road, by the years overhauled.

   Green on the hillside, green in the hedgerows,
   Spring calls without as the class drones within,
   Youth with its head bent low over schoolbooks,
    Ending a chapter, but yet to begin.

     There goes the bell!
    And the mem'ries come crowding,
   Gathered like sheep to the fold, in the quad;
   Triumphs, disasters, something of either,
   And personal failures known only to God.

   Blue summer skies with white clouds a-sailing;
    Far round the field rings an echoing shout;

Crack of the bat as the ball rises upwards,
Hope for a vict'ry, fear of a rout.

There goes the bell!
And the mem'ries are homing,
The sad and the joyful,
The fleet and the lame,
Homing on Buckland, timeless and ageless,
Evermore changing, ever the same.

## A New School Song

I'm afraid I have to own up to the fourth.

It arose quite by chance. At a speech day, the guest speaker (who was himself an old boy) drew attention to the school song, printed above – Brereton's version. Thinking out loud, he wondered whether or not it might be time to compose a more modern one. With that in mind, he offered to arrange a sort of competition; entrants would submit their idea of a new school song, and he would bestow some kind of distinction or reward on the one he thought the best.

That set me thinking. I got out Brereton's song, and wondered whether a new song could be devised which offered new sentiments, but which maintained a connection with the past by preserving the scheme of the original – the number of verses, the length of the lines, the idea of a chorus, and so on. At the same time, one had to take note of the changes that had taken place in over 150 years – the number of foreign students, and fact that the school is now co-educational, the regular provision of bursaries to assist suitable pupils who can not afford the fees – and so on.

I am not an old pupil of the school, but, as Archivist for seventeen years, I like to think I have become fairly well acquainted with it, and I dare to hope I have absorbed something of the spirit of the place.

Anyway, here is what I produced:

## A New School Song

No matter your nation, your colour, your creed;
No matter how local, no matter how far;
No matter your riches, no matter your need –
You can all be at ease with the person you are.

So long as you're willing to help and to share;
So long as you're willing to grapple and strive;
So long as you're willing to lead and to dare –
You can all make the most of just being alive.

May your newly-found friends see you over the tears.
May your memories soften the wind and the rain.
May you see what you gained with the wisdom of years.
May you all want to come back again and again.

*Chorus*
Then read, reap, and take your own small share of Devon,
To guide you through life, and help you choose your Heaven.


I sent it in, but nothing came of it. Pity.

## 21. You can't beat a good story

### It doesn't really happen like that

DID YOU KNOW THAT it is now nearly fifty years since James Bond burst into our cinemas? Now the whole world knows him – 007. He is up there with Jesus, Mickey Mouse, Muhammad Ali, and Harry Potter. And he has one advantage over the others: we don't, most of us, particularly want to be a religious leader, a cartoon animal, a boxer, or a wizard. But we might often fancy ourselves as a spy – well, half of us anyway – the glamour, the guns, the girls, the gadgets, the travel, the tuxedo – what an image!

The reality, as we all know in our more down-to-earth moments, is far different. The life of a spy can be obscure, seedy, unpleasant, often mind-crushingly dull, and often too exceedingly dangerous. If you want evidence, I think I can supply it with a bit of West Buckland history. Because one West Buckland old boy (or rather Devon County School old boy) became just that – a spy. At least that is what the evidence shows.

He had a good career at the School – honours in the then equivalent of GCSE and A-Levels, and 2$^{nd}$ in Drawing in the whole of England. He won a national scholarship. In 1882 he entered the Civil Service Examinations, and was placed 9$^{th}$ in the whole of England. He was selected for the Foreign Service, and was posted in the end to Berbera, a grubby coastal town in Somaliland, the back of beyond of North-East Africa. He was officially listed as an accountant. An accountant. He was sent on what was called a 'special mission', and died, it was announced, of malaria in June, 1901.

Now – why on earth was a boy with a scholarship in Drawing recruited into the Foreign Service? Or was it simply on the strength of the fact that he was clever – 9$^{th}$ in the whole of England? And why was he sent to Berbera, as an accountant? And why did a seedy little town like Berbera, whose economy was almost nil, *need* an accountant? And what was the 'special mission' he was sent on?

And – *and* – when he died, why did his mother receive a personal letter of condolence from the Foreign Secretary, Lord Landsdowne himself? And why did the news of his death take six years to leak out into the local papers? Yes, exactly. It smells, doesn't it? But if he really was a spy, he wasn't a very likely one, was he? And he didn't have a very James-Bondish sort of life – or death – did he?

*Nearly off the Record*

You could say the same about the Second World War. The most unlikely people were recruited to be spies, or saboteurs, or secret agents. Far from being tough guys with degrees in Oriental Languages, some of them were women, and very ordinary women at that. Young women too – 29, 23, 21. So at least one of them was only three years older than you in the Upper Sixth.

And they didn't apply to become spies; they just volunteered for what they were told was 'special duties'. Any one of them could have come from a school like this (if it had had girls then). They were trained intensively in parachuting, map-reading, wireless operating, explosives, shooting, killing. So – yes, if you like – that was exciting. It was certainly different.

Only at the end of their training were they told that they were to be parachuted into German-occupied France and Holland and Belgium, to spy, naturally, and to help with the Resistance. You have all seen films about these people – the drama, the waves of orchestral music, the glamorous heroines, the hairsbreadth escapes, the tricks played on 'ze veray stupid Gairman fawcess'. The truth was not like that.

The 'veray stupid Gairmans' had in fact penetrated part of the British code system. They knew the spies were coming. Many of these young women were arrested as soon as they landed, or soon afterwards. They were transported to concentration camps, including one specially designed for women, where experiments were conducted the details of which have no place in a school morning assembly. They were tortured, and later hanged, injected with lethal drugs, gassed, or shot in the back of the neck. We know this, because some of their German guards gave evidence after the War.

I repeat – these were young women, ordinary young women, although their German guards testified that they conducted themselves with great courage and dignity when the end came, so perhaps they were not so ordinary after all. But some of them were barely older than some of you. And they had no idea what was in store for them when they volunteered. So – not much of the vodka and martini there, was there?

Do I mean that something like that could happen to you? No, of course not. Why am I sure? Because you know what happened to them. And you know why it happened. If you don't, your History teachers will tell you. And, when you become fully adult, you will see to it that it will never happen again.

## Straight Talking

WHEN I WAS A schoolboy – going back a bit now – we often used to talk between ourselves about teachers – which seems normal enough, considering the amount of time we spent with them during a working week. One of the topics we discussed was the business of keeping order: why did some teachers get played up, and others exert total control? Why did we never move a muscle with one man (it was a boys' school) and play merry hell with another – honestly, some of the things people got up to. . . . maybe in another assembly.

Anyway, was it age? Was it height? Was it sheer animal strength? Was it a sense of humour? Was it a sharp tongue? Was it pure scholarship? Was it brain power? And so on.

There are lots of answers to this question, and I don't know which is the best, but there is one which, over the years, has impressed me.

Think. What do you expect a teacher to do? Exactly – teach you something. If he gets across to you the simple fact that he is in the business of making you learn, you will put up with almost anything. Why? Because his message is clear, and he works at getting it across all the time. He is consistent; he is reliable. Even if he is a monster who regards all schoolchildren as the lowest form of animal life, you don't mind because you always know where you are – in the wrong. And you go on from there. And you usually know much more when he has finished teaching you.

In other words, you are comfortable with him. You know the set-up; you know it won't change; you know that, because he is getting you to learn, and helping you to do so, he is on your side. In a word, you trust him. If he gets things done, you trust him; and if you trust him, you get things done.

Relationships like this are not built easily; both sides have to work at it, and each side has to give the other side the benefit of the doubt. But this trust and confidence, if it can be built, often turns out to be biggest dividend of the whole business. Two stories:

When I was teaching full time – going back a bit once again – like most other teachers I had a tutor group. The usual mixed bag – very mixed – this was a comprehensive school. There was one girl I remember – let's call her Wendy. She was bright – no genius, but bright. Happy too. She was prompt; she was polite; she was smart – a credit to any school. In fact, I remember once writing on her tutor report: 'The biggest compliment I can pay this girl is to say that she has never needed me.' So we never had much business to conduct.

Then, one morning, Wendy came into the tutor room, breathing fire and brimstone. There had been an incident – I forget what it was, but everybody knew about it – and everyone was talking about it. And she had got the impression that another member of the tutor group had been very unfairly treated, and that maybe I was responsible. She came straight up to my desk, with eyes blazing, and, without any preamble, said, 'You can't do that!'

Luckily, I was able to convince her that I was not to blame, and that no great injustice had in fact been done. But the moral of this story, I think, is that she was clearly cross, and in effect said so, yet she felt confident enough in our relationship to be able to say what she said without fear of reprisal. And I felt sure enough of her not to take any offence. I think we both came out of it with a certain amount of credit. But the real hero of the story is trust. We both trusted each other.

Second story. I spent three years in a college studying history. There was a college shop, which sold absolutely everything from string to Gordon's gin. The man who ran it was Bill Cornwell. He had been a college servant for years, so long that he had become part of the college furniture. He knew the name of everybody.

The Master of our college was a powerful personality. I can't think of anyone I have known who was half as eminent as he was. He was a Nobel prize winner; a Life Peer; President of the Royal Society; and a member of the Order of Merit.

One day some unexpected guests called on him. He went to his pantry – no drink left. So he left the Master's Lodge, went to the college shop, and asked Bill for a bottle of gin. (Everybody had an account; you didn't have to pay on the spot.) Bill duly provided it. The Master picked it up, and was leaving, when Bill said, 'Excuse me, Master, but where are you proposing to go with that bottle?'

The Master, caught at the door, explained, rather shamefacedly, that he was taking it to the Lodge for some guests.

Bill drew himself up and said, 'Master, as long as I am a servant of this college, no master will be seen walking to the Lodge carrying a bottle. Now you put it down on the counter like a good gentleman, and I shall see that is immediately delivered.'

And he did. And it was. You see? Bill felt sure of himself and of his position. The Master understood at once that, with Bill, it was a question, not of rudeness, but of pride. Total trust, and total respect, on both sides.

In any organisation – say, like a boarding school – with so many different kinds of inhabitants – each with its own position and its own pride – it is not success, or riches, or fame which make it thrive; it is trust and respect.

## Listen to the Band

ONE OF THE THINGS that makes the Queen unique is that, every year, she has not one birthday but two. One of the things that makes me unique is that I am the only person in this hall who has done National Service.

The Queen has her own private birthday – her real birthday – on 21$^{st}$ April. The nation celebrates her official birthday early in June, with a colourful ceremony called Trooping the Colour. I did two years' service in the Army.

What have these two facts in common – my national service and Trooping the Colour? Well, surprising as it may seem, I once trooped the colour. I was the young soldier who carried that flag around the parade, just as you see on the telly every year.

Of course there are certain differences – I don't want you to get the wrong idea. The parade I was in was not in England, and I was not in the Brigade of Guards. But I did carry the flag. It is called the Queen's Colour, and every regiment in the Army owns one. And not only in England. I am talking about the days when England had colonies.

I served in Kenya with a regiment called the King's African Rifles. Most of the sergeants and officers were white; the ordinary soldiers were black – or should I say varying shades of black and brown according to which tribe they belonged to. You'll see the point of the colour element in a minute.

Things went roughly like this. Sections of three battalions were drawn up on the parade ground. Each battalion was dressed in pale khaki, and they each wore a bright sash round the waist according to their battalion. The Fourth Battalion wore green; the Seventh wore yellow; the Third – us – wore red. It was a long time ago, and I am guessing, but I should reckon that there were about three or four hundred men out there, in three rigid straight lines.

I stood on the very edge of the parade ground – not grit as it is on Horse Guards Parade. Just plain grass, but hard, and very well mown actually. Around me were five African sergeants and sergeant-majors. They were known as the Escort to the Colour.

When the time came, the band struck up, the whole parade was ordered to present arms as a compliment to the Colour, and I gave the command to march on. Our job was to reach the very middle of the parade, where they had left a gap for us, then do some pretty fancy drill movements to get us into the front rank, facing forwards like the other 394. When everything was still, and the band had stopped, I then had to give the order for the colour party – my lot – to present arms like everybody else.

This was the crunch. The band was silent. The parade was silent. The whole crowd was silent. In the next few seconds the only voice that was going to be heard was mine – and it had to be audible to every single person on that field. Remember a parade of three or four hundred soldiers and hundreds of onlookers. So this is what happened. [And I really bellowed it:]

'Escort to the Colour – PRES –E-E-E-NT. . . . ARMS!!'

Like that. [Very quietly.]

That was one memory of that day. For the ear. The second was for the eye. The parade ground, as I said, was grass – bright green. The sky was a dazzling tropical blue. The sun shone. In the background was the second highest mountain in the whole of Africa – Mount Kenya – rearing up 15,000 feet, a great cone of black rock and blinding snow. It looked so close it was like shaking hands with the Matterhorn. Add to that the shining pressed pale khaki of the askaris' uniforms, the great contrast of their black and brown skins, the reds and yellows and greens of their sashes. They looked magnificent. The whole scene was a symphony of colour. Unforgettable.

There was a third memory. As you know, they do a lot of drill in the Army. Right turn, left turn, quick march, slow march, slope arms, present arms, and so on. It can get rather wearisome. Especially when you are practising for a big parade – hour after hour, day after day. Sweating and stamping, turning and wheeling, all with heavy rifles. And then, one day, close to the big one, they bring in the band.

You have no idea of the magical effect that band has. It is loud, it is lively, it is confident, it is playing just for you. And only for you. The lift it gives to the spirits is indescribable. Suddenly you are not tired and fed up; suddenly you are the Grenadier Guards, the Gurkhas, the Paras, the French Foreign Legion, the American Marines, all rolled into one. You feel absolutely terrific. You know – you just *know* – that you are going to dazzle them all.

I didn't like everything they made us do during National Service, but I shall always be grateful that, just a few times, they got me to march to a band. That moment when they first strike up – for you – you cherish for the rest of your life.

*The Archives of an Archivist*

## Chopin Manuscripts and Crocodiles

ONE DAY IN 1967 the Headmaster of West Buckland, Mr. Leslie Stephens, received a letter from a French nobleman, the Count of Panouse. The Count said that his son was keen to improve his English, and asked if he could come to the school as a paying guest, and possibly receive some private lessons as well – in English. The boy was also a keen sea scout, and was learning Russian as a second foreign language.

Mr. Stephens replied to the effect that the Count's son was indeed welcome, and that his, Mr. Stephens', wife, would be happy to give him some English lessons. Alas, nobody in the school was learning or teaching Russian, and the chances of sea sports in the middle of Exmoor were a trifle limited. The Count replied that that was all right; his son was keen to join in whatever lessons and games the school had on offer.

He came, and stayed a month. In his letters home, he told his father that he was 'interested by his new life' and that he 'very much admired the countryside'. We have no record of how the boy managed with understanding the finer points of cricket, and we don't know how the History teacher got round the problem of the guillotine in his lessons on the French Revolution.

But father was delighted with the boy's visit, and offered his hospitality to the Headmaster and his wife if they should happen to be near his chateau during their holidays. Mr. Stephens replied gallantly that he and his wife would be pleased to drop in should they happen to be passing.

And that was that. All the letters went into the file. But in this old file there were two more documents – cuttings actually.

The first was about the composer Chopin of all people. Frédéric Chopin. Apparently, according to the *Daily Telegraph* of November, 1967, two original Chopin manuscripts – waltzes – had been discovered in the library of a French chateau not far from Paris. . . . That's right, in the chateau of the Count of Panouse. The waltzes were well known, but the manuscripts had long since disappeared.

So – imagine the scene – the great composer, accompanied by his lover, Georges Sand (she was a writer who used a masculine name to sell her books). There he was, after a splendid dinner, strumming on the grand piano in the great chateau drawing room, with the firelight flickering romantically on the silver candlesticks. And Mlle Sand leans over, strokes his cheek, and says, 'Oh, Frédéric, you improvise so beautifully.

– 223 –

You should write some of these things down.' And he did. And then they had a row in the morning, and went off and forgot them.

The second newspaper cutting could not have been further away from either Chopin or Devon boarding schools. It was about the Count again, and was dated May, 1968. It announced that the Count was going to open an African game reserve in the grounds of the chateau. An illustration depicted lions, elephants, crocodiles, giraffes, panthers, rhinoceroses, gazelles, and wild boar. So – some spread.

The Count was apparently quite famous for this sort of thing. He had already opened his estate to the general public, and had also started up a zoo. French aristocrats who opened zoos and game reserves could not have been very numerous, so it seems very likely that the Count was the subject of a well-known story that went the rounds at about this time.

In this story, the owner of the chateau declared that he was going to offer a prize of a million francs to anyone who was willing to swim the moat which surrounded the chateau. There was just one other detail: the moat was filled with man-eating crocodiles.

The grand opening day came. Thousands gathered, round the moat naturally, but nobody seemed willing to take up the Count's challenge.

So the Count made another announcement over the public address system: '*Mesdames et messieurs, je dois vous expliquer.* I say again, a million francs, to be paid at once to the lucky man. And – in addition – the chance to meet any lady of his choice. *Any lady you like.*'

The crowd fell silent. Suddenly there was a splash, and there was a man swimming for his life, with a fleet of hungry crocodiles in pop-eyed pursuit. He made it, but only just; one of the crocodiles got a consolation prize of a pound or two of leg.

The Count went to visit the man in hospital, taking, of course, the million francs. Remembering the second half of the bargain, he said, 'Now, who do you want to meet?'

The man turned away in weary disgust.

'I mean it,' said the Count. 'I know everybody. I can arrange it with anyone – Cheryl Cole, Lady Gaga, Ann Widdicombe. . . . ' [Here you can insert the name of any current celebrities you like.]

The man turned towards him. 'Did you say anybody?'

The Count nodded. 'Anybody.'

'Actually,' he said, 'there is one.'

'Who?' said the Count. 'Just give me the name.'

The man looked directly at him. 'I don't know his name, but I should like to meet the man who pushed me in.'

All this in a dog-eared buff file in a school archive – French nobleman, country chateau, sea sports on Exmoor, Russian as a second language, Chopin manuscripts, panthers, giraffes, and crocodiles. You see? You never know.

## Flowers for a Soldier

I THINK IT IS safe to say that the Second World War was the greatest event of the twentieth century. It upturned the world; it caused the death, altogether, of fifty-eight million people. *Fifty-eight million.* Its influence remains part of our lives. There are people going around today who bear on their forearm the identification numbers tattooed by the Nazi guards in the concentration camps. Turn on the television; go to a bookshop; sit in a cinema – you still can't move for material about it. Like it or not, you have to live with it.

You have to put up with grandad – or, more likely these days, great-grandad – going on about it – what he did, what happened to him, where he went, what he saw, people he met, narrow escapes he had. It may be a yawn to you, but you have to remember that it was not a yawn to him. He lived through the greatest event of a whole century; it would be amazing if it had *not* made a mark on his life. He can't help it; that is what it made him; that is what he is.

Perhaps what is really amazing is that the people who did *not* live through the Second World War are still hypnotised by it. Not only the old codgers – everyone else. There is, even now, no shortage of material to feed their curiosity: Government documents are released; secret hiding places are discovered; bits of Spitfires are dug up; private papers and photographs are discovered in the lofts of dead pensioners.

And still the stories come. Some of course are awful; some are funny; some are sad; some are touching; some are inspiring; some are nearly unbelievable. And some don't fit into any category.

I came across this one in a book about Exmoor during the War. You wouldn't think that the War could reach out into the back of beyond like North Devon, but it did.

This story is about an American army camp up on Exmoor, in the Brendon Hills. It may be a mite difficult to take in now, but, in the years of preparation for D-Day, the Liberation of Europe, there were American army (and Air Force) camps all over the place.

Anyway, near this camp, in a small cottage, lived a man who worked for the local council, looking after the roads. He didn't go to the camp, but of course he knew about it. One day he heard that two American soldiers ('G.I.'s', we used to call them) – two American soldiers had died there. Young men, healthy, well trained, fit – but they had died. Pretty unusual. Nevertheless, the Army had a method for dealing with these sad events: they buried them in temporary graves, and at the end of the war they would have the coffins transported back to the United States, to the place where their families lived, and they would be given a permanent resting place. It was common practice.

However, when he found out about it, this roadman could not get it out of his mind. He thought constantly how lonely those graves must be, on the edge of a military camp up in the Brendon Hills, thousands of miles from their grieving families. Grieving especially for sons who were so young.

One day he picked some flowers from his garden and went over to the camp. At first of course the sentries suspected him: what was a stranger – a civilian at that – doing in a secret Army base? He was taken to some officers and told to explain his business. But when he did – and showed the flowers – everything changed. He was escorted to the graves and allowed to lay them.

The story spread fast. The roadman was invited to come back whenever he wanted to lay some more flowers. When he did, he was met with smiles all round the camp.

This went on for quite a while. The roadman became a familiar face to everyone. When the war came to an end, the officers told him when the coffins were to be moved and flown back to the United States. The roadman went to work again: when the coffins were placed on the plane, they had bunches of Canterbury bells from the roadman's garden resting on them.

That was not the end of the story. After the soldiers had left Brendon, an American officer approached the roadman, and told him to dig in a certain spot on the local common, near the camp. He did, and unearthed a tin containing money, and a bible which had belonged to one of the dead soldiers. Later again, he received a message asking him to call at the Trustee Savings Bank in Taunton. He did that too, and found that an account had been opened in his name, with a hundred dollars in it. There was a note. It said that the money was 'an expression of thanks' from the unit to which the dead soldiers had belonged.

That was not the end either. A short while afterwards the roadman received a parcel from the parents of one of the dead soldiers. In it was a letter of gratitude and a gold watch.

It was still not the end. The roadman had not known the soldiers' names when he laid the flowers. It turned out that one of them had the surname Farmer. The roadman's name was Ernest Farmer. They did some research, and discovered that some of Ernest Farmer's ancestors had emigrated to America, and their descendants and the roadman were distantly related.

Two years after the war, the American Mr. and Mrs. Farmer came to England, and they visited Ernest Farmer. So a family was reunited. All as a result of two tragic early deaths. And all because a kindly man had picked a bunch of flowers.

So there. If ever you should feel like doing something kind, do it.

## 22. Assembly Philosophy

### Take Your Pick

HENRY FORD, AS YOU know, made motor cars. According to an old story, one day his production manager came to see him to discuss the new model that the factory was bringing out. He said to the great man, 'What colour do you want us to do it, sir?' Ford said, 'Paint it any colour you like so long as it's black.' Not much joy in that.

In History lessons I often made the point that the majority of marriages in the old days did not involve much romance. Very often you had to marry the person you were told to marry. The class usually recoiled in shock and disgust. How uncivilised. How barbarian!

What am I talking about? I am talking about choice. You are all raised to worship at the altar of the great god Choice. Choose your menu at lunch-time. Choose your GCSE subjects. Choose your future partner in life. Fancy having your marriage arranged for you. How stupid. People today have total freedom to choose, and so they should. Now examine the present divorce rates; they are much higher than they used to be in the bad old days. Is there a connection?

Stuff and nonsense, you say. You can choose to get married; you can choose to get divorced. The point is not about marriage and divorce; it's about freedom. It's about choice. That is the really important thing.

So what do we have? Take crisps. Once upon a time, if you wanted some, you went and bought a packet of Smith's crisps. That was it – Smith's or nothing. We have progressed: now you go to the supermarket, and there is not a drawer of crisps, or a shelf of crisps, or a counter of crisps; there is whole aisle of crisp packets, of every conceivable size, shape, taste, and texture – all made to seem different by the addition of chemicals which, if you understood them, would probably turn your stomach.

Do you want sweets? Cereals? Asian food? They have aisles full of them too. Wherever you turn – toys, tee-shirts, mobile phones, computer games, jewellery, watches, foreign holidays, ball-point pens – you are swamped with alternatives. Computer screens burst with 'menus' and 'options'. Look at the television. By the time you have decided which of eighty-nine channels you want to watch, it's time to go to bed. Dammit – even your exam questions now are 'multiple choice'. Not just 'choice', or 'free choice', or 'open choice', but 'multiple choice'. It has to be 'multiple'.

Choice, choice, choice. Of course, you say; that's what makes our lives interesting. We are intelligent human beings, in a civilised society; it is our right to choose – everything. Oh really? Well, before you get on your high horse, consider this.

Did you choose your mother? Did you choose your father? Your sisters and brothers? Did you select from a long United Nations list the country you were born in? Did you look at an Ordnance Survey map and choose the county, the town, the village? The climate? Did you choose the language you spoke first? Did you choose your height, the shape of your face, the tone of your complexion? No. Nobody asked you what you wanted. There you are, said God: that's the deal. You have life; now get on with it.

You're stuck with it, aren't you?

This may also apply to your school, your class, your house, your teachers. Was there a whacking great aisle of them to choose from? Did you even choose your first teddy bear? Or did you wake up one morning and find him there on the bed? But you loved him. Gave him a silly name too, didn't you? – Goober, Dimby, Bar-bar, Pollypot. Wouldn't go anywhere without him.

And you spend a much bigger part of your life with parents and teachers than you do with cereal packets and crisps. You spend *all* your life with how you look.

Please note too that this works both ways. You don't get any choice of teacher; they don't get any choice of pupils. They are stuck with you too. They can't walk down an aisle of new kids and say, 'No, I won't have her; she looks as if she will never learn her irregular verbs.' Or 'I'll have him; I reckon he'll be good at Maths; he's got circular glasses'. Or 'No, I'm not having him; he's got dark eyebrows and he frowns – bound to be a trouble-maker'.

It's the same with parents. They may want a child to love and to rear, but, when the moment finally comes, they have no idea what's going to pop out. Tall? Short? Chatty? Silent? A treasure? A pain? They're all up against the genes. It's the genes that call most of the shots. So parents, like teachers, have to get on with it. We all have to lump it.

So – is choice really the be-all and end-all? Look at all those things you just have to lump. Then look again; they're mostly – well – pretty all right, aren't they? They all put up with you. They don't mind you grumbling now and then. And what, realistically, could you put in their place? You might have a job to think of something better.

## Being Rude

ALL OF YOU KNOW what it is to be rude. Some of you have been rude to other people; some of you have had other people be rude to you.

I suggest that there are two types of rudeness. Let us call them 'nasty rude' and 'funny rude'.

Take the 'nasty rude' first. It is blindingly obvious that this is wrong. At its mildest it can be misery-making; at its worst it can be evil. At one end is the playground teasing and the sending of abusive text-messages; at the other it is a government-inspired wholesale campaign to belittle, and ultimately destroy, an entire race.

Bad. No question about that. The trouble is that, because of this nasty rudeness, we have perhaps become afraid of the whole idea of rudeness, and try to tailor our lives, and other people's, so that we can not ever be suspected of rudeness. You can't complain about West Indian burglars or Pakistani hooligans in case somebody calls you a racist.

So – we must never, then – *ever* – be rude, in any way. And that, I think, deprives the world of a great benefit. I am talking now, not about 'nasty rude', but about 'funny rude'.

Take the circumstances you know best – school. 'Nasty rude' sets out to destroy the atmosphere in the classroom; 'funny rude' – cheek if you like – adds to it. It brings surprise, novelty, humour, and enjoyment. It helps us all to get through the lesson better.

'Give you an example. You don't know, so I'm going to tell you, that in the French Revolution – in 1793, to be precise – King Louis XVI was executed on the guillotine on 21$^{st}$ January. Well, one of my classes knew that, because I had taught it to them.

So, on the morning of 21$^{st}$ January, I walked into the classroom, wrote '21$^{st}$ January' on the board, and said, 'What is the importance of that?' Total silence.

I said, 'This is a History lesson. We have been doing French history for three weeks. What happened on 21$^{st}$ January?' More silence.

In desperation, I said, 'Now come on, think. What great event happened on this very day 182 years ago?'

A dark voice came from the back of the room: 'Many happy returns, sir.'

Very rude. But beautifully timed, and very funny. The point was that that boy felt safe enough with me to be rude like that. He had clearly been paying attention. And the humour was greater than the rudeness. So we all had a laugh.

And how about this? I was once a games teacher. I used to coach hockey. One day I was out on the field with a group of fourteen-year-olds, and I was lecturing and hectoring and nagging, and they were pretending to be grumpy and argumentative and questioning my credentials. So I put on my fiercest expression, and said with mock severity, 'You should pay proper respect. I would have you know that I have been playing hockey for twenty years.'

Quick as a flash, one boy remarked innocently, 'You must have taken up the game very late in life, sir.' The game collapsed for twenty seconds, but everyone played better afterwards.

It was, I think, a splendid illustration of a great truth about teaching (stand by: trade secret coming up) – namely, that the classroom, or the games field, is not primarily a drawing room or a debating chamber or a playground. Nor even a workshop. It is an arena. Think about it: there is one of you; there are twenty-five of them, most of whom are not exactly dying to be there. They put up with you; you do your best to survive them. Relations are conducted in a permanent state of friendly, undeclared war. You win some; you lose some.

The occasional bit of cheek is like oil; it lubricates the lesson.

Now, all that is rudeness and cheek face-to-face, as you might say. It works just as well at a distance. Take a war. If you make jokes about the enemy, it helps you to stop being afraid of him. In the First World War, the English soldiers used to call the Germans 'Fritz'. In the Second World War he was 'Jerry'. In the Napoleonic Wars the French were 'the Frogs'. It was almost friendly. Indeed, soldiers on both sides knew full well that soldiers everywhere had the same rotten life. They shared the same mud, the same cold, the same danger, and the same general awfulness. The chaps on the other side were 'our friends the enemy'. As in the classroom, you put up with each other. You learn tolerance.

Look at all the jokes about other nations, whether they are friends or enemies. We call Americans 'Yanks' and they call us 'Limeys'. We used to call Australians 'Diggers'; they call us 'Poms'. We can all live with that.

I am sure the Irish can live with all our jokes about them. Like the one about the English Olympic bobsleigh team who crashed going down on a practice run because they met the Irish team coming up.

It goes on everywhere. The French have Belgian jokes. The Germans have Polish jokes. The Russians have Armenian jokes. One day Radio Armenia came on the air, and announced that they had an apology to make. 'We regret to inform you that yesterday we said that half the members of the Russian Government are idiots. This was a mistake, and we apologise. In fact, half the members of the Russian Government are not idiots.'

A bit of cheek, a joke, a laugh helps you to get through life, to get through a war, to get through school. We are all in it together, and a teacher's task is to help you recognise that. Teachers don't set out to make you like it. They set out to help you get through a job of work, and to take pride in having done so. Liking it has nothing to do with it. Liking it is a bonus. A Latin teacher I knew had his own joke about this, his own bit of cheek. He used to say that it doesn't matter what you teach boys and girls so long as they don't like it.

## **Being Worried**

DO YOU EVER WORRY? I bet you do. I defy anyone to claim that they have never, ever, worried. I worry. I have worried about whether I was going to get this assembly right.

We agree, I'm sure – worry is a pain. So what we do? You have to do something. What did I do? I changed my script. I revised it. I rewrote it. If necessary, I could have scrapped it altogether and written something else. It wouldn't be the first time. Have I got it right at last? I don't know. Anyway, it's a bit late now.

What do *you* do about worry? Or should I say, 'What do you *do* about worry?'

Well, you use your gumption, for a start. You get ahead of it if you can; you hit it before it gets going. For example, if you are worried about what nasty things people might do and say at the party, don't go. If people like that are going to it, it'll be a rotten party anyway. If you still want to go, then you must be expecting to enjoy yourself, so what are you worrying about?

Then there is the Biggles philosophy. Ever heard of Biggles? The daring fighter pilot whose adventures sold in their millions to generations of schoolboys? Biggles was the commander of a Spitfire squadron in the Battle of Britain. His new young pilots, understandably, got frightened and worried. So he would say, 'Think. When you are up in the sky, one of two things is going to happen: you will be all right, or you will not be all right. If you are all right, there is nothing to worry about. If you are not all right, one of two things will happen: you will get shot down, or you will not get shot down. If you are not shot down, there is nothing to worry about. If you are shot down, one of two things will happen: you will crash or you will not crash. If you do not crash, there is nothing to worry about. If you do crash, one of two things will happen: you will survive or you will not survive. If you survive, there is nothing to worry about. If you do not survive, you will be dead, and you will not be here to worry. So why worry?'

That was all to stop worry coming in the first place. If it works, fine. But what do you do when it arrives without you realising? And you turn round, and there it is – there.

Well, there is the champagne method. There was a bishop who was never worried by a huge pile of unanswered letters He said he used to open a bottle of champagne. By the time he had finished drinking it, he didn't care whether he answered the damn letters or not.

Yes, I know, all very amusing. But let us be practical. And realistic.

Say you are worried about something that is not going to happen for a month. Why worry for the next thirty days? It won't make any difference. The time to worry is the thirtieth day, and then you *must* think of something. It's odd, but, very often, when we really *have* to think of something, we do.

Again, if you are worried about not passing an exam, because you have not done enough work, well, do some work, for God's sake. If you don't, your worry is entirely self-inflicted, and you don't deserve any sympathy.

Another idea is to imagine the very worst possible thing that can happen, and ask yourself whether it really would be so terrible. Suppose you fail that music exam. So what? You can always take it again. Suppose the boy doesn't ask you to go with him to the disco. Have you got two heads or something? Can you not find another boy to go with? Boys (and girls, for that matter), are like London buses. Never run after them; there is always another one coming along behind.

The trouble is, simply, thinking. If something is getting you down, it usually means that you have been thinking about it too much. So you find something that stops you thinking. You have to find something to do that you like – really like. If it means listening to trash music or playing with Lego, then listen to trash music or play with Lego; it will take your mind off the worry.

Then again, think what worry means. It means that your brain is working overtime. So give your body something to do to counteract it. What am I talking about? Exercise. Hard work, sweat, aches and pains, running, swimming, chopping down trees. You can't worry while you're puffing and blowing, have you noticed? You will feel better for it. And that good feeling eats away at the worry.

Another suggestion is to have a second worry in reserve. When the first worry starts to get you down, switch to the second one; you can't worry about two things at once.

I said just now that we must be realistic. Well, of course it is possible that a worry is so bad that all our tricks for dealing with it don't work. The load is too big. What do you do then? You have to get somebody to help you carry it.

Don't be ashamed of being worried, and don't be ashamed of asking for help. If you got toothache, you wouldn't be ashamed of that, would you? And you wouldn't be ashamed of going to the dentist. You wouldn't struggle on in silent agony, afraid to speak, almost unable to think.

Same with worry. Think of it as mental toothache.

And think of the great trump card in your hand: your great trump card is that you are young. Well, play your trump card. You are surrounded by people who want you to be happy. Adults like helping the young. The world is full of parents, relations, friends, neighbours, teachers, counsellors, doctors, psychologists, chaplains, priests, child-liners. There ought to be *somebody, somewhere.*

Don't try and be tough and pretend that there is no such thing as worry. You are fooling nobody. You wouldn't try to cross the road by pretending that traffic does not exist, would you?

The minute you talk about it, it's like releasing a pressure valve; things start to get better. By the time you've finished talking, you sometimes wonder what the Hell you were worried about in the first place. Like having that bad tooth out. Once it is gone, you find it difficult to imagine what the pain was like before.

For the third time, be realistic. Worry is a fact; face it; do something. Take precautions. Take a break. Take care. Take some medicine. Take heart. But don't take fright. And don't take out the white flag. God gave you something besides your body and your brains; He gave you a mind – to cope with things. Well, get on and cope. If you can't cope, cope with *that* by getting somebody to *help* you to cope. Coping is not easy; it's a struggle. God does not promise that you will win; but He does promise that you will take pride in having made a fight of it.

## **Putting Something Back**

ASSEMBLIES ARE A BIT like the sun; they just come up. Like lunches, lessons, games, exams. You accept them. Other things 'come up' too – prizes, awards, medals, help, advice, interest, encouragement, somebody being there. You accept all that too. You may say, 'Well, why not? Our parents have paid good money for it.' Well, yes, that's true – but it is only half a truth. I put it to you that a lot of what 'comes up' does not figure in a School end-of-term bill or a balance sheet. What am I saying? I'm saying that a lot of people do a lot for the School with no expectation of payment, or even of recognition. And often the most unlikely people.

Take a look at this gentleman. [I showed a large portrait photograph of him.] If you are close enough, you don't need me to describe him. But those further away will need me to say that, with the peaked cap, the red tabs, the medals, the white moustache, and the other paraphernalia, he looks the typical elderly army officer of a bygone age – the archetypal 'old buffer'. And we don't take old buffers seriously, do we?

He was a brigadier, actually. Brigadier Michael Rookherst Roberts. Seeing him like this, in his most distinguished get-up, it is hard to imagine that he was once a small, very new boy. He was born in 1894, and came here in 1905, from Ilfracombe. Stayed till 1912. This is what he did in between.

He was a holder of a Shepard Law Scholarship, he passed the then equivalent of the 16+ and 18+ exams, and the Entrance Exam for the Royal Military College at Sandhurst. He played cricket and football for the School, won his colours at both, and in 1912 was top of both batting and bowling averages. He won the Donegal Badge for Shooting, he was Athletics Champion, and, just for good measure, he won a couple of *Exmoors*, the second one in record time. He was President of the Debating Society, Head of School, and, of course, a holder of the Fortescue Medal. He appears to have been pretty popular too, because Old Boys years later were referring fondly to 'Mickey' Roberts; you don't usually get names like that if you are not liked.

You will see his name in the Karslake, on three of those boards up on the wall.

He went into the Army, naturally, just in time for the First World War, in which, among other things, he was gassed on the Western Front and won the MC. After the War, he stayed in the Army, and ended as a brigadier in the Gurkhas. He served throughout the Second World War, and won the DSO. He began a second career as a writer, and was the author of four volumes of the official history of the War against Japan. In 1960, he was elected a Fellow of the Royal Historical Society. He was also Chairman of the Gurkha Brigade Association.

During all these years, he regularly attended all sorts of Old Boys' functions, and served as President of the Old Boys' Association twice. He also sat on the Board of Governors, and was its Chairman for several years. When he gave up that office, he served as Chairman of the Friends of West Buckland, an organisation devoted to raising funds for the School. He found time to be a Committee Member of the Governing Bodies Association of Public Schools, and to come down in 1949 to present the prizes at Speech Day. When he died in 1977, he had been associated with the School for 72 years.

During the whole of that time, everything he did for the School was done without payment, or indeed any expectation of payment. He did it because he wanted to. He was grateful to the School; he wanted to put something back.

You may be sitting there and thinking, 'Yes, that's all very well, but we can't all be like good old Mickey Roberts.' Yes, that's true. You can't all win the *Exmoor* twice, or come top of the batting averages. But you all have the capacity to put something back, if you feel like it.

Not right now, of course not. You are all still on the receiving end. It's all still coming up every day, like school lunches and the pat on the back. And many of you will say, when the last day comes, 'Right – I'm off.' And you will be, all of you.

But somewhere along the line, you will pause now and then to remember. You will get curious about the Old West Buckland Association, because you hear that one of your friends has joined. After a while, you will just happen to be passing, and you will drop in just to see how the old place is getting on, and tell yourself that things are not what they used to be. You attend an Old Members' Dinner; you buy a raffle ticket; you lend a hand at a School fete. And that's how it all begins.

What are you doing? You are putting something back. You are doing what Brigadier-General Michael Rookherst Roberts did. And you won't care tuppence whether people think you're an old buffer or a has-been or some relic from the previous century. Look around you – there's another Mickey Roberts down there somewhere – maybe several of you. And you will all do it for nothing.

## Being a Professional

FOR MOST OF MY working life, I was a History teacher. In the last two years the History dried up, and I taught General Studies instead.

I would not have chosen it, but it was on my timetable, and I was a professional, so I did it.

How did I go about it? By doing what I always did. I planned my lessons. I set the homework regularly. I collected it on time. I marked it, and I returned it on time. I tried to make my lessons interesting. At the very least tolerable.

Why? Because I was a professional. It was my job to create a classroom atmosphere in which pupils could listen and learn. It was my job to try and arouse their interest. It was my job to offer them something that they might find worthwhile. It was my job to keep them busy. It was my job to offer them the chance of the satisfaction that comes from a task well done. It was my job to set an example, to lead, to take the initiative. The subject, to a certain extent, was irrelevant.

Naturally, no headmaster would have turned me loose in a classroom with a subject I knew absolutely nothing about. Imagine me surrounded by test tubes and electric terminals and anatomical specimens. But, if I was considered sufficiently knowledgeable in a subject, then a headmaster had a right to expect me to teach it. Liking it had nothing to do with it.

I think it is the same with the receiving end of the process. Liking a subject – as a pupil – has little to do with it either. You are there to work. I think the teachers you most respect are the ones who *get* you to work. Naturally, if you do happen to like the subject, that is a bonus. But it is the work that comes first. You only have fun if you are working first. If you are not working first, you don't. Well, not the right kind of fun. If you have the wrong kind of fun, it means the teacher can not keep order, and you lose respect for him, and, sometimes, for the subject too. It is the work that comes first.

At the school I went to, it was these professionals – real professionals – who won most of our respect. They were the ones who always set the homework. They were the ones who always marked it, always gave it back on time. They were the ones who made demands on us, not the ones who made allowances for us. They were the ones who said they were going to do something, and did it. We didn't mind them being odd, or peculiar, or eccentric, because they taught us something. We didn't even mind them being grumpy, so long as they were grumpy all the time. Then you knew where you were – in the wrong.

They were always the same. There is nothing worse than a teacher who is as nice as pie one day, and behaves like a bear with a sore head the next.

We knew nothing about these men, except that they came into the classroom every day and made us do some work. Was it miserable? No. We still had some fun. But the fun came out of the work. Work doesn't come out of fun. I had a Latin teacher who understood very well that Latin was not a likeable subject, and that children were not there to enjoy it. He made no apologies for Latin being hard. With the same confidence, he taught Greek too, which was even harder.

Our games teachers were the same. Not even games were games. You were there to learn how to play cricket and hockey. If you were good enough to get into a school team, you were expected to work even harder.

Think about it. It is all about lumping it, isn't it? You don't choose your teachers; you have to make the best of them. You know – 'Oh, God, guess who we've got for French – Miss Clingbine.' And you're stuck with Miss Clingbine for a whole year.

It is the same for teachers; they can't choose their pupils. *You* have to put up with just one teacher at a time. Teachers have to put with twenty, twenty-five, thirty at a time. Nobody asked them if they wanted you. We all have to lump it. Thank God we have some work to do; it takes our minds off some of the awful people we have to work *with*.

It is the job that counts every time. Being professional. In one of my previous schools, I was a housemaster. As you know, part of the work involves competing in a house championship. As housemaster, it is your job to make sure that your house officials do *their* job by putting out teams for all these competitions. They are expected to do something towards the organisation and coaching of these teams too, aren't they?

Well, one year, I had a boy coming through the sixth form who looked as if he might make a good house captain. Tall, smart, bright, polite, well-behaved, reliable, busy – he had all the makings. I asked him if he would like to be house captain. He said yes.

Then I spelt out some of the implications of *being* a house captain, especially the bit about coaching games teams. His face fell slightly.

'But I'm not interested in cricket or hockey, sir.' (He wasn't very good at them either.)

I repeated, 'Do you want to be house captain?'

He said, 'Yes, sir.'

'Then,' I said, 'if you become house captain, *it is your job* to be interested. You *will* be interested. Now – do we have a deal?'

Yes, we had a deal. He duly made himself interested, and, so far as I remember, we had a successful year.

Being professional. Look out for professionalism wherever you go.

What is it? I suggest it is having respect for your work. It is teaching your pupils to have respect for the work. It is having respect for fellow-professionals doing the same work. It is a correct level of correct behaviour, both to your pupils and to your colleagues. It is simply *having* colleagues. Not friends, or mates, or family, or neighbours, or team members – colleagues. (There's a difference.) It is ensuring that no action of yours brings your work into disrepute. If your work places you in a position of power or privilege or trust, it is ensuring that nothing you do takes advantage of that power or privilege or trust. It is never allowing your performance to fall below a certain standard, regardless of how you feel at the time. Whether or not you like the goods you are handling is immaterial; it is your job to deliver them.

It is the same for both teachers and pupils. Whether you are doing the homework or marking it, the only way to self-respect and satisfaction is to deliver the goods.

## Never Won Anything

IF YOU HAD A pound for every time you clapped for a win, a medal, a first prize, a commendation, for any one of dozens of distinctions and successes won by somebody else, you'd be a rich person, wouldn't you? But you don't; all you get is tingly hands.

This is particularly hard to take if you have never had anybody clap for something you have done yourself. But we can't all come top of the class, can we? We can't all come first in the race. We can't all be selected for the county. We can't all win prizes, lead the pack, head the cast, captain the jolly old team. Sheer arithmetic. You can't have a winner if you don't have several losers. You can't come top unless a lot of people come middle or bottom. You can't have a captain if you don't have a team in the first place.

It means of course that there are going to be an awful lot more also-ran's than there are winners. Isn't this a bit unfair? Well, perhaps it can look like that. But look at it another way. Could you really have a world where we all cross the line at the same time? Where we all come top of the class? Where we all get medals? Where everybody gets fifteen A-stars at GCSE? Where everybody gets a fat job, marries a dreamboat, and lives happily ever after? You have all been alive long enough to know that that is not going to happen. And if it did, life would become unliveable.

Educational authorities understand the problem, and do their best to arrange enough activities to ensure that as many people as possible succeed at something while they are at school. So they do try.

Nevertheless, one has to accept the likelihood that there will be some pupils who are coming up to their day of leaving, and they have never won a race, a competition, a prize, a colour, or a medal. Not even a damn raffle.

There may be some here right now. When they get out of bed on the good side, they might shrug and say 'what the hell'. When they get out of bed on the wrong side, the situation can look a bit depressing, and they might be tempted to look forward to the day of leaving as the day of liberation.

The trouble is that, when we are down, we tend to look at the underside, not the topside. But the glass is not only half-empty; it is half-full too. Before you write off your schooldays, have a little think.

For a start, you are far more numerous than the golden boys and girls. You are the majority. You are the world. You are the foundation, the ballast, the bedrock of society. You are the millions of tiny crustaceans who between them make the great white cliffs. You provide the background against which the winners can stand out. You are the mirror in which the light of the stars is reflected. Without you there would be no winners; without you there would be no stars.

Education is about more than getting fifteen grade A's. Games are about more than coming top of the batting averages. By the same token, school is about more than success. Of course success matters, but it is not necessarily the be-all and end-all.

So what are you missing out in your calculations? Quite a lot of things, possibly.

Such as? Well, you don't need to be a genius or superman to collect friends. And you will find that you can keep some of them till you're ninety. You don't have to be brilliant at something – a game, a subject, a hobby – to conceive an affection for it, and to be happy working or playing at it for the rest of your life. As the author G.K. Chesterton said, 'If a thing is worth doing, it is worth doing badly.' If you give anything affection, respect, and loyalty, it will repay a hundred times over.

There will be a lot of things you will not notice until they are gone. Familiar faces, favourite places. Rules to break. Plans, plots, jokes, adventures. Help and interest from people who have simply been around all the time you have been here. People you can trust.

You have come to expect a good example from those put in authority over you. You have taken for granted a life of general order and discipline, a standard of decent behaviour, a level of good manners, a correct way of doing things. Whether or not you have enjoyed it all the time, the fact remains that, for the duration of your stay here, you have belonged somewhere. Such a feeling of security is not easy to come by.

Smaller things too – lying out on the grass on a sunny day during the lunch-hour and putting the world to rights; gossiping in the tuck shop; knowing that the *Exmoor* is awful, but knowing too that all the other wimpy schools haven't got it and couldn't do it.

So – yes – you will take something away with you, and it won't all be relief. You may not tumble to it straight away; it will sort of creep up on you. You will realise that most of us are ordinary; that's what 'ordinary' means. You will twig the fact that education, as the man said, is what you have left after you have forgotten everything you learnt at school. And you will work out the riddle that self-respect is what you have left, what you fall back on, after everybody else has been given the prizes.

'My Mum thinks a triple jumper is a thermal sweater for the cricket season.'

## 23. Little Tributes

ONE OF THE SATISFYING features of the Archivist's work is that, when a member of staff moves, or retires, it often falls to him to write something about them to go into the school magazine. If the member in question is part of a school department – say, the Modern Languages Department – then it falls to the head of that department to do it. If it is the head of department himself who is going, the job is taken on either by somebody senior to him, or, quite often, by a colleague in that department.

That still leaves quite a fair number of leavers who do not fit easily into the usual categories, and that's where the Archivist comes in.

Of course, this section does not cover everybody who left during the Archivist's term of office, and it would be a mite daunting to read if it did. What I *hope* it does, though, is to give a flavoursome dash of the sort of work these people do, and the quality of their service. One can criticise the independent schools for many things, but one feature of them that seems to rise above criticism is the fact that they can boast an extraordinary number of staff who have served for a very long time, and who have taken little notice of the usual hours of work laid down in their contracts. They are one of the adornments of the independent school world.

Quite often these little tributes can throw up a host of details about such people which have nothing to do with their qualifications for their job or their manner of performing it. They are people of many parts.

It is, as I said, always satisfying to write such pieces.

Let us start with

## Rosalie Priscott

[This was written when she retired in 2002.]

EVER SINCE 1979, ANYONE with a query about salary, expenses, departmental accounts, games funds, or indeed any topic related to finance, would, sooner or later, have to see Rosalie. Anyone who had failed to sign an invoice, forgotten to mention a couple of impromptu guests' lunches, neglected to fill in an expenses form, or simply slipped up with their sums, would, sooner or later, hear from Rosalie.

A discreet note would insinuate itself into the enquirer's or the sinner's pigeon-hole, and the minuscule handwriting would either explain the answer to the question or itemise the full and embarrassing extent of the dereliction of detail. If you went to see her, a quiet and measured voice would spell it all out in words of even fewer syllables. You would come away either wondering how you could have been so obtuse as to imagine that there was a problem in the first place, or burning with shame at your mortal sins.

Teachers as a breed are not good accounts managers. It is thanks to patient, vigilant, meticulous ladies like Rosalie that they are not considerably worse.

As the Presiding Judge, Grand Inquisitor, *obergruppenführer*, and Pooh Bah of the Bursar's Outer Office, hers is not a familiar face to pupils, and her work is even less well known to them, but what she does is vital. The coins and the notes she records represent the red and white corpuscles in the school's bloodstream; get the balance wrong, and the whole body of the school could wilt. Put simply, the health of the school derives partly from the fact that you rarely, if ever, catch Rosalie out in a set of figures.

As with so many other non-teaching members of staff, there is much more to Rosalie than meets the eye – gifted pianist, busy music teacher, willing accompanist, Justice of the Peace, brass band enthusiast, and cat-lover. So we expect her retirement to be a busy one, as all the best retirements should be.

She can take pride not only in the gratitude and respect of her colleagues, but also in having maintained with honour a fine family tradition: over eighty-odd years, no fewer than ten other members of her family have served the school.

*Nearly off the Record*

## Guy Hopson

GUY WORKED FOR NEARLY twenty years at West Buckland. He had not always been a teacher; for many years before that he had served as a district officer in the colonial government of Kenya. He had plenty of stories about that.

He taught Economics and Politics. Probably more, but I did not know about those; it was before my time. But I did work with him when he set up the teaching of General Studies in the Sixth Form. For several years he was a housemaster. He did all the usual things that good schoolmasters do, which is a great deal more than the syllabus.

Before very long, he had become, unquestionably, a 'character'. Stories stuck to him like glue – the half-extinguished pipe that had a regular habit of igniting his breast pocket; going to sleep in the middle of an Economics lecture – his own. And so on.

He possessed a combination of charm, eccentricity, integrity, and conscientiousness which the majority of pupils found not only worthy of respect, but also endearing. When he died before his time, only in his fifties, many of them were visibly shocked and moved.

I was asked to contribute a memory of him (for a magazine piece, I think it was), and this is what I wrote. You will understand from the above that it is far from a complete appreciation – just a snapshot, a reminiscence:

Guy and I worked together at the old Barnstaple Grammar School for a couple of years, in the English Department. When the school went from grammar to comprehensive, and so took in a majority chunk of children who would normally have gone to the old secondary moderns, I fancy that coming across a 'county', frightfully well-spoken, laid-back personality like Guy (Oxford University and all) must have been, for them, quite a culture shock.

He was just a little bit of a handful for the head of department too. This lady was a spinster of the old school (to coin a phrase) – a scholar, highly intelligent, dedicated, and very conscientious. I don't think she had much experience in the handling of mavericks like Guy. It was not that he was lazy or inefficient or ineffective; it was just that he did not do things in the way she was prepared for. You always got the feeling that she lived on tenterhooks, in constant apprehension about what Guy would do next – or not do (he could at times be somewhat forgetful).

Guy, as a district officer, had been concerned for the welfare of those in his charge, and was equally concerned about his pupils, but it did not show in the ways that this lady was used to. In the absence of those regular ways, she was tempted to conclude that he was, shall we say, not as responsible as she felt he should be. I don't think she ever quite made up her mind about him.

He was of course the soul of courtesy when dealing with her, and would not have hurt her for the world, but I think he knew he disturbed her, and in the privacy of his own soul, he must have enjoyed a chuckle or two about it.

So you could add to the list of charm, eccentricity, and integrity the qualities of mischief and kindness – all in all a pretty rare mix.

## Lady Margaret Fortescue
## 1923-2013

INDEPENDENT SCHOOLS WITH A long history tend to accumulate some useful advantages along the way – well-publicised traditions, aristocratic connections, gifts, endowments, scholarships, legacies, land – all sorts of things which can be turned to the benefit of pupils who come along later.

West Buckland is not especially famous, rich, fashionable, or in any way 'cool'. But it does have one particular asset – or sheaf of assets – which can be summed up in one word – Fortescue.

It was the second Earl Fortescue who made available the land for the accommodation of the school in 1860. It was the third Earl Fortescue who, together with his lifelong friend, the Revd. J.L. Brereton, pioneered the idea of a new type of secondary school – designed specifically for the 'middle classes'.

New schools, especially pioneering ones, need care and attention – and devotion – and money. As the years went by, each head of the Fortescue family willingly took up the burden of these worries – sometimes very big worries (the school nearly closed three times).

The fourth Earl and the fifth Earl continued this tradition. Tragically, the young man who would have become the sixth Earl was killed in the War. But there was another member of the family to take up the reins and continue the tradition of support – Lady Margaret Fortescue. And she held those reins for 55 years, in fact ever after her father's death.

So, for 155 years, the Fortescue family has given the school its interest and goodwill. It has made available the fruits of its prestige, experience, and general 'clout'. It has given constant vindication of the idea that privilege carries with it responsibilities.

Lady Margaret did not regard herself as some kind of nursemaid or Lady Bountiful or Fairy Godmother. She expected the school, by and large, to fend for itself. But she accepted that privilege taught you to be a benefactor. Being a benefactor was not some kind of special virtue; it was something that you just did – like shutting the gate. You were there – in case.

Not every independent school has a family of six generations of willing aristocrats (and more to follow) just up the road who are so committed to it and proud of it. West Buckland is one of the lucky ones. And, in this year of her death, it is proud to state that it owes a great deal to the service and example of Lady Margaret Fortescue.

# Robert Moor
# 1978-2014

TWO OF US WROTE this: myself, and Chris Allin. I had been a head of History in my previous school. At West Buckland, I worked with Robert for several years, as joint assistant masters in the History Department under somebody else, and later when he was head of that department. Chris came as a junior in the Department, and rose to become its head when Robert moved to other duties. But he, Robert, continued to work in the Department, so we had the odd situation in that all three of us had been a head of History, and both Chris and Robert had worked with each other as head and assistant, and vice versa. It says a lot for Robert's character that he was able to work in each role with consummate ease and total lack of friction.

It seemed fitting, then, that Chris and I should write this piece together.

Robert has given loyal and impeccable service to the school for 36 years. That in itself is quite an achievement. But he is a great deal more than a holder of the Long Service and Good Conduct medal.

He is a history teacher of remarkable breadth, and depth, of knowledge, and his dedication to the subject remained unabated right up to his final weeks in his post. He was kind and considerate to every colleague who joined the department, giving generously of the fruits of his wide experience, and boosting morale when necessary. Moreover, he was equally supportive when our roles changed, and he was a member of the department of which one of us became head. He was always available, without ever intruding or imposing his ideas.

Right to the end he enjoyed bringing History alive in his classes – even as far as dramatic, if slightly freethinking, 'reconstructions' of great characters or dramas from the past. He had the great history teacher's knack of being memorable. A departmental questionnaire among his Year 7 pupils brought to the surface, many times, the word 'legend.'

Not only did all pupils enjoy *him*; he counted himself lucky that he had been able for so long to be among *them*, and his love of the subject shone through all his teaching.

Particularly appreciative were generations of sixth-formers, whose budding careers he watched over with great care and shrewdness. He possessed the good schoolmaster's gift for judging a pupil, and seeing potential which might have escaped a less experienced or perceptive colleague. He guided hundreds of boys and girls through the bewildering maze of mysteries surrounding university entrance. He may not have taken them there, but he showed them which way to go.

Outside the classroom he was just as much a force. He was guardian of the Phoenix Society for years, and many a time and oft held them with a two-minute speech which nobody minded going well over the two minutes. He ran the school second teams in both cricket and rugby. For all his mild manner, he was not put off with second-best output or half-hearted effort. His skills as cricket umpire have been valued, and will, we hope, continue to be on offer.

Squeezed into his bulging portfolio have been scores of duties, chores, odd jobs, schemes, projects, and general business, which he performed with such quiet efficiency that a casual observer would have been tempted to think that there was no job involved; it just happened. Well, it didn't; it came about because Robert made it come about.

Equally present in a similarly quiet way has been his beloved Jane, a long-serving houseparent. As with Robert, hundreds of pupils over the years have been grateful for her kindness and for simply being around.

It was a clear sign of their devotion that, when Jane became ill with a kidney complaint, Robert donated one of his own. We wish them both well in a long retirement.

It has been a pleasure working with him, and we shall miss him.

## Known to one and all

IT IS A FEATURE of many schools like West Buckland that, besides being the beneficiaries of gifted and long-serving teachers and administrators, they have the knack of retaining the services, often over an equally long period, of the humblest of employees in a wide variety of the humblest of positions. But such is their devotion and reliability and consistency that they become part of the very fabric of the school, acknowledged, respected, and ultimately cherished. Over the years, their service becomes, in the memory, pure gold. In that memory, they become unique, and inseparable from any old pupil's recollection of their schooldays.

A common trait they possess, apart from their virtues, but springing from their virtues, is the fact that everyone knows them by their Christian name. In fact, I venture to suggest that nine pupils out of ten, if pressed, would have to admit that they did not know Sylvia's surname, or Gerald's, or Keith's. Possibly quite a fair proportion of staff too. Old Boys are the same. I have never heard one of them use their surnames in conversation with me. But, when those Christian names are mentioned, they all smile.

Sylvia Ridd came to the school when she was fifteen years old. Ridd is her married name. But I have no idea what her name was when she came. Even the Archivist does not know her maiden name. She started work here as a chambermaid, and worked in the Headmaster's House. That is, the great central block, which, originally, comprised the entire school – classrooms, dormitories, offices, outside toilets and all.

The rooms must have been pretty forbidding places, and the staircases were of stone (they still are). Rooms in old houses always seemed to be so lofty. Big houses, that is; I am not talking about lowly cottages (which of course housed the vast majority of the population). Keeping them warm must have been a constant problem. All right, so the people who lived in them were usually better off than average, and could afford coal, but the fireplaces were not exactly expansive. It is surely no coincidence that beds were surrounded by thick curtains, or that people slept not only in flannelette nightshirts but nightcaps as well. One of the regular chores of the chambermaid must have been keeping up the supply of fully-charged hot-water bottles.

And this went on until relatively recently. Central heating did not reach the dormitories till 1987, and did not reach the Headmaster's house till nineteen *ninety*-seven.

So young Sylvia was kept busy. And, quite likely, cold too.

Maybe then, it is no wonder that she soon found work in the kitchens.

Well, it may have been a warm option, but it certainly was not a soft option. Anyone who has worked, in any capacity, in surroundings where food is prepared and served will confirm that. And when you think of the almost total absence of the host of labour-saving devices that today grace the modern kitchen, you can begin to get some idea of what Sylvia's average day was like.

It says a lot, then, for her industry, persistence, and stamina that she learned the trade on the job, and rose in the end to become the Chief Cook, or, in today's parlance, Catering Manager, knocking up meals, as the years went by, for four, five, six, and finally nearly seven hundred hungry pupils. And that means not only the main meal of the day, but breakfasts, teas, and everything else.

As the years went by, and the school expanded, it also implied 'refreshments', and sometimes full meals, for droves of hungry parents, visitors, governors, members of masonic lodges, and I don't know what else.

When she really pushed the boat out, and laid on her famous salads and desserts, it was a mouth-watering experience – whole salmon, cold roasts, meringues and pies and pavlovas as far as the eye could see.

Her presence behind the hotplate at regular mealtimes became as normal to the children as the clock on the wall.

She chalked up fifty years in all, and would have been happy to continue. But a ruling at the time insisted that sixty-five was the 'cut-off' point, and, reluctantly, Sylvia left.

We have a new catering manager now, and very good he is too. But that does not stop one looking back fondly to Sylvia and her hotplate and her pies and her pavlovas.

Gerald Parker did fifty years too. Fifty-one actually. He too came to the school when he was fourteen or fifteen. He had had a dreadful start in life. I'm not sure of these details, but I believe he was born nearly blind, and an orphan. He partially recovered his sight, but it was never good, and it was a later decline in it which forced him to retire. And *he* didn't want to go either.

By that time, he had secured, or had been provided with, a small cottage in nearby East Buckland. Every lunchtime after he had retired, I was told, he was sent a hot meal from the school. And guess who arranged that.

It is quite likely that, because of his background, he came to regard the school as his home. He certainly devoted his life to it. Generations of boys remembered him ringing the bell first thing in the morning. At mealtimes he practically took root in the Karslake Hall. He is remembered as an immovable adjunct to the proceedings on *Exmoor* day, when he provided the traditional ration of hot pea soup. It may not sound very exciting, in bald statement like that, but, when you have just completed a six-mile walk and a nine-mile run in the wind and the rain, it can take on a completely different character.

His eyesight may have been a mite dodgy, but there was nothing wrong with his memory. Tradition again has it that Gerald could recite nearly all the Saturday football results after, presumably, having heard them on the BBC News. Interesting to sport-minded boys, and vital to those staff who had been having a flutter on the pools. (Who knows? Perhaps the boys did too.)

Memory was also Keith's strong point. He was one of the maintenance staff. All right, sweeper if you insist. (When he finally left, the staff presented him, besides his official leaving gift, with a shiny new broom.) He knew a mind-boggling number of boys' names. Instant recall too. Mind you, he could be trifle uncertain about staff names; I was, at various times, 'Eric', 'Derek', and 'Mr. Er – '. But it was close, close. And he did get the 'Berwick' sometimes.

He loved a chat. He listened to everything you had to say, and took you up on it. Getting away from Keith was a great exercise in one's powers of diplomacy. The story has it that, when there was a charity fund-raising event once, they persuaded Keith to go in for a twelve-hour sponsored silence. Probably not true, but it occasioned many a chuckle.

And the joke of course is on us. That is why it was not unkind.

These people were ordinary people, but were made extraordinary by their very unobtrusiveness and capacity for permanence, and by the clear fact that they were devoted to the school. Old pupils and staff did not remember their weaknesses, or, if they did, they made allowances for them; they smiled simply at the memory of them.

## 23. What do you actually do?

### Life under the dust

SOMETIMES PEOPLE SAY TO me, 'What do you *do* up in the School Archive?' The way they say it implies that whatever it is, it can't be very exciting. The very fact that they say 'up' in the Archive suggests that wherever my office is, it's a bit distant and remote, so it doesn't affect anybody much. They know I work with records from the past, so it must be a bit dusty, musty, and fusty, and therefore pretty generally boring.

Well, I've got news for you. Of course it's not screams all the time; every job has its boring bits. But, also like other jobs, the Archive has its interesting bits as well. Why? Because you meet so many interesting people, and you come across so many sides of life – some sad, some touching, some amusing. A bit of everything. It's all there if you have ears to hear and eyes to see.

Take Ernest Harries. He arrived to become Headmaster here in 1907. He was a bachelor, and he brought his mother to live with him. She had been born before Victoria became Queen, but she became such a force in the School that she was included in the formal photographs of the Staff.

In 1918, Harries decided, at the age of fifty, to get married. Who was his bride? The sister of one of his head prefects. And his brother, the School chaplain, married another sister – of the same head prefect. As both bridegrooms were priests, they married each other, if you see what I mean. When he died, his ashes were buried beside those of his mother in East Buckland churchyard. His wife was later buried beside them, only five months short of her hundredth birthday, in 1985.

You will also find buried there a teacher called Hugh Darvill. A shy man, and a bachelor (another bachelor), he had given sterling service to the School during the terrible time of the First World War, especially during an epidemic of scarlet fever – once the scourge of boarding schools. He was also best man at the Headmaster's wedding.

But he did not enjoy good health himself, and died suddenly in 1920. The School naturally moved to inform his family. But despite all their efforts, they failed, and no single member of it came to his funeral. So they had to put him in East Buckland churchyard as well.

Think about it. No wife, and not good at relationships; working in a place like West Buckland, before the days of regular motorised transport;

poor health did not allow him to take part in sporting activities. But at least one could usually look forward to seeing one's family in the holidays. This man had none. Or at any rate none that wanted to come to his funeral. How sad.

On the edge of the churchyard is a large gravestone inscribed with the name of an ex-pupil of the school, who had recently gone up to Cambridge University. The School magazine stated that he died in 1892 'after a short illness'. But the grave is oddly placed. All the other graves are orientated east-west. This one is orientated north-south, and the stone is right up against the boundary wire. The suggestion therefore seems to be that he took his own life. Suicides were not allowed to be buried in consecrated ground. So they got the stone in the churchyard, up against the wire, but the grave itself is outside. Did this unhappy young man find that he could not cope with university life away from the comforts and consolations of home? Did he choose his own way of dropping out?

One last illustration about death, but an equally touching one. An Old Boy had died. His wife had written to the OWBA to give the news. She ended her letter by saying, 'He was a gentleman who always treated me as a lady, and I am proud to be his widow.'

But there are cheerful things too. Take the orange faces. During the Second World War, the Government had been advised that if you painted your window panes blue and your light bulbs orange, this would confuse the German bombers. So the School did. An Old Boy remembers that when the lights were switched on at night, a dormitory full of boys' orange faces was, he said, 'the most disgusting sight you ever saw'.

What about the Headmaster's batting average? We had a Head who in 1898 scored 7 centuries. His total for the season was 1,285, in only 15 innings. His average was more than twice of that of the greatest cricketer playing at the time, Dr. W.G. Grace.

There was the organist who wore purple socks, the cook who used to wallop cheeky young waiters with his ladle, the fairy who caught fire. Remind me some time to tell you all about the French nobleman, the Chopin manuscripts, and the crocodiles.

It's all there – underneath the dust, in between the faded covers, lingering in the dog-eared files. All it needs is a little bit of imagination to let it out.

## **Interview technique**

Round about the middle of the 1990's, the master then in charge of the Sixth Form, Allan Cameron, decided that it might help university candidates who had been called for interview to be given a sort of dry run-through of the process. There was no chance of our being able to anticipate the questions that they might be asked, but we could give them a taste of the *pressure* of interviews, and at the end of the practice session make some suggestions as to what mistakes to avoid, and as to how they might improve their performance.

Mr. Cameron knew an ex-teacher who lived locally, and who had wide experience of conducting such interviews – Mrs. Rosalind Kriteman. She readily agreed to help. But he needed a second mind on the matter. Or, if you like, two heads were better than one. And he seemed to think that a school archivist (another retired teacher, and part-time writer) might have something to offer. So he asked me if I would be willing to share the job. I took a deep breath and said 'Yes'.

As the years, and the interviews, passed, Mrs Kriteman and I became, I hope, more proficient, or at any rate more experienced. We learned to work together. We liked to think we were developing a sort of nose for promise. More and more, at the end of a session, we found ourselves in agreement about a candidate's potential and chances of success.

Then Mr. Cameron asked me to take this a stage further, and offer some comment not only on composing the Personal Statement, which every candidate has to send off with his application, but on preparation for the interview itself. So the candidates were wheeled, *en masse*, in and invited to lap up a dollop of good advice.

As I delivered it in the form of a lecture, I thought it might make it clearer if I set it out as a batch of notes – thus:

These notes are simply to help you to show your best. The pressure is not only on you; it is on them. They have to find the best people to keep their universities up at the top, and they don't have very long in which to do it. You're hoping; they're looking.

Have the basic answers ready – why are you there? How badly do you want to go/work there? That sort of thing.

Surely you just go in there and answer their questions, don't you? That's like saying that rugby is easy; you just run faster and tackle harder than the other side. A bit more to it than that.

**1. Be ready** –
 - examine motives – long-term drive or recent impulse? A/S results? Parental expectation?

- what have you found out? – re city/college/faculty/course (how many of you brought pen and paper here? Who did research on me?) – eyewash in the personal statement – 'I like to think of myself as somebody who is always looking for new options and opportunities in a wide range of activities'. Well, don't we all? Who's going to say 'I'm an old stodge who sticks to what he is familiar with'? Or – 'I am a caring person'. Ugh! Or jargon – 'friendship skills', 'upsizing', 'meaningful relationships'. Far too many situations are 'challenging', which the applicant of course 'welcomes'. Just precisely what is an 'interpersonal relationship skill'? **Talk English.**

**2. Talk detail** – which is better? – 'I like animals'? or 'I had a go at shearing'? 'I leap at the challenge of outdoor activities' or 'I hold an instructor's certificate after a course in sailing in the Aegean Sea'? Give them hooks to hang questions on.

**3. Offer something.** Don't expect them to do all the work. Interviews are two-way traffic.

a) Newspapers – if only the headlines. Something to talk about. . .
   OR
   A book, film, TV programme, anything. Try and slip it in. All the steering need not be theirs. What are you good at? Again, steer it. Think of the story of the farmer's son who didn't have any books in the house to talk about, and who talked about ploughing competitions – and was absolutely fascinating.

a) Be ready to talk outside your subject – are you good, even interested, in anything else?

b) Foreign students – use your 'foreign-ness'. You have gifts and perceptions which are beyond the range of your English counterparts. But show respect too for the West. After all, you want the education they have to offer.

d) Have questions to ask them. It shows you've done some thinking, given them attention.

**Think about it** – however badly – it will show. It will certainly show if you haven't. The most relaxed and focussed are the ones who have done the most preparation. If you want to make it look easy, work hard. Sweat at it a bit beforehand. If you want to be cool, you have to get hot first.

## 4. Make their search easier
a) What do you think they are looking for? Have you got it? How do you show it?
b) What makes you think you are a good candidate? How good do you think you will be three years down the line? They know you will do well at 'A' Level; will you do equally well at Finals in three years' time?
c) Get to know yourself – how good are you with people? With strangers? With the opposite sex? (Girls and male interviewer, and v-v.) Do you talk easily, too little/too much? Get your friends to tell you – if they dare. Waving hands, tossing hair. Can you improve? What makes you think you are different?
d) What makes you think *they* are different?
e) They like to know that you rate them highly.
f) Play losing tricks first – e.g. non-bender, only child, many house moves, new to area.
g) If you were an interviewer, what would *you* ask you?
h) Again, **think** about all this – don't expect to find a set of pat answers. But – if you have thought, **it will show** – unconsciously, the best way. (Don Thompson, the 50-kilometre walk, and the kettle in the bathroom.)

## 5. General
a) Have respect for the system – it's all there is, and you're stuck with it.
b) Respect for English, the nuts and bolts of it – spelling, punctuation (the candidate for Vet. St. who couldn't spell 'veterinary') Writing smart counts.
c) Looking smart counts too. What is 'smart'? Suggest wholesome, tidy, understated, easy. Never mind your precious 'freedom' to wear what you like; remember the overall strategic object.
d) They have only 30 minutes. Give them credit for knowing their job.
e) Accept the hoops – don't let precious pride interfere with willingness to jump through them. Suggest happy medium between cap-twiddle and smarty-pants.
f) Do your thinking the week before, not the night before. *It will show.*

Ready for anything – nice/nasty; easy/hard. Whatever is happening, they will be talking to you, so – **LISTEN** – and **respond**. Give your native wit a chance to work. Don't be afraid to come clean if you don't know. It makes you human.

Is this a set of instructions? No. We make no claim to omniscience ot to infallibility. But give us credit for our experience. However, the situation always changes, and we are human. If you think you know better, go ahead and do it your way. It's your life. But please, for the fourth time – **think about it.** They are doing their best; help them. This is an opportunity, not an obstacle course. A chance, not a trap.

## What might be the collective noun for archivists?

BEFORE I BECAME A school archivist, I was a schoolmaster for nearly forty years. People think that being in the classroom all that time – any time – makes you somehow insulated. 'Ah, yes, teachers – well, of course they don't live in the real world, do they?' People also say it about monks, film stars, old age pensioners, pretty well anybody, till the currency of the comment becomes worthless.

The statement is ridiculous anyway. We all live in the real world – milkmen, international bridge players, night nurses in a hospital, politicians – you name it. Whoever we are, it is *our* world, and it is very real to us. And it is a complete world, with drama, variety, problems, crises, boredom, worries, anything you care to think of.

People who look in on other people's lives nearly always get it wrong, because they see only glimpses, moments, instants. From these unpromising ingredients, they build, very quickly, a great cliché world, and they use it to apply every time they come across that life again.

What, for instance, do they know about teaching? Only what they gained from a casual glance through the single transparent pane of the glass in the classroom door. From this they come to the conclusion that all a teacher has to do is stand in front of thirty children, say, 'Take out your text-books and turn to Chapter 14.' What do they know about bankers? Only that they raise the charges on current accounts, and pay themselves enormous bonuses. By the same token, politicians do nothing but make pompous speeches and get given directorships which offer them huge salaries for doing practically nothing. Film stars live garish life styles, get paid obscene salaries, appear on chat shows, and divorce each other. And archivists get dust all over their faded, baggy suits, because they spend their time in some lofty cubby-hole under the eaves poring over faded yellow pages which nobody has read for centuries, or is likely to read ever again.

And here I have a sort of confession to make. When it was suggested to me that perhaps I might like to become an archivist, one or two images like that did flit past my mind's eye. All right, I was a teacher, so I had some practical idea of what a school archivist's life and work might consist of. But I was in for quite a few surprises.

A teacher deals normally with pupils and other teachers. An archivist can find himself involved with academic staff, true; but he will also, at various times, negotiate with clerical staff, maintenance staff, pastoral staff, ground staff, catering staff. Before he has been in the job very long, he will discover that he needs several members of these various 'staffs' to do him a favour. That's one lesson.

Another is to do with casual visitors. Teachers normally do not have time for such duties; it is as much as they can do to squeeze a formal appointment into an average day's timetable. An archivist, on the other hand, can be deep in a task he has been hoping to tackle for several weeks; the telephone goes, and he is told that an Old Boy has just dropped in by chance. He has not been back to the school for 45 years, and would the Archivist please meet him and show him around; dig out evidence of his time at the school; listen to his reminiscences; and generally give him the treatment. It goes with the territory.

Another problem is to do with knowledge. People, as I said, don't know much about what an archivist does. One or two I have spoken to even look a little blank at the word 'archive'. Most of the pupils have little or no idea of what it is, where it is, or what it does. Before very long I came to realise that a large slice of my activities was going to come under the heading of 'Public Relations', or, if you like, 'Publicity'.

Then there was the small matter of finding out where the 'archives' actually were. Before I became the archivist, there was no archive. I had to locate, then collect the ingredients from offices, cupboards, dusty corners and lofts (oh, yes, there was dust there all right). And it wasn't just those yellowing documents I spoke about; it could be, and was, photographs (of course); cups, medals, and other trophies; venerable volumes from the past; in fact anything from old governors' minutes to ancient sporting caps and blazers, from a celebrity's cricket bat to a set of cadet band equipment (complete with bass drum).

I found that I needed to negotiate with a wide range of people in order to obtain basic furniture, a telephone, a computer, a scanner, even a budget. So that expanded my range to include technical staff, cleaning staff, bursary staff, cadet staff, and anybody else who would listen to my tale of woe.

I made myself available to give assemblies, so that pupils would at least have heard of me, and so that they would know what I looked like.

I never dreamed at the outset that I would be giving speeches and addresses to parents, the old pupils' association, the Exmoor Society, the relevant masonic lodge, and local cultural and recreational clubs.

Much less could I have foreseen that I would, in time, have three books about West Buckland in print. More meetings – local society secretaries, publishers, the local press and local magazines. The list seemed to grow every year.

And I still had only the same four hours allocated. That was, and is, what I am actually paid for – four hours a week. (Incidentally, I discovered later that some school archivists did not get paid – full stop.)

It followed, then, before very long, that I wasn't going to get done a tenth of what, ideally, needed doing. I got yet another surprise when I began to attend annual meetings of the Schools Archivist Group. This was the brain child of a very resourceful lady archivist at Harrow School. When she set it up, she was able to assemble a membership of 5. Now, less than fifteen years later, that membership has grown beyond 250, including schools in South Africa and Bermuda. As I said elsewhere, school archiving is a growth industry.

These meetings do several things. Obviously you hear talks from seasoned professionals in subjects like document preservation, computer skills, digitisation, archive organisation, and a host of other topics. They inform and depress in equal proportions. You feel that it is all knowledge that it would be useful for you to have; and on the other hand your common sense tells you that will never master the techniques, raise the money to buy the gadgets, or have the time to put them into operation.

But you meet other school archivists, naturally, and you soon discover that many of them feel exactly as you do – inadequate. Once again, it is lowering and uplifting. You come away from all these prestigious establishments (we have had conferences in Harrow, Eton, Blundells, and Charterhouse, for instance) feeling, as I said, inadequate. But you also feel uplifted because you have met and talked to a host of people who, like you, are manfully doing their best in circumstances very similar to yours.

Many of them too were totally without experience, like me. We gleaned our knowledge from the shavings and debris on the workshop floor of mistakes, failures, frustrations, and incomplete projects. Also, like me, some of them operated in a school which had never had an archive before.

Hence the last, somewhat wry, surprise. There was one laurel we could lean on: whatever we may have been able to accomplish (however humble) represented a distinct advance on what had existed before. So we have done *something*.

## **Getting on the telly**

THE LATE FRANKIE HOWERD, who, like many comedians, was a notorious worrier, was once asked if, after a particularly difficult show with a particularly difficult audience, he had ever contemplated suicide.

'No,' he said at once, and paused. 'But I have often contemplated murder.'

Which only goes to show that you never know what is going to happen.

I thought, when I took on the task of creating a school archive, that I would be involved with books, bottom drawers, junk, and dust. Well, I was, but it soon became clear that there was a lot more to it than that. Like Topsy, it sort of growed.

For example, the Headmaster would say to me, 'Berwick, I have to make a speech to an Old Boys' dinner next week. Dig me out something about the early days of rugby in the school, please.' So I did.

Or the School Press Officer would ask me to provide a little documentary background to something she wanted to do for the local paper. Or a member of staff would request some material on a historical topic for one of his classes.

This set me thinking: if I was going to make the Archive a going concern, I needed to develop what the experts call an 'image', a 'profile'. I had to make people aware that the Archive was there. And a way to do that was opening up. So I started taking assemblies; I put regular bulletins on the Common Room notice board; I took the initiative in providing more material for the local press – about school celebrities, unusual coincidences, anniversaries.

Our Press Officer was successful in extending our press coverage, so people started reading more about us. One of those new readers was somebody connected with the television industry. He was involved with a programme called *Collectors' Lot*. As the title suggests, it was about collections. They could be collections of anything – match-boxes, Dinky cars, teddy bears, ancient foundation garments – I suspect, the more *outré* the better.

Anyway, this BBC person got the idea that what was in the West Buckland Archive might provide ammunition for another 'collection', and he approached the School about a possible programme.

It was as well that we didn't get too excited. For a start it wasn't going to be a whole programme, just part of a programme, and not a very big part at that. And it wasn't going to be enough for the School Archivist to take the viewer on a guided tour of the School's most attractive memorabilia. We had to have a celebrity. Did we have a celebrity on the books?

Yes, we did – Brian Aldiss, the writer. Good. The team duly arrived – the cameraman, the 'other-duties' boffin, the Familiar Face as the Presenter, and Brian Aldiss himself (whom they had persuaded to come to Devon all the way from Oxford – for a fee – they didn't offer one to the School Archivist).

I was asked to lay out a selection of our collection on a large table in the School library, with a carefully-angled background of venerable bookshelves groaning under the weight of suitably impressive tomes. While I was doing this, Brian Aldiss was interviewed about his time at the School, and he took the Presenter round the older buildings that he remembered.

When it came to my turn, I joined the Presenter and cameraman before the bookshelves, and was asked questions about the history of the School and about the Archive and its genesis. Then, to my horror, and with the camera still running, he said, 'Now talk about what you have on the table.'

I said, 'What – just like that?'

'Just like that.'

'Suppose I make a mistake.'

He saw the look on my face, and leaned forward. 'Mr. Coates, when our editors have finished with what you have said, believe me, it will be seamless.'

So that's what we did. It is difficult to estimate or remember how long I spoke for. When I had finished, the Presenter got up and left me to the cameraman, who needed some close-ups of the documents and other things I had referred to in my – what shall we call it? – my 'address'.

And that was it.

When the programme went out, it was a third or fourth part of a half-hour slot – on a weekday mid-afternoon – so peak viewing. The Presenter set the scene. Brian Aldiss got the lion's share, with his reminiscences. The Archivist was introduced and given some cursory questions. Then I did my piece, such as it was. The rest of the time was taken up with the Presenter nodding at carefully-spaced intervals, and with some splendid close-ups of the Archivist's index finger.

Fame indeed.

## Beginning to be a School Archivist

IT MAY COME AS a surprise, but school archiving is a growth industry. And a relatively new one. Probably the result of two things:

One – the computer revolution. Suddenly – well, in the last two decades – the compiling of lists and catalogues and inventories has moved away from the devoted retired accountant sitting at his kitchen table of a winter's evening with a clapped-out typewriter, and it has migrated to an office (or a cubby-hole) in the more remote reaches of an ancient building which has a few spare rooms which nobody can think of another use for.

Even more recently, the digitising craze has struck. There are firms now who will collect all your documents and pictures and put them on a computer for everybody to 'download' – they will 'digitise' them. Funny how quickly we get used to the new jargon. I bet very few people who are now school archivists (they are mostly retired teachers, parents, and general friends of the school in question) would have claimed familiarity with this jargon twenty, even fifteen years ago. Well, they're all the rage now. If you're not digitised, you are simply not with it.

So that's the first reason – computers. The second in the realisation by independent school headmasters (and headmistresses) that having an archive could be good business. Or should I say an *organised* archive. Every school has an archive if you mean various piles, boxes, folders, cupboards, trunks, shelves, nooks and crannies scattered all over the place, and nobody who stumbles across their contents has the heart to throw them away.

That is no use to anybody. But collect them all up; put them in a single corner, shed, office, or disused laundry room; appoint an archivist to look after them and bring some system to the job; and you have the potential for a Resource.

Notice that, in a higher paragraph, I referred to 'independent' schools. To the best of my knowledge, state schools are not attracted to or involved in this activity. Perhaps it is because not many of them have any kind of venerable history. Maybe nobody there thought it was worth preserving anything. I once worked for a comprehensive school headmaster who decided to scrap the First World War Book of Remembrance because, he said, it dwelt too much on the past, and who was interested in the past?

But independent schools, for the most part, *do* have a lengthy history, some up to half a millennium. And they have to balance their books. State schools are by definition funded by the government; independent schools, also by definition, have to finance themselves.

So – make the equation. If you create an archive, it becomes at once a useful 'resource', as I said, for the teaching activities of the school. But, more to the point in this context, you forge a new means of making contact with ex-pupils. At the very simplest level, they are suckers for looking up their old activities in the yellowing pages of the school magazine. At another level, the archive can be the inspiration of shows and exhibitions of the school's past history; it can run a website for the information and amusement of old pupils; and, at the most sophisticated level, it can offer computer contact with any part of the school's history, which can be 'downloaded' – for a small fee of course. Interaction is, I believe, the word. One way and another, it can revolutionise (and has in many cases already done so) the richness of contact with old pupils. Once you have made contact, you can inform, welcome, and entertain.

Put crudely, it can be nice little earner. Pupils who take the trouble to come back to visit, or who tap into the website, do so because they are well-disposed towards the school, and so are willing to be informed about schemes, trips, projects, building programmes, theatrical performances, concerts, and I don't know what else. Well, you're half-way there, aren't you?

Now, what has all this to do with me? Well, the search is on for school archivists. Very few schools can afford a full-time archivist, and I daresay not many can afford a properly-qualified one. (Though this situation is now beginning to change; more professionalism is seeping into the business.) However, in the early days, school archivists were recruited from retired teachers, businessmen, professionals of most kinds, and anybody else who liked the school, and had a few hours a week to devote to it. Because they are mostly comfortably off, they don't expect much in the way of salary. If they are not qualified, they can not command a professional level of remuneration. Some do not get paid at all, and do it for the love of it.

But many of them don't know much about it to begin with. And here, at last, I get to the point. Somebody (I forget who) asked me to set down a few comments, for a beginner, about setting up and running a school archive.

It would probably make a professional curl his toes if he read this, but I am not a professional, and I was a beginner, like the people I was writing this for. I didn't know about sliding bookshelves and paper preservation and chemical damage to flimsy records, but I did know something about starting from scratch, about living from hand to mouth, and about learning on the job.

When I began, I had a table, a chair, two expired filing cabinets, and a faded three-foot bookshelf. Oh – and a brand-new soft brush which had been purchased by a thoughtful bursar (which gives you some idea of how other people thought about the job). No lockable cupboards, no telephone, no computer (of course), and therefore no scanner or printer, and no budget. And I was left to get on with it.

So, in that sense, yes, I did feel eminently qualified to write what follows.

This memo is the fruit of ten years' performance of and musings on the work of School Archivist. I am not professionally trained. I came to the post with no previous knowledge of the work. But I did have over forty years' experience of teaching, a lifetime's interest in History, varied experience in lecturing and games coaching, several published books to my credit, and knowledge of the Armed Forces through an Army commission.

Its various sections may reflect only my strengths and preferences, and is by no means intended to appear definitive.

No two schools will have the same situation. Some will have a vast archive, already half-organised; others will have nothing but a couple of huge dust-covered trunks in a dormitory loft. Obviously, the total amount of the archive material will have something to do with the length of the school's life. Some will have benefited from the efforts of one or two dedicated and imaginative history teachers who have already awakened governors, staff, and pupils to their own heritage; others will have to start from total ignorance, or scepticism, among their colleagues, never mind their pupils. So the following remarks are never going to be universally applicable. Anyone searching for relevant help or ideas must use his common sense to pick and choose.

I had to start from scratch. Not only did I have no experience or professional training; there had never been a school archive where I worked as a part-time History teacher. I was given an office about twelve feet by nine. I had a desk, a chair, a table, a half-height, three-foot bookcase, and two time-expired filing cabinets with no locks. No cupboards, no phone, no computer, scanner, or printer. And no budget – nothing.

If ever necessity was the mother of invention, it was in this case. But it did provide freedom of a sort; having no knowledge of the rules, I could freely break them. Having no-one to help, I was a committee of one (I was responsible only to the Headmaster, and, as our archive was very much his brain-child, I was sure of support and interest). And, whenever I was assailed by feelings of inadequacy, I was comforted by the constant self-reminder that whatever I was doing represented a considerable advance on what had existed before.

So – what does, or can, or should, an archivist do?

1. Find out what you have, and where it is. Tell colleagues who you are, and what you are looking for. It is surprising what will turn up from departmental stock cupboards and elsewhere; often the previous

*The Archives of an Archivist*

guardians will be only too pleased to get rid of it.
2. Concentrate it in your room/office/store. If you haven't got a place, get one. And get one on the premises, as close to the heart of things as you can. Ideally in administrative headquarters. And get a prominent notice on the door. An archive must be central, it must be known, and it must be accessible. An archive off site is at best a bind to have to visit, at worst a distant repository for relics nobody knows about or is remotely interested in.
3. Do the obvious unfolding, dusting, cleaning, and preservation that needs doing at once.
4. Make commonsense divisions into Documentary, Visual, and Physical.
5. This process will make you familiar with the main features of your collection. You will note the highlights and valuable pieces which require special treatment.
6. Once the collection is complete – or as complete as it can be at the time; you will always be discovering or be given additions – turn to the business of Storage, Recording, and Presentation. Remember that looking after the past does not mean just putting it away in a safe place; it means putting it out as well for everybody to enjoy. An archive that isn't there isn't worth much.
7. So – make the resources of the archive as available as possible, subject of course to the needs of security, confidentiality, good order, and completeness. An archive is not a library. Don't let originals out; don't let documents go off the premises. However fervently a member of staff assures you he will see that it will be tenderly cared for, it often is not. Availability and constant care: an archivist will have to decide for himself how to balance these two opposing needs.
8. It hardly needs saying that confidential records must stay confidential. Valuable relics need protecting. At the very least, get a lock put on the door.
9. Offer the archive's stores and facilities (assuming you have been able to acquire some) to colleagues and Old Members for pupil projects, private research, and so on. If your office is big enough, have a few small desks and chairs for people to work there; try and get them to come to you. It is all part of making everyone aware of you.
10. Which leads to the question of Profile. Tell everybody who you are and what you do, and where you can be seen and talked to. Keep regular patches on notice boards in the Common Room, the Quad,

pupil common rooms – prominently labelled 'Archive' – and put up regular items of interest – an old photo, a funny letter, an exam paper from way back, anything (copies of course). People love sepia photographs. Another way of getting people to talk to you is to put up, say, a group photo of about twenty years before, and invite staff with long memories to identify the faces.

11. Get an 'Archive' section inserted into the school's website, and update it as often as you can. Make sure that the website explains how anyone can contact you.

12. Establish, and maintain, a good relationship with the school press officer. Feed him/her with tasty morsels from school history which can be worked up for items on local radio or in the local paper – even further afield. We were able to take this so far once that it secured the school a place on a Channel 4 collectors' programme – cameras in the school, a Familiar Face, and everything. Keep your eyes open for an impending centenary or other significant anniversary and make something of it.

13. If you have no budget, think of ways to raise some modest funds for the archive – e.g. making and selling Christmas cards using images from the archive. For instance, I discovered an amount of old blazer material in a cupboard, which an Old Boy was happy to buy to have made up – into a blazer of course.

14. If you do get given a budget, maintain a regular account of expenditure. Keep contact with the Bursar's Office. In fact, set up and maintain good relations with all sorts of people that a teacher normally would not see much of – the Bursar, the Bursar's Secretary, Reception staff, the Ground Staff, the Maintenance Staff, the Catering Staff. You would be surprised how many people you are going to need to do favours for you.

15. Make up a folder of unusual photographs which reflect striking features of school life which would not necessarily find their way into a prospectus, and leave it on a table in a potential parents' waiting room.

16. You will probably come across old books and folders in bad condition. Find a good bookbinder and get them re-bound. (That is, if you have a budget.)

17. And if you haven't got a phone and a computer by this time, start agitating to get them. This is where bursars and other important

functionaries may come in useful (the higher the rank the better).

18  At the outset, it would pay you to establish a clear chain of command. If possible, don't get tacked on to some department or other; you will be the poor relation. If you were, as I was, set up directly by the Headmaster, make sure that your line of responsibility is *to* the Headmaster, *direct*.

19  Maintain contact as much as possible with Old Members. Go to gatherings, speech days, old boys' dinners. Be seen. Be interested in their reminiscences; you never know what bonus will drift your way perhaps months later. You will soon find, for instance, that, when an Old Boy visits out of the blue, you will be the one to receive him, take him to the archive, show him his old magazines, take him round, discuss modern projects, give him lunch, and generally make a fuss of him. They are often thrilled to bits to have somebody who gives them their undivided attention. It can pay dividends in all sorts of ways. For this reason, the Development Director is another functionary whose goodwill and co-operation you will benefit from nurturing. You can also be very useful to them. Use it.

20  Be prepared to talk about your work. For instance, over the years, I have given talks and speeches to Parents' AGM's, Leavers' Dinners, Old Members' Dinners, masonic lodges, the local rotary, and local historical societies. I 'do' a school assembly once every term.

21  Be prepared to write about your work. I have provided copy for articles in local press and magazines; I contribute regularly to the School magazine; I have written articles for local and national quarterlies; and I have published three books about my work based on the archive.

22  Sooner or later you will have to compile a database of every pupil, past and present. That is, assuming that you have by now wheedled a computer out of the Bursar or the Headmaster (here again, direct access is so important – and here again a central position is so vital – so that you can bump into and talk to important people regularly and easily). This is a huge and daunting task, and you will probably have to be content with nibbling at the problem as time and chance permit.

23  Try and talk to fellow-practitioners. There is now a nation-wide society of school archivists – the Schools Archivists' Group. And they are run by a remarkable lady who has been the Archivist at Harrow School. You will find it comforting to discover that school archiving is a growth industry. You will also find it comforting to meet other

people who feel as inadequate as you do, because there is so much to do and not enough time in which to do it.

A few suggested 'don'ts' –
1. Don't get too interested. Old documents, books, and pictures are fascinating (if you didn't find them fascinating, you wouldn't be doing the job). But always bear in mind the work's limitations. The chances are that you will be part-time, and very part-time at that. Always keep an eye on the clock. You will never get done all the things you hoped to do that day, but there will probably be one or two that simply have to be done. Make sure you allow yourself enough time to do them.
2. Don't get too sidetracked by individuals who want you to do something which has a wearing tendency to elongate.
3. Don't play all your tricks at once. If you have stumbled across a real winner, it often pays to use the drip-feed technique. Remember, it is your job, or part of it, to generate interest.
4. Don't let anyone borrow originals. If they want a copy of a photo, you are the one who gets it for them, not them.
5. Don't worry about feeling inadequate – nobody in my experience in school archiving feels adequate. You just do the best you can. You will feel like young mothers meeting other people's babies; every other infant is a precocious *wunderkind* who is light years ahead of the backward little bumpkin in your own arms. You will find, in the magazines and hand-outs, the press articles, the conference minutes, the book faces, the twit chatter, the bleats, tweets, logs, and blogs, news of every kind of sophisticated material, technique, and practice which you can't operate, can't understand, or can't afford. Do not let it concern you; remember that your school archive is not a showpiece of glittering modernity; it is a means of enhancing the life of your school. If that involves a bit of bumble and index cards and paper clips and office stool, so be it. Know and accept the limitations on your knowledge, your time, your facilities, and your budget, and keep in mind not only what is realistically possible, but what is realistically needed. One thing for sure: you cannot do the job if you are miserable about it. Don't worry; just look back at what you had when you started, and look around at what you have now. What was there before? What have you put there?

And what have you been doing in such an enterprise? You have been doing what a school archivist is supposed to do: you have been tending the school's roots. As I said before, and have no shame in saying again, 'Without roots, nothing grows.'

## The finished product

In November, 2008, the school celebrated its 150<sup>th</sup> anniversary. Naturally, there were big junketings laid on for the occasion. Perhaps the biggest was a huge service of commemoration in Exeter Cathedral. Everybody connected with the school was there – pupils, staff, governors, distinguished old members, undistinguished old members, oldest old members, ancillary staff of every description (it was an assistant groundsman who carried one of the celebration candles), local aristocrats and benefactors – absolutely everybody.

I was asked by the school chaplain to write a sort of final postscript reading: this.

'On their last day at school, pupils become leavers, and we look back at the process of educating them.

'What has made these leavers? The School, that's what – teachers, technicians, secretaries, cooks, nurses, cleaners, mowers, sweepers, lessons, laboratories, examinations, broken rules, tall stories, scandals, traditions, friendships, crushes, trips, worries, parties, shows, games, gossip, good days and bad days, high days and holidays – they are what we are.

'It is a common practice in France to put on their war memorials, under or above the names of the fallen, **"Les enfants du village"**. "The children of the village." They do not mean children; they mean the lusty, brave, loyal, devoted young people who belonged there and who wanted very much to do something which would reflect credit on the place which had nurtured them, and who wished to do their best in whatever circumstances life was to place them. **Les enfants du village.** The tone is not patronising; it is tinged with fondness and pride.

'Well, then, these leavers – all 150 years of them – are the School's children; they are what we've got and they are what we have made of them. For better or worse, they are – unavoidably, irretrievably, and ungrammatically – us. And West Buckland is happy to settle for that.'

### THE END

*The Archives of an Archivist*

www.ingramcontent.com/pod-product-compliance
Lightning Source LLC
Chambersburg PA
CBHW050554170426
43201CB00011B/1695